LifePrints 2

ESL FOR ADULTS

TEACHER'S EDITION

Judy Veramendi
Robert Ventre Associates, Inc.

with

Allene Guss Grognet
Center for Applied Linguistics

and

JoAnn (Jodi) Crandall
University of Maryland - Baltimore County

Vocational Resource Center
HUTCHINSON TECHNICAL COLLEGE
Two Century Avenue
Hutchinson, MN 55350

New Readers Press

ISBN 0-88336-045-4

Copyright © 1994
New Readers Press
Publishing Division of Laubach Literacy International
Box 131, Syracuse, New York 13210-0131

All rights reserved. No part of this book may be reproduced or transmitted in any form or by any means, electronic or mechanical, including photocopying, recording, or by any information storage and retrieval system, without permission in writing from the publisher.

Printed in the United States of America

9 8 7 6 5 4 3 2 1

Table of Contents

Introduction: Using *LifePrints* 4
    Student Performance Levels 20
    Scope and Sequence 22

Preliminary Lessons 24

Unit 1	**Getting a Job**	28
Unit 2	**On the Job**	42
Unit 3	**Making Choices about Money**	56
Unit 4	**Driving a Car**	70
Unit 5	**Having a Good Time**	84
Unit 6	**Discovering Patterns**	98
Unit 7	**Wash and Wear**	104
Unit 8	**What the Doctor Said**	118
Unit 9	**Going to School**	132
Unit 10	**Becoming a Citizen**	146
Unit 11	**Getting Used to a New Land**	160
Unit 12	**Discovering Patterns**	174

Tapescripts 180

Index of Functions 191
Index of Structures 192

Introduction: Using *LifePrints*

Welcome to *LifePrints*. This introduction to the Teacher's Edition will help you understand the rationale behind the program and the relationship among its various components. It will also explain the methodology inherent in the units of this Teacher's Edition (TE) and give you a step-by-step guide to conducting the suggested exercises and activities.

There are eight major sections in this introduction:

    I Philosophy/Principles of the Program
    II Principles of Second Language Acquisition
    III Creating a Learner-Centered Environment
    IV The *LifePrints* Program
    V Developing Literacy and Reading Skills at Level 2
    VI Features of Student Book 2 Lessons
    VII Testing and Assessment
    VIII Classroom Management

The core of the introduction is section VI, which describes the activities and exercise types for developing oral/aural language and reading and writing at this level.

I

Philosophy/Principles of the Program

LifePrints begins with the premise that adult language learners bring diverse life experiences that are rich sources of sharing in the ESL class. These experiences, together with the learners' current needs and desires, form the basis for learning the new language. By tapping into familiar roles and experiences, *LifePrints* allows such learners to see their past experiences as valuable in their new environment and helps them sustain their dignity during a time of transition.

LifePrints also assumes that adults enter the ESL classroom with a life-centered or task-centered orientation to learning. Adults perform many different roles in their daily lives. They are worker, spouse, parent, friend, citizen, and more. These roles often become sources of their self-identity. The role of student may be a new and frightening one to many adult ESL learners. They do not necessarily want to learn *about* the English language; they want to learn to *use* English in performing their various adult roles. For them, English is not an end in itself; it is a tool with which to do something else. Adult ESL students are fully functional, at least orally, in their native language. *LifePrints* gives them the ability to start transferring to a new language and a new culture what they have done and can do as adults.

The organizing principle of *LifePrints* is not language; it is context. Language learning is contextualized in the everyday life experiences of immigrants, their neighbors, their co-workers. The lives of the characters in the book are entry points into the lives of the individual adult learners, and the lessons immerse the learners in situations where they can hear and see and practice language that is relevant to contexts in their own lives. The linguistic and cultural skills presented in the pages of *LifePrints* are transferable to real contexts in the lives of adult ESL students.

Another principle of this series is authenticity. What would a native speaker hear or say or read or write in a given context? What communicative role do English-language speakers play in a given situation? Are they primarily listeners, as when a doctor is giving them medical advice? Or are they speakers, as when giving someone directions to the library? Are they readers, as when looking up a telephone number? Or are they writers, as when completing a work log at the end of their shift? Or do they combine skills, like listening and writing when taking a telephone message, or reading and writing when completing a form? Learners are asked to practice only those linguistic skills that are authentic to the contexts or roles in which they will find themselves using English.

II

Principles of Second Language Acquisition

The acquisition of a second language is a complex process, representing a delicate balance between the learner and the learning situation. There is no single way in which all learners acquire another language. Many factors pertaining to each learner come into play, including age, preferred learning style, previous education, first language and its similarity to English, and motivation. The teacher has little control over these factors. What the teacher can do, however, is shape and reshape the language-learning environment so that all learners have the greatest opportunity to acquire the English language skills they need to function as adults.

Throughout this introduction, we use the terms *acquisition* and *learning* interchangeably, irrespective of the cognitive processes involved. Some researchers and teachers contrast these two terms, assuming that they represent two different psychological processes. They apply *acquisition* to "picking up a language through exposure, using subconscious processes" and *learning* to the "conscious study of a second language." Other researchers and teachers argue that a sharp distinction between *acquisition* and *learning* is theoretical, not real. In both the acquisition and learning modes, basic principles underlie curriculum development.

These are some of the principles that guided the development of *LifePrints:*

- **The goal of language learning is communication in both oral and written form.**

  Learners should emerge from the language-learning classroom better able to understand and make themselves understood, as well as having greater facility in reading and writing English, than when they entered the classroom. Without being fluent in English, they can communicate on various levels, as described in the Student Performance Levels document (pages 20–21).

- **Communication is a process, not a sequence of memorized patterns or drill and practice exercises.**

  Function is more important than form. That is, what the learner *does* with language is more important than what he or she *knows about* language. Errors are therefore a necessary step in language acquisition. What is being communicated should be the focus, not the accuracy of what is said or correctness in the form of language. This is not to say that form—grammar, punctuation, and pronunciation, for example—is of no concern. Teachers need to focus on form, but at the right time in the learning process and in terms of furthering meaning. Too much attention to form too early will inhibit rather than encourage communication.

- **Language is most effectively learned in authentic contexts.**

  Contexts should reflect the world in which learners are expected to communicate in English and, as much as possible, they should come from the learners themselves. A corollary to this principle is that language is best presented not as isolated sentences or words but as meaningful discourse. The learning of grammar should also emerge from authentic contexts and should comprise a process by which learners discover patterns in language they already know and use.

- **Comprehension precedes production.**

  Learners need time to listen to language and to absorb what is happening in a variety of communicative situations. They need many and varied opportunities in which to be exposed to spoken and written English, using visual clues such as pictures, film, and video, and realia (things from the real world that learners can see and touch).

- **Production of language, both oral and written, will most likely emerge in stages.**
  Beginning language learners will respond first nonverbally, then with single words, then with two- or three-word combinations, later with phrases and sentences, and finally, by linking sentences together to form discourse. Although students should be encouraged to progress in their language learning, they should not be forced to produce language beyond their ability.

- **Key to student participation is a low anxiety level in the classroom.**
  For adults, language learning is by its nature an anxiety-laden pursuit. The more the teacher and the textbook focus on "doing something with language"—for example, solving a problem, finding new information, describing a thing or situation, or buying a product—rather than on "learning language," the more likely students will be to engage in the process of "acquiring" language. *LifePrints* will help the teacher establish a learning environment in the classroom where students can actually function in English through task-oriented activities.

- **Linguistic skills should be as integrated as possible.**
  Adults interact with others and with their environment by using all their senses. By integrating listening, speaking, reading, and writing in meaningful, interesting, and interactive activities, *LifePrints* simulates the processes in which adults interact with their environment. The term *whole language* has been used to describe this integration of skills. In the following pages we present some particularly effective listening, speaking, reading, and writing strategies. We suggest that these strategies be used together whenever it is feasible and authentic to do so.

III

Creating a Learner-Centered Environment

If language learning is to be successful, the learners' needs, not the grammar or functions of language, must form the core of the curriculum. Before discussing the creation of a learner-centered environment, we ought to look at who our learners are. Adult ESL students are a diverse group, ethnically, linguistically, and culturally. Some are immigrants, some are refugees, and some were even born in the United States. Some are newcomers, while others have lived and worked in this country for a long time. Some had strong academic preparation in their native countries but have weak oral skills; some have strong oral skills but weak or nonexistent literacy skills; and some have problems both with oral interaction and with reading and writing in English. Often these students are grouped in the same classroom, so teachers will have to focus on the language needs of each type.

- Learners who have had academic preparation in their native countries must develop the practical oral language skills necessary to function in everyday life in their new cities or towns, to express their ideas in English, and to work in an English-speaking environment. These adults, who are likely to be newcomers to the United States, may even be comfortable with some reading and writing in English. Literacy in their native language is a part of their lifestyle, and they can use that literacy as a tool in learning a second language.

- Learners who have lived and worked in this country for a number of years have some oral English interaction skills, and they may have developed cultural coping strategies for living and working here. They may have limited formal education in their native countries or in the United States. Their literacy skills in any language may be low or nonexistent, and their academic and study skills may be lacking. Many of these learners come to the ESL classroom looking for programs that upgrade their oral English skills, as well as for literacy skills that prepare them to benefit from academic, vocational, or job-training opportunities.

- Learners who are new to the United States, and who lack both oral and literacy skills needed to access information, express ideas, and solve communication problems in English, are also likely to lack cultural coping strategies. They need strong developmental programs that help them acquire the language, literacy, and cultural skills necessary for learning and working in this country.

In addition to background, each adult comes with his or her preferred learning style. In general, *learning style* refers to one's preferred patterns of mental functioning. At least 20 different dimensions of learning style have been identified, far too many to detail here. Some people prefer to learn by watching, listening, and reflecting on their observations. Others are more comfortable learning by using abstract conceptualization, analyzing, and then acting on an intellectual understanding of the situation. Others learn best by doing and by active experimentation, while still others learn from feelings and specific interpersonal experiences. What this means for teachers is that a variety of strategies must be built into lessons so that all learners can draw on their preferred learning styles.

Teachers can use *LifePrints* to help learners with varying learning styles to observe, question, infer, and brainstorm—all activities that imaginative learners find useful. Full-page illustrations with prompt questions ("What's happening here? What do you think will happen next?") and semantic webbing are examples of activities that are effective with visual learners. Analytic learners can find patterns, organize, identify parts, and classify through activities such as using English to create charts and graphs. Commonsense learners can problem-solve, predict, experiment, and tinker with language. Dynamic learners can integrate, evaluate, explain, and reorganize the learning. In short, teachers using *LifePrints* can choose from a variety of activities that are consistent with students' learning styles and with their own. Research has shown that teachers tend to teach from and to their own learning style, so they should be aware not only of learners' needs but also of their own preferences and behaviors.

Creating a learner-centered environment is at the core of *LifePrints*. *Learner-centered* means that learners are in control of their own learning and direct what happens in the classroom. It also means that the curriculum is communicative-based rather than grammar-based and that language lessons center on relevant aspects of learners' lives. Finally, a learner-centered classroom calls for a collaborative effort between teacher and learners, with learners always playing an active role in the learning process. It is perhaps easier to describe than to define the learner-centered principles that guided the development of *LifePrints*.

- In an adult learner-centered class, learners and teacher become partners in a cooperative venture. The teacher creates the supportive environment in which learners can take initiative in choosing what they want to learn and how they want to learn it. This does not mean that the teacher has given up control of the classroom. The teacher must structure and order the learning process, guiding and giving feedback to learners in such a way that learners have the right amount of freedom. Too little freedom, as in a traditional teacher-centered curriculum, will stifle learners; too much freedom will make learners feel that the teacher has abandoned them.

- What happens in the language classroom should be a negotiated process between learners and teacher. The content and sequence of *LifePrints* lessons do not preclude the use of the program in a learner-centered curriculum. Indeed, the program is a starting point for classroom interaction and for student generation of adult learning materials. The language presented and practiced in *LifePrints* is based on issues, situations, and contexts that language-minority adults have expressed as crucial in their lives. Many of these same issues and situations will also be important in the lives of the learners in your class. The participatory process means that teachers must know their students and ask them what they think and what they want to learn and do.

- Problem solving occupies a good portion of any adult's life, so it is not surprising that problem-solving activities are a necessary part of learner-centered curricula. Problem-solving exercises are prominent in *LifePrints*. In beginning units, learners are asked what they would say or do in a particular situation, or about their own experiences in similar circumstances. Later on, they are asked to present the pros and cons of a situation, to negotiate, or to persuade. Learners are also asked to generate problem-solving and simulation activities from their own lives. By presenting and solving problems in the classroom, learners become confident of their ability to use language to solve problems and to take action in the larger social sphere.

- The traditional roles of the teacher as planner of content, sole deliverer of instruction, controller of the classroom, and evaluator of achievement change dramatically in a learner-centered curriculum. When the atmosphere in the classroom is a collaborative one, the teacher becomes facilitator, moderator, group leader, coach, manager of processes and procedures, giver of feedback, and partner in learning. *LifePrints* lends itself to these roles, giving suggestions to the teacher for whole-class, small-group, paired, and one-to-one activities.

- In managing communicative situations in a learner-centered environment, teachers set the stage for learners to experiment with language, to negotiate meaning and make mistakes, and to monitor and evaluate their own language-learning progress. Language is essentially a social function acquired through interaction with others in one-to-one and group situations. Learners process meaningful discourse from others, and they produce language in response to other human beings. The teacher is responsible for establishing the supportive environment in which this can happen. This does not mean that the teacher never corrects errors; it means that the teacher knows when and how to deal with error correction and can help learners understand when errors will interfere with effective, comprehensible communication. *LifePrints* introduces and then recycles vocabulary, grammar, and functions. This helps both learners and the teacher in the monitoring and correcting process.

IV

The *LifePrints* Program

The *LifePrints* Program is composed of four separate but linked components for each level:
(1) the Student Book (SB)
(2) Audiotapes (▣)
(3) the Teacher's Edition (TE), and
(4) the Teacher's Resource File (TRF).

The Basic English Skills Test (BEST) is an optional feature of the *LifePrints* Program, providing a means for assessing placement and progress of adult ESL learners.

Encompassing three levels, *LifePrints* is designed to enable adult learners who have little or no oral and/or written competence in English to handle most everyday survival, social, and job-related situations independently, using oral and written English. Student Book 1 is designed for adults at Student Performance Levels (SPLs) 0–1; Student Book 2 for those at SPLs 2–4; and Student Book 3 for those at SPLs 5–6. A description of the SPLs appears on pages 20–21 of the Teacher's Edition.

Student Book

Each Student Book follows a set of characters as they live, work, and study in a given community. Their lives and experiences become the stimuli for learners to talk and write about their own lives and experiences. As language proficiency expands from level to level, so does the number of interactions with people from diverse backgrounds.

There are 12 units in each Student Book. Ten (Units 1–5 and 7–11) focus on content, for example, housing, health, shopping, cultural adjustment, and employment. The other two (Units 6 and 12) focus on the grammar (structures) that learners have used in the preceding five units. A full Scope and Sequence for each Student Book, covering functions, structures, culture, and life tasks, is included in the Teacher's Edition for that book.

These are some of the features of all three student books:

- Authentic language use.
- Adult contexts relevant to the lives of learners, their families, and friends.
- Visual stimuli for language learning, where appropriate, and a progression from visual to text-oriented material. While effective for all language learners, this progression taps into the natural learning strategies of low-literate individuals who often use visual clues in place of literacy skills.
- An emphasis on paired and group work, because learners acquire language through interaction with others on meaningful tasks in meaningful contexts.
- A whole language orientation, integrating listening, speaking, reading, and writing, to reflect natural language use.
- Activities that help students transfer what they learn in the classroom to the world they live in.
- Grammar learning as a discovery process, with a focus on understanding the rules for language that students have already used and internalized. The discovery of rules is contextualized and at the discourse level whenever possible.
- An integration of new cultural skills along

with new linguistic skills. *LifePrints* recognizes that adults need to understand and acquire a layer of cultural behaviors along with language. The situations presented help learners explore cross-cultural beliefs, attitudes, and values, and to compare and contrast expected behaviors in their native countries with expected behaviors in the United States.

Audiotapes

Because *LifePrints* learners are asked to engage in active listening, not to read conversations, there are no written dialogues in the student books. Instead, the audiotapes, an integral partner with the student books, offer real listening opportunities by providing all conversations on tape. In keeping with authentic language, they offer authentic listening practice, exposing learners to different voices and relevant listening situations in which learners will find themselves. Learners are given the opportunity to listen to a conversation several times, to ask questions about it, and to develop strategies for understanding what they hear. Most important, learners are not forced to produce language they are not yet ready to produce.

Teacher's Edition

The layout of the *LifePrints* Teacher's Edition allows for a full view of each student page, along with the purpose of the lesson, materials needed, warm-up, presentation, and expansion activities. For each unit, the *learning objectives* are listed and categorized by linguistic functions, life tasks, structures, and culture. Key and related vocabulary are also provided for easy reference. Following is a description of the learning objectives sections in the TE, with suggestions on how to use them.

1. **Functions.** Functions focus on what people want to do with language or what they want to accomplish through oral communication. Functions can be categorized in different ways. The functions in *LifePrints* relate to *personal matters,* such as identifying oneself and one's family, and expressing needs or emotions; *interpersonal matters,* such as expressing greetings and farewells, expressing likes/dislikes and approval/disapproval, persuading, and interrupting; and *giving and seeking information* by, for example, reporting, explaining, describing, asking, clarifying, and directing. An index of functions for this level of *LifePrints* appears on page 191.

2. **Life Tasks.** Life tasks refer to coping skills required to deal with aspects of daily life in U.S. society, such as shelter, employment, food, clothing, transportation, and health care. The life tasks included in *LifePrints* are listed in the Scope and Sequence. It should be noted that when put into the statement "The learner will be able to . . . ," these life tasks become functional life skills or competencies, correlating with adult competency-based curricula such as the California Adult Student Assessment System (CASAS).

3. **Key and Related Vocabulary.** For every subject or topic, some vocabulary is key, or content-obligatory; that is, without those words, one cannot discuss the subject. Other vocabulary is related, or content-compatible; these are words that modify, describe, or complement the key vocabulary. For each *LifePrints* lesson, the most important key and related vocabulary is listed. At a minimum, learners should be able to *understand* these words in context. The subject matter and the proficiency level of the class usually determine whether the teacher should expect learners to *use* this vocabulary actively in conversation.

4. **Structures.** Although grammar is not isolated for practice in each lesson, certain structures are primary and appear frequently in the lesson. Many of these structures are brought together in Units 6 and 12, where learners are asked to discover patterns of grammar and then to practice the structures in new contexts. To help teachers give explanations where necessary, notes in the Teacher's Edition focus on the important features of a particular structure. The Scope and Sequence lists the primary structures for each lesson, indicating whether they are introduced for the first time or are being recycled.

5. **Culture.** Items inherent in the subject matter of the unit that are cross-cultural (for example, family, shopping, medical care, gender roles, and child-rearing) are noted in the Teacher's Edition. There is often a crossover between cultural points and life tasks. We suggest that, whenever possible, learners discuss cultural similarities and differences so they can reflect on ways of doing things in their native culture and of performing the same tasks in U.S. society, without making value judgments in either case.

Besides outlining the objectives for each lesson, the Teacher's Edition gives detailed suggestions for the teaching of each Student Book page. We use the word *suggestions* because the steps presented are meant as guidelines, not as absolutes. After considering the needs and learning styles of the students in your class, as well as your own teaching style, you might blend them with the suggested steps for teaching the lesson. To feel comfortable with each student page, make your own lesson plan; include, along with the approximate timing, a "grab bag" of possible whole-class, small-group, paired, and one-to-one activities. Gather any needed materials well beforehand and, if you have time, practice-teach the page (without learners) to get a feel for the flow of the lesson, for monitoring your own speech, and for noting what you think might be difficult points for the learners. Suggested teaching steps include the following:

1. Teacher Preparation and Materials.

Gathering materials is an important step, so the TE suggests the materials and any special preparation needed for the lesson. Most lessons require a cassette player for the listening activities, but other equipment and supplies may be needed as well. A language course that is contextualized in survival situations must rely on pictures and real objects to convey meaning. Building a *picture file* for the first time will take some work; however, after you have gone through the book with a class once or twice, the file will need only periodic updating. Highly visual magazines, mail-order and other catalogs, and newspaper advertisements and Sunday supplements are good sources of illustrations for survival situations. Pictures of houses; the insides of clinics/hospitals and various workplaces; items in grocery stores, supermarkets, and department stores; and people interacting in both everyday and problem situations are examples of visuals for your file. Include pictures that can be used for sequencing and strip stories. In some cases you will want to cut and mount the picture before class; in others you will want to have learners look through a magazine or catalog to find items as part of the class lesson. From time to time, the TE also suggests asking learners to provide pictures as out-of-class work.

For some units you will also need realia. An empty milk carton, an aspirin bottle, a soiled piece of clothing, a bus schedule, or a hammer and screwdriver can make the difference between learners really understanding and internalizing language and having only a vague idea of what a word or concept means. Particularly at the beginning and intermediate levels of language learning, the gathering of materials is a crucial step in the teaching process.

2. Warm-up.

The Teacher's Edition gives suggestions for getting the class started and for eliciting concerns, information, and questions from the learners. Casual conversation with the whole group or a few learners, or small talk on a given topic, can be an icebreaker. Movement, chants, dances, and songs can both stimulate and relax learners so they are ready to attend to class business. The most important part of warm-ups for adult learners is tapping into their prior knowledge and experience, and using their backgrounds to prepare for the lesson topic. Brainstorming activities that involve both learners and teacher in generating vocabulary, multiple associations, and illustrations on a specific topic can set the tone for the entire lesson. Warm-ups help learners organize information about a subject, while lowering their anxiety level and getting them to use the English they have already acquired.

3. Presentation.

This section is the heart of the Teacher's Edition in that it gives step-by-step suggestions for each page. It includes:

- Suggested language for asking questions and eliciting information. "Teacher talk" often gets in the way of the learners understanding what they are supposed to do. In giving instructions, teachers sometimes use more complex grammatical structures than the learners can handle. Or they may talk too long, causing learners to lose track of what they are supposed to do. The suggested language in the Presentation section helps teachers avoid these pitfalls.
- Suggested activities or exercises. These activities—often introduced by "Have learners work in small groups to . . ." or "Elicit from learners . . ." or the like—will help the flow of a lesson, though others can be substituted or added. You may need to adapt activities to the needs and proficiency level of the class, as well as to the characteristics of the learning site and your teaching style.

- Suggested teacher modeling and demonstration. Remember to model and/or give examples whenever possible. In activities such as completing interview grids, your asking a question first will make learners feel more comfortable approaching their classmates.

4. Expansion/Extension.

By giving suggestions for additional classroom practice, this section answers the common teacher lament, "I've finished the Student Book, so what do I do now?" It functions as an idea bank both for whole-class exercises and for activities specifically geared to certain types of learners. The more advanced learners are challenged to be creative with the language they have acquired and to try out new language; slower learners are given opportunities for more work in problem areas. Some of the expansion exercises draw on the Teacher's Resource File, or TRF (see below). Others are variations of activities already done in class. Still others help move the language lesson from the classroom to the world outside, asking learners to do something new and immediately useful with the language they have acquired.

The Teacher's Edition also gives less experienced teachers insights into what might be going on when a student or a class is faced with learning a certain function or structure. These insights come both from research into second language acquisition and from classroom practice. It helps teachers to know that when learners continually make mistakes with a certain structure, it is not because they haven't presented the structure correctly or given enough practice with it, but because, as research and experience have shown, the structure is acquired late and will remain a problem even for advanced learners. Similarly, it is helpful to know that, according to classroom experience, a particular exercise works better in small groups than with the whole class, or that learners must be at an intermediate language level before they can be expected to be aware of certain features of language, such as register. The *LifePrints* Teacher's Edition is designed to be used effectively by both experienced and less experienced teachers.

Teacher's Resource File

The Teacher's Resource File (TRF) extends the Student Book by giving teachers a wide variety of reproducible complementary activities. Only so much text can fit in a Student Book, so the TRF for each level offers exercises, simulations, problem-solving activities, and games relevant to the themes of individual units, as well as generic games or game boards that can be used at any time. Because of the match between the Student Book and the TRF at each level, the Expansion/Extension sections in the Teacher's Edition often refer to specific TRF activities. Though an optional feature of *LifePrints,* the TRF is a resource that teachers can use over and over again, saving countless hours of planning and materials preparation.

Basic English Skills Test

The Basic English Skills Test (BEST), another optional feature of *LifePrints*, assesses listening, speaking, reading, and writing in life-skills contexts. It contains two distinct parts: a one-to-one structured oral interview, which uses picture stimuli, and an individual or group-administered reading and writing section. The BEST can be used both as a placement tool and as a progress test. Its scores are correlated with the Student Performance Levels (SPLs) of the Mainstream English Language Training (MELT) Project, as are scores on the California Adult Student Assessment System (CASAS). For a description of the SPLs, see pages 20–21.

V

Developing Literacy and Reading Skills at Level 2

Level 2 of *LifePrints* is designed for learners at Student Performance Levels 2–4. At SPL 2, learners can understand and express a limited number of simple learned phrases, and they have some literacy in English. At SPL 4, learners are beginning to move away from learned phrases, both orally and in writing, and are starting to create language on their own. If we use the analogy of climbing a flight of stairs, learners moving from SPL 2 to 3 will take steady steps, one by one. Those moving from SPL 3 to 4 will take leaps as well as steps, sometimes relying on learned phrases but also trying new combinations of words and grammar that they have not previously learned.

In reading, students are moving from "learning to read" to "reading to learn" (or do). Literacy skills at Level 2 are taught and practiced in meaningful but controlled contexts from the beginning pages. In early lessons, learners are exposed to want ads, job applications, safety notices, and consumer information. In other lessons, they are asked to deal with labels and charts and graphs, pay stubs and budgeting, and excerpts from driver's manuals and insurance brochures. Learners relate charts and graphs to information in paragraph form, and make choices about reading strategies, e.g., skimming or scanning to obtain information or instructions.

For learners at Level 2 who may still be at a lower literacy level, the Student Book stimulates reading and writing by relating the visuals in the book to the meaning being conveyed in writing. Pages are designed so that learners can focus on visual representations of thoughts or vocabulary, can relate what they are hearing on the tapes to clear pictures of situations or people, and can work with materials in grids and other graphic formats.

In writing, learners are asked to complete forms, take notes, and transfer oral information, such as interview data, to written form. They are also asked to put their experiences and personal histories into writing. Those with more literacy can take the lead in cooperative writing activities, while not excluding students with less literacy. The Level 2 reading and writing activities can accommodate learners at different points in the literacy continuum, helping to form a community of learners in the classroom.

Two approaches to the teaching of reading are currently prominent: a skills-based model and a strategy-based model. In a skills-based model, the learner is asked to focus on pieces of language, for example, first sounds, then words, then phrases. Phonics-based instruction, such as decoding, is a skills-based model for teaching reading. In a strategy-based model, the focus is on both comprehension and production. Whole language is a strategy-based model. *LifePrints* draws on a whole language model, with reading, writing, and oral language being mutually supportive components of a communications system that focuses on meaning. Literacy that focuses on meaning gives adult learners new ways to understand and to control and participate in the new environments in which they find themselves. It also enables them to tap into their background knowledge and to express something from their past.

While *LifePrints* adopts whole language strategies, some phonics instruction may be of value. English does use an alphabet, which means there is a sound-symbol correspondence, and phonics may help learners visualize the written form of words they have already acquired orally. The important point to remember is that all skills must be a part of, not separate from, meaningful communication. The following section describes in more detail *LifePrints* activities that develop reading and writing, as well as listening and speaking, through a focus on meaning.

VI

Features of Student Book 2 Lessons

1. The Setting and the Characters

The units in *Lifeprints* reflect the lives of real adults doing real tasks in a community. Level 2 is set in the Los Angeles metropolitan area. In the first unit we meet Tony Martino, an Italian immigrant who is the owner and chef at Pizza Time, a small restaurant in a typical Los Angeles strip mall. We also meet Kim Lee from Korea, a waitress in the restaurant, her husband Joon, and Isabel Santos, a Salvadorean woman who is the restaurant's cashier. The other major setting in Level 2 is Seacoast Industries, where Joon works. We interact with his co-workers and their families. They include Monroe Bonner, an African-American machine operator; Olga Kovacs, a Hungarian refugee who is the receptionist in the Personnel Office; and Ramón Fernández from Mexico, Joon's supervisor.

2. First and Last Pages

The first page of every lesson is a full-page visual that introduces a main theme. It also taps into previous knowledge and experience, and into the vocabulary learners might already possess. By asking questions such as "What do you see?" "Where do you think they are?" "Was it like that in your country?" "What's going on?" and "What are they thinking?" the teacher elicits or provides vocabulary, gives learners a chance to answer and ask questions about a visual stimulus, helps learners to explore what they already know, and "hooks" them into the lesson. At this point, the teacher will want to write the vocabulary on the board and/or prepare a set of word and picture flash cards that can be used throughout the lesson.

The last page of every lesson gives learners a chance to make the connection between new information and language they have learned in a given unit, what they already knew, and their life beyond the classroom. They are asked to use and stretch their reading and writing skills by doing something authentic with language: completing a form, taking notes, writing notes, writing about their own experiences, following and giving written directions, and so on. The last page also gives learners a chance to review vocabulary, connect it with what they have learned, and extend it to new situations outside of class.

Between the first and last pages, a variety of language presentations and exercises introduce and give practice in listening, speaking, reading, and writing holistically, that is, as interacting parts of a complete system. There is no set pattern. Authentic language situations often call for one skill more than another. For instance, a visit to a doctor's office, as in Unit 8, elicits listening and speaking practice primarily, while participating in a citizenship class, as in Unit 10, requires more reading. The flow of Level 2 follows the situation and the language needed to cope in that situation. In general, though, learners are asked to reflect on their individual experiences and to express their opinions. Particularly in Think and Talk about It exercises, learners are asked not only to describe but also to comment on situations from their frames of reference. They are also asked to use critical thinking skills to analyze, compare, classify, predict, and hypothesize about a given situation. Sometimes they are asked to justify their answers. Learning and practicing the language related to these skills is a major focus of Level 2.

3. Activity and Exercise Types

The Student Book contains various exercise and activity types, including question-answer, matching, charts and graphs, identification, interview, fill-in, labeling, and Venn diagrams. Activities or exercises are also suggested in the Teacher's Edition for each page—for example, using graphic organizers such as semantic webs and Venn diagrams; doing a Total Physical Response (TPR) activity; using a substitution drill; playing games; role play; and creating a story. The following are short step-by-step instructions for many of the exercises and activities that appear either in the Student Book or in the Teacher's Edition. Instructions for many other activities that are used in Level 2 are presented in Teacher's Edition 1 and are not repeated here: Total Physical Response (TPR), Listen and Do, Chain Drills, Structured Interviews, Substitution Drills, Paired Exercises, Role Play, Language Experience Approach (LEA) Stories, Dialogue Journals, and Strip Stories. Instructions that are self-evident, as for matching and question-answer activities, are of course not included.

Listening/Speaking Activities

Until recently, listening was considered the passive skill and speaking the active skill in aural/oral communication. We now see that good language learners are active participants in the listening process, not just passive recipients. Level 2 listening activities, in which learners must respond with action or demonstrate comprehension, help learners start developing strategies for active listening. They are also effective lead-ins to the Level 2 speaking activities.

- **Semantic Webbing**

  Semantic webbing is a form of graphic organizing in which learners and teacher work together to make connections between ideas they group together and the vocabulary inherent in those ideas. Besides being an excellent whole-class warm-up activity, semantic webbing builds vocabulary by asking learners for information and language they already possess and linking that information and language with new vocabulary. Moreover, learners can use the webs throughout the unit for both oral and written work. An example of a semantic web appears below.

Steps for Using Semantic Webbing

1. In the center of the board, write a word or phrase referring to the topic of the unit. Be sure learners understand the word by asking them for an explanation, description, or examples.

2. Ask learners for related vocabulary, trying to elicit the unit's key words. Organize the words into categories, as in the example on page 13.
3. Have learners copy the web in their notebooks. Keep a copy for class use.
4. Refer to the web during the unit, adding vocabulary where appropriate.

Variation

Semantic webs also lend themselves to small-group activities, with the same stimulus being used by each group. Then the whole class can compare the webs for similarities and differences, and come up with a composite web.

- **Venn Diagrams**

  The Venn Diagram is another graphic organizer that can help learners store and categorize new information. Venn diagrams are good for comparing and contrasting.

  ### Steps for Using Venn Diagrams
  1. Tell the class that you are going to put the information you are discussing into three categories: same/different/either-or. You designate the topic headings, such as jobs that can be performed only during the day (e.g., gardener); jobs that can be done only at night (e.g., night watchman); and jobs that can be done at any time (e.g., factory worker). See below for another example using a different topic.
  2. Elicit learners' contributions to each of the categories. As they give you the information, write their "same" answers on the left side of the board; their "different" answers on the right side, and their "either-or" answers in the middle.
  3. Draw two intersecting circles around the lists so that the "either-or" column appears in the intersection. Have learners copy the diagram in their notebooks. Keep a copy for class use.
  4. Refer to the diagram during the unit, adding to it when appropriate.

Venn Diagram

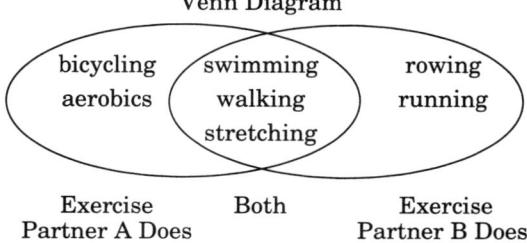

Exercise Partner A Does   Both   Exercise Partner B Does

Variation

Venn diagrams can also be used with parts of speech, for example, words that are verbs, nouns, or both.

- **Time Lines**

  Time lines are graphic organizers that allow learners to sequence and display events chronologically. They give meaningful practice with tenses, most commonly in the past and present, but also can be used to extend events into the future. Time lines are good devices to use with such functions as sequencing, hypothesizing, and cause and effect.

  ### Steps for Using Time Lines
  1. Draw either a horizontal or a vertical line on the board. Write time markers appropriate to the topic at each end of the line, e.g., year, time of day, last week, yesterday.
  2. Elicit information from learners, such as "When did you work in the bicycle factory?" "When did you leave Korea?" and "In what year did you come to Los Angeles?" As learners respond, mark points on the time line, writing information on one side of the line and the date, time, etc., on the other side. Information can be of a personal, historical, or hypothetical nature.
  3. Have learners copy the time line in their notebooks. Keep a copy for class use during the unit.

  ### Variations

  Make a time line from information collected through a guided interview about a learner's work history or an oral report on a diet and exercise plan that learners give to the class. Have learners make individual time lines from listening activities, e.g., stories you read them or directions or information. A flowchart is another variation of a time line. Instead of events in time, it shows progression, sequencing, and cause and effect related to an event or process.

- **Continuous Stories**

  In continuous stories, one utterance builds on another, so learners have to listen carefully to what has just been said. Continuous stories are good motivators for students to be creative with language and to express thoughts and feelings. They can be started with either an oral or a visual stimulus.

Steps for Using Continuous Stories

1. Have learners look at one of the illustrations in their book or some other picture. Have one group (or you yourself) give the first line of a story that relates to the picture.
2. Have the next group give the second line, and so on, until you or the learners declare the story finished.
3. Have volunteers try to remember and retell the entire story in order.

Variations

You can start a continuous story without an illustration by giving the first line of a story with which the class is familiar. You can also use a game format, allowing each group a certain amount of time to give its line of the story. If they respond with an appropriate next line, the group wins one point. There can be a five-point bonus for retelling the story correctly. The group with the most points wins. Another variation is to give each group a short amount of time to change the ending to the story. See how many "resolutions" the class can develop, and have them vote on the best ending.

- **Information Gaps**

These are pair or small-group task activities in which each learner or group has some crucial information that the partner or other group members do not, and together they must complete a task. These are excellent communicative activities, because the task cannot be accomplished without asking and answering questions. The emphasis here should be on task completion, or the acquisition of information that learners can use in some way, not just on exchange of information for the sake of random question-and-answer practice.

Steps for Using Information Gaps

1. Inform the pairs or groups about the task or objective. For instance, they have to locate all the stores in a shopping mall.
2. Give each pair or group different, incomplete information for the task. For the task above, give each learner a different, incomplete map of the mall.
3. Tell learners that they cannot show their information (map) to anyone, but must ask and answer questions, e.g., "Where is the department store?" When their partner or a group member responds, they fill in their maps (or worksheets) with the missing information.
4. When learners think they have all the information, they compare their maps (or other product) with each other. If they have asked the right questions, and have understood and recorded the answers correctly, their completed versions should be identical.

Variations

Give one learner a simple picture and have him or her describe it to a partner or small group. The other learners must re-create the picture. The closer the re-creation is to the original, the better the language task was performed and received. This is a good activity for mixed pairs or groups in which one learner has more productive language than the other(s). For another variation, give paired learners partial and different information on a chart and ask them to complete their charts by asking and answering questions without looking at their partner's paper.

Reading/Writing Activities

After learners go through the initial process of learning to read, they then read to learn or to do. Along the way they also learn to write, and the writing in turn helps them to read. As literate persons, they will read for information, meaning, directions, and/or pleasure.

- **Learner-Produced Picture Books: A Class Library Project**

It is very important for ESL learners to realize that they can write in English, as well as read. Having learners produce books that then become part of the class library can help accomplish this. Learners might produce books that go with the topics of the units (for example, Working in My Native Country, Getting Medical Help in My Native Country, Thoughts about Becoming a Citizen, and Folktales from My Native Country).

Steps for Using Learner-Produced Books

1. Distribute or have learners bring in "picture" magazines such as *National Geographic* or *Life*, as well as mail-order catalogs and the like, which can be cut up.
2. Have each learner find a picture of interest, clip it, and mount it on a sheet of paper.
3. Ask learners to write something about the picture on another sheet of paper. Provide help as necessary.
4. Correct what the learners write to make it comprehensible; that is, do not necessarily

correct every mistake, but enough so the message is clear.

5. Have learners produce clear, neat, corrected copies of what they wrote.
6. Repeat this activity throughout the course. Near the end, have learners assemble their pictures and written work into books for the class library.

Variations

Have learners develop a cultural resource library. Ask them to find pictures or bring in photographs from their native countries and then to write about those countries and about the visuals in particular. You might have learners write and illustrate folktales from their native countries. Developing books can also be a group project, with a learner at a higher level of language and literacy acting as the group leader.

- **Process Writing**

  Anyone learning how to write, and along the way becoming a better reader, must be given the opportunity to write freely. As with oral language, the focus needs to be on communication and on the development of ideas, but in this case by means of the written word. Good writers produce many drafts before they consider their work final. Learners need to have the same opportunity and to have feedback from both their peers and their teacher. At Level 2 learners are beginning to generate new language, both orally and in writing. So as not to get discouraged by the struggle to put their thoughts on paper, it is important for learners at this level to realize that writing is a process, even for native speakers of English, and that while the final product is important, so is the process.

  ### Steps for Using Process Writing

  1. Use the Student Book writing exercises or choose another topic. Group discussions are helpful in identifying potential topics.
  2. Write ideas related to the topic on the board, perhaps using a semantic web (see page 13). This *prewriting* activity helps learners to focus and recall vocabulary.
  3. Have learners write freely for a few minutes. This is the *drafting* part of the process. Encourage low-literate learners to draw a picture or to simulate writing as best they can.
  4. In pairs or small groups, have learners *share*, *read*, and *discuss* their drafts. At this time, circulate among the groups. You may provide other questions for learners to consider in their writing and help them expand or elaborate on what they have written. For learners who are new to literacy, you (or a peer) can help them put pictures into words or form their letters more precisely. However, at this stage the focus should be on content.
  5. Have learners *redraft* and *revise*, focusing specifically on the purpose of their writing and on their audience.
  6. Have learners *edit* their work for a final version, paying attention to form or whatever portions of the mechanics of writing they are capable of handling. At this writing proficiency level, it is acceptable for the teacher to function as editor. You can change spelling and punctuation for and/or with the learners.
  7. Have those learners who wish to do so read their work to the entire class, display it prominently where other learners can read it, or publish a class anthology. This final *publishing* step is important, because it establishes each learner as an author.

- **Round-Robin Writing**

  This is a written version of Continuous Stories, described on page 14. The basic idea is to get learners to read what someone else has written, and then add to it, so that the information or story flows in a logical manner. This is an excellent way to elicit not only creative writing but also written directions or instructions where sequencing is important.

  ### Steps for Using Round-Robin Writing

  1. Have learners look at one of the illustrations in their books or at some other picture. Ask individuals (or pairs) to write a sentence or more about the picture. The same or different pictures can be used.
  2. Collect the writing (and picture, if necessary) and pass it on to another learner or pair.
  3. Have the second learner or pair read what the first has written and then add to the writing. Continue this process three or four times.
  4. Have the last individual or partner read the story or information to the whole group.

Variations

Place large sheets of newsprint around the room. Using a picture or oral stimulus, ask groups of learners to start a story or other written information and then to continue clockwise, adding to the next newsprint sheet. Continue until each group has written on every sheet. The last group reads the story aloud. In another variation, learners can each, in turn, respond in writing to a pre-specified set of questions. When completed, this guided writing activity can form a story or a description of something.

This is by no means an exhaustive list of exercises and activities. You will find that, as you use them, some will be more comfortable to you and your learners than others. You will also find yourself inventing your own variations.

4. Structures

In *LifePrints,* grammar is a discovery process in which learners are exposed to and use structures in context in the thematic units and then, in Units 6 and 12, focus specifically on a portion of the grammar they have used in the preceding five units. Not all the structures presented in the thematic units are emphasized and practiced in *Discovering Patterns* (Units 6 and 12). Those that are selected are structures that learners should be able to use actively. If you feel that your learners need or want practice with other structures, you can of course add exercises. At Level 2, learners should be ready for some overt grammar practice. If you feel that some of your learners are not ready, you can skip Units 6 and 12 and focus on their special needs. Learners will be practicing structures throughout the text, and you may want to point to some patterns as you go through the units. The Index of Structures on page 192 indicates where structures are recycled through the thematic units. In Level 2 the emphasis should be on communication over accuracy, on function over form.

The exercises in the *Discovering Patterns* units of Level 2 are not only contextualized but are as visual as possible, with the illustrations adding to meaning. You can extend and vary these exercises with transformation drills, that is, by asking learners to change utterances from one grammatical form to another. For instance, you can ask learners to add tag questions to statements, or to change direct speech into reported speech. The Teacher's Resource File also includes activities that focus on grammar. Do not expect the learners to have control over grammar at this stage. We can look at grammatical control as a continuum, from no control at one end, to the control of a native speaker on the other end. Learners at the lowest end of Level 2 will have some control of very basic grammar. Some learners will have more control, but still be very inconsistent. Your students are likely to be at different points on this continuum throughout Level 2. (See the Student Performance Levels, pages 20–21.)

5. Vocabulary

Vocabulary is best taught in context, as part of communicative listening, speaking, reading, and writing activities. Isolated lists of vocabulary items that learners memorize do not lead to meaningful use. New words and phrases become internalized to the point where learners will use them in new situations after multiple opportunities for use. Vocabulary-building and internalizing activities include semantic webbing, matching words to pictures, labeling, TPR, and other types of exercises that require following directions. To elicit known vocabulary at the beginning of a unit, use illustrations and realia, with such prompt questions as "What is this called?" "What are they doing?" "Where are they?" "Do you know another word for that?" and "Is it a (object) or a (object)?"

As learners progress through the units, recycle vocabulary from previous lessons and help them start recognizing synonyms and antonyms. Keep on display in the room semantic webs and lists that learners have made, checking off vocabulary that they seem to have mastered. This gives beginning learners a powerful tool for seeing how much they have learned. Prompt learners to use new vocabulary in LEA stories and to read those stories several times as you go through the units. As learners gain more and more vocabulary, have them see what familiar words they can identify within new words. There are many ways to exploit each activity for its potential to reinforce vocabulary.

6. Culture

Language and culture are integrally bound, so learning a new language means understanding a new culture. Culture is the institutions and shared behavior patterns of a society. But it is also the values, attitudes, and beliefs that underlie the institutions and behaviors. How we think about family is culture-bound. So is our attitude toward work, gender roles, competition, and medicine. All these factors are touched upon in Student Book 2. From the beginning units, learners are asked to reflect upon their experiences in the United States in terms of what things were like or how they did things in their native countries. You as the teacher are the guide in helping learners understand cross-cultural situations. Start from learners' native cultures to help them explore their new one. Both you and the other learners in the class can learn much.

7. Pronunciation

There are few overt pronunciation exercises at Level 2 of *LifePrints*. Like grammar, pronunciation deals with form, not function. Teachers can devise listening/speaking activities (using minimal pairs *[pat/bat]*, for example) to practice sound discrimination or production for situations where pronunciation gets in the way of meaning or where students appear to be having trouble. The following are examples of meaningful pronunciation practice for Level 2.

- You may want to point out intonation patterns and have learners practice them, particularly when it comes to the difference between questions and statements.

- You may want learners to recognize two- versus three-syllable words, particularly in sentences or longer discourse. You can also have them mark the stressed syllables.

- You may want to have learners identify and write the contracted forms they hear in a given conversation or reading. Sometimes you may want them to write a full form that they hear as a contracted form, and sometimes you may want them to convert a contracted form they hear to the full form.

- You may want learners to listen for and identify the plurals of regular nouns they hear in a given conversation or reading.

- Similarly, you may want learners to listen for and identify the past tense forms of regular verbs (/d/, /t/, or /id/) as heard in context.

In providing examples of natural speech, the audiotapes are good models of pronunciation. In general, attention is better devoted to fostering communication than to working on pronunciation.

VII

Testing and Assessment

Testing is a part of teaching, and while no formal end-of-unit tests are included in *LifePrints*, you should use performance-based techniques to see that learners have progressed in the outlined objectives. Checklists are an easy way of showing progress over time. The summary pages for each unit in the Teacher's Edition can be used as checklists. Additional items on an *aural/oral checklist* might include: uses level-appropriate words/phrases to respond verbally to spoken language; uses extended speech to respond verbally to spoken language; initiates conversation; has increasing control of grammar; and participates in small group/paired activities. A *reading checklist* might include: recognizes appropriate sight words; responds to comprehension questions; recognizes words in context; shows evidence of skimming; shows evidence of scanning; can read LEA story aloud; and can retell story. For *writing*, portfolios that include learner writing over time can indicate progress by displaying a range of writing tasks, as well as growth in vocabulary, fluency, and mechanics of writing. At this level, it is more important for learners to be able to perform, to show you what they can do with language, than to pass formal tests.

In addition to checklists, learner-generated learning logs can be a form of self-assessment. Learners can keep separate pages in their notebooks labeled: Things I Learned This Month; Things I Find Easy in English; Things I Find Hard in English; Things I Would Like to Be Able to Do in English. Learners should make an entry on one or more pages every week. Every three months or so, go over the logs with learners, showing them how much they have learned and noting their ambitions so that, whenever possible, you can individualize instruction.

VIII

Classroom Management

Level 2 of *LifePrints* is more heterogeneous than either of the other levels since it encompasses students who still rely mainly on learned phrases, as well as those who are truly generating language. Some of you will also teach in open entry/open exit situations. Others will have impossibly large classes with learners both below and above Level 2. *LifePrints* strongly emphasizes pair and small-group work. While pairings and groupings will not solve all classroom management problems, they offer many advantages. When the entire class is actively engaged in pair or small-group work, everyone is communicating. For a learner who is uncomfortable speaking in front of the entire class, for instance, pair work offers an audience of one. Small-group work allows that same learner to contribute what he or she can, relying on others to both add and stimulate.

Pairings are of three types: random, voluntary, and assigned. It is a good idea to vary pairings so learners get to work with different members of the class. *Random pairs* are generally formed by asking two learners who are sitting next to each other to work together. Random pairs can work together for active listening practice, conversation, completing various exercises, cooperative writing, and reviewing each other's work. When learners form *voluntary pairs*, they are likely to gravitate toward a classmate with whom they feel comfortable. Often this is someone who speaks their native language, so expect to hear some non-English conversation in the classroom. You should use voluntary pairs when the task is such that English must be produced, as in the preparation of dialogues to present to the class, the creation and ordering of strip stories, and interviews outside of class that require interaction with native speakers of English. *Assigned pairs* are usually based on proficiency levels. If you pair learners with similar abilities, they can work together at the same pace on various activities or they can correct each other's exercises. At other times, assigning partners of different levels is helpful, because the more advanced learners who are also in the process of language learning can quietly help the less advanced. Both learners benefit. The less advanced are generally not threatened, and the more advanced gain valuable practice and self-esteem. It should be noted that this type of informal peer tutoring is the normal practice in many educational situations around the world. It is part of many cultures for one learner to help another.

In moving from pair work to small-group work, you will be much more involved in forming the groups. Heterogeneous assigned groups usually stay together to complete a task, and if they are working well together, they may remain together for the entire unit. Groups of four to eight work well for cooperative learning tasks. With the groups, specify roles that are required. There needs to be a leader to organize the group, to keep it on track, and to see that everyone participates; a recorder to write down the results of the group; and a reporter to report to the class. These roles can be assigned by you or self-assigned by the group. For a group to be heterogeneous, literacy level comes into play, especially for the role of recorder.

In managing a pair or group activity, you will find that your role changes. First, in your lesson planning you will need to create reasons for the two or more learners to cooperate. Much of that has already been done for you in *LifePrints*. Second, you will need to move around the classroom, paying attention to what each pair or group is doing, rather than orchestrating from up front. Third, for assessment purposes, you will need to focus on what each learner in the pair or group is doing so you can provide appropriate feedback and evaluation.

Most of the exercises and activities geared to pairs and small groups can easily be converted into *one-to-one situations*. Wherever the ■ icon appears in this Teacher's Edition, you will find a suggestion for adapting group and pair work to a one-to-one exercise. In working with one learner, the tutor plays several roles: those of teacher, facilitator, *and* fellow learner. Classroom management per se is not a problem, but varying the learning situation is. The burden for performing must be shared by the tutor and the learner. If learners feel they must be talking all the time, their affective filters will be high. If teachers feel they must be in charge all the time, they will tire quickly. By doing exercises and conversation activities together—provided that learners have their own listening, reading, and writing time during the tutoring session—learners and tutors will set a comfortable learning/teaching pace.

In going through this Teacher's Edition as you teach the units, note on the TE pages or in a notebook what worked and what didn't work, and why. This will help you in teaching with *LifePrints* later on. Good luck to you and your learners.

Allene Guss Grognet
JoAnn (Jodi) Crandall

Note: *In the following pages, italicized sentences generally indicate suggested questions and other language for the teacher to use. Sentences in regular type (usually in parentheses) generally indicate responses and other language that learners can be expected to produce.*

Student Performance Levels

	GENERAL LANGUAGE ABILITY	LISTENING COMPREHENSION	ORAL COMMUNICATION	BEST SCORE	CASAS SCORE
0	**BOOK ONE** **No ability whatsoever.**	**No ability whatsoever.**	**No ability whatsoever.**	0–8	N.A.
I	• Functions **minimally, if at all,** in English. • Can handle only **very routine entry-level** jobs that do not require oral communication, and in which all tasks can be **easily demonstrated.**	• Understands only a few **isolated words,** and **extremely simple learned** phrases (What's your name?).	• Vocabulary limited to a few **isolated words.** • **No control** of grammar.	9–15	165–185
II	**BOOK TWO** • Functions in a **very limited way** in situations related to **immediate needs.** • Can handle only **routine entry-level** jobs that do not require oral communication, and in which all tasks can be **easily demonstrated.**	• Understands a **limited number** of very **simple learned** phrases, spoken slowly with frequent repetitions.	• Expresses a **limited number** of **immediate** survival needs using **very simple learned phrases.** • Asks and responds to very simple learned questions. • **Some control** of **very basic** grammar.	16–28	186–190
III	• Functions **with some difficulty** in situations related to **immediate needs.** • Can handle **routine entry-level** jobs that involve only the **most basic oral communication,** and in which all tasks can be **demonstrated.**	• Understands **simple learned** phrases, spoken slowly with **frequent repetitions.**	• Expresses **immediate** survival needs using **simple learned** phrases. • Asks and responds to simple learned questions. • **Some control** of **very basic** grammar.	29–41	191–196
IV	• Can satisfy **basic survival** needs and a few **very routine social** demands. • Can handle **entry-level** jobs that involve **some simple oral** communication, but in which tasks can also be **demonstrated.**	• Understands **simple learned** phrases easily, and **some** simple **new** phrases containing familiar vocabulary, spoken **slowly with frequent repetitions.**	• Expresses **basic survival** needs, including asking and responding to related questions, using both **learned** and **a few new phrases.** • Participates in basic conversations in **very routine social** situations (e.g., greeting, inviting). • Speaks with **hesitation** and frequent pauses. • **Some control** of **basic** grammar.	42–50	197–205

	GENERAL LANGUAGE ABILITY	LISTENING COMPREHENSION	ORAL COMMUNICATION	BEST SCORE	CASAS SCORE
V	**BOOK THREE** • Can satisfy **basic survival** needs and **some limited social** demands. • Can handle **jobs and job training** that involve following **simple oral and very basic written** instructions but in which most tasks can also be **demonstrated**.	• Understands **learned** phrases easily and **short new** phrases containing familiar vocabulary spoken slowly with **repetition**. • Has **limited** ability to understand on the telephone.	• Functions independently in most **face-to-face basic survival** situations but needs **some help**. • Asks and responds to direct questions on familiar and some unfamiliar subjects. • Still relies on **learned** phrases but also uses **new** phrases (i.e., speaks with **some creativity**) but with **hesitation** and pauses. • Communicates on the phone to express a **limited** number of **survival** needs, but with **some difficulty**. • Participates in basic conversations in a **limited number** of **social** situations. • Can occasionally clarify general meaning by simple rewording. • Increasing, but inconsistent, control of **basic** grammar.	51–57	206–210
VI	• Can satisfy **most survival needs** and **limited social** demands. • Can handle **jobs and job training** that involve following **simple oral and written** instructions and diagrams.	• Understands **conversations** containing some **unfamiliar** vocabulary on many **everyday** subjects, with a need for **repetition, rewording, or slower speech**. • Has **some** ability to understand without **face-to-face** contact (e.g., on the telephone, TV).	• Functions **independently** in most survival situations, but needs **some help**. • Relies less on learned phrases; speaks with **creativity**, but with **hesitation**. • Communicates on the **phone** on **familiar** subjects, but with **some difficulty**. • Participates with **some confidence** in **social** situations when addressed **directly**. • Can sometimes **clarify** general meaning by **rewording**. • **Control** of **basic grammar** evident, but **inconsistent**; may attempt to use more difficult grammar but with almost no control.	58–64	211–216

Information taken from the Mainstream English Language Training (MELT) Project, of the U.S. Department of Health and Human Services.

Scope and Sequence

NOTE: Items with a bullet (•) are *introduced* in Level 2. It is assumed that learners are familiar with all other functions and structures. All functions and structures may be recycled throughout the book.

UNITS	FUNCTIONS (• *introduce*)	STRUCTURES (• *introduce*)	CULTURE	LIFE TASKS
Preliminary Lessons	Expressing greetings; introducing oneself/others; giving/getting personal information; asking for clarification	*Wh-* questions; present tense; past tense; present continuous tense	Greetings and introductions in the U.S.	Responding to personal information sight words; self-evaluating language needs
1. Getting a Job	Asking/answering questions; expressing ability; expressing likes/dislikes	Modal: *can*; *wh-* questions; past tense; • *Have you . . . ?*; • *used to* + verb	Ways of finding a job; how to dress and act at an interview; equal employment opportunity	Identifying personal goals; reading job notices; interviewing for a job; filling out forms
2. On the Job	Requesting assistance; following directions; • understanding safety requirements; asking for clarification; • making small talk; • giving reasons/explanations	Positive/negative imperatives; sequence words; modal: *can*; present continuous tense; past tense	Safety rules; written and unwritten company rules; relationships with co-workers and supervisors; place of small talk	Performing on the job; using the telephone; talking to co-workers; understanding written communications in the workplace
3. Making Choices about Money	Giving reasons/explanations; • asking for/giving advice; • dealing with numbers (budgets, costs); comparing/contrasting	• Comparative adjectives; • modals: *would, could, should*; adverbs of frequency; • negative questions; • *if/then* statements; modals: *can/can't* (possibility); intensifiers: *too, very*	Alternative forms of payment: cash, credit cards, checks; advertising and sales; shopping in the U.S.	Shopping; budgeting; applying for credit; making choices about payment options; figuring costs
4. Driving a Car	Expressing needs; • expressing intention; following directions; • reporting past events; describing problems	Past tense; imperatives; • conjunctions: *but*; • past continuous tense; prepositions of place/direction	How and when to report accidents; traffic rules in the U.S.	Getting a license; traffic tickets; reading graphs; completing forms
5. Having a Good Time	Expressing preferences/pleasure; describing events/objects; comparing/contrasting; • inviting; • accepting/declining invitations	• Tag questions; • demonstratives: *these, those*; • *while* clauses; descriptive adjectives; • future tense: *going to*; past tense	Vacations and recreational activities; U.S. holidays; leisure in the U.S. and in native countries; seasons	Choosing leisure-time activities; participating in sports; planning for recreation; getting information

UNITS	FUNCTIONS (• introduce)	STRUCTURES (• introduce)	CULTURE	LIFE TASKS
6. Discovering Patterns				
7. Wash and Wear	Comparing/contrasting; asking for information; expressing needs; expressing preferences; following directions	Verbs: regular past tense; verbs: irregular past tense; verbs: past continuous tense; adjectives: comparative; modals: *can, could, would, should* Comparative adjectives; • future tense: *will*; imperatives	U.S. department stores and discount stores; sales and discounts; U.S. sizes	Buying clothing; caring for clothing; examining the cost of clothing
8. What the Doctor Said	Reporting; following directions; clarifying; • interrupting; sequencing; • identifying causes; describing symptoms	*Wh-* questions; past tense; adverbs of frequency; imperatives; sequence words	Medications; prenatal care; health care; preventive medicine; diet and nutrition; causes of and treatments for stress	Talking to a doctor; following medical directions; completing a medical history
9. Going to School	• Expressing concern; • expressing agreement/ disagreement; asking for clarification; describing problems; reporting successes	• Modals: *must, may; if/then* statements; future tense: *will*	Expectations of children in U.S. schools: behavior, attitudes; special school programs; grade levels of U.S. schools; adult education in the U.S.	Understanding the U.S. school system; understanding expectations of students; understanding parental rights and responsibilities; talking to a child's teacher; reading a class schedule and course descriptions
10. Becoming a Citizen	Reporting; • persuading; expressing agreement/disagreement; clarifying	Past tense vs. past continuous tense; • reported speech with *that; wh-* questions; modals: *can, should, must;* tag questions	U.S. history and government; civic duties	Learning about U.S. history and government; understanding civic duties; becoming familiar with the immigration categories and citizenship requirements
11. Getting Used to a New Land	Reporting past events; • expressing surprise; comparing/contrasting; expressing emotions; • expressing embarrassment	• Adverbs of time; adverbs of frequency; prepositions of place; descriptive adjectives; • *when* clauses	Customs in the U.S. and in other countries; stereotypes; American immigrant groups; male and female roles in different countries	Expressing feelings about being a newcomer to the U.S.; understanding and describing multiculturalism in the U.S.; different countries; dealing with embarrassing moments
12. Discovering Patterns		Verbs: future—*going to* and *will; if/then* clauses; verb + infinitive and verb + *-ing;* reported speech with *that;* tag questions		

Preliminary Lessons

Summary

The two preliminary lessons are designed to welcome learners to the classroom environment and to provide review or practice with the basic English skills taught in *LifePrints* Level 1. The activities can be adapted for one or two class periods. These lessons give the teacher time to assess learners' strengths and weaknesses in verbal expression, vocabulary, structures, and written skills. If learners have a great deal of difficulty with the preliminary lessons, it may indicate that the learners are inappropriately placed at Level 2 in this series.

Objectives

Functions
- Expressing greetings
- Introducing oneself and others
- Giving and getting personal information
- Asking for clarification

Life Tasks
- Responding to personal information sight words
- Self-evaluating language needs

Structures
- *Wh-* questions
- present tense
- past tense
- present continuous tense

Culture
- Greetings and introductions in the United States

Vocabulary

Key words:

address	name
clothing	native country
date	(numbers 1–100)
date of birth	people
food	places
health	shopping
job	Social Security number
language	telephone
(letters A–Z)	

Related words:

banana	now
bread	nurse
chicken	pants
clinic	post office
coat	rice
cook	school
drugstore	secretary
eggs	shirt
every day	shoes
farmer	sometimes
hat	supermarket
hospital	sweater
last week	teacher
mechanic	yesterday
milk	

Preliminary Lesson A

Purpose: To give practice in giving and getting personal information; to assess listening, speaking, reading, and writing skills

Teacher Preparation and Materials

1. Map of the world; pushpins
2. Copies of the chart used for Presentation #4
3. Index cards with personal information words: *name, address, telephone, Social Security number, date, date of birth;* tape
4. Copies of a personal information form that asks for name, address, telephone, Social Security number, date of birth
5. Multiple sets of index cards with words: *supermarket, hospital, post office, clinic, school, drugstore, shoes, hat, pants, sweater, coat, shirt, banana, milk, chicken, eggs, bread, rice, teacher, secretary, farmer, cook, nurse, mechanic*
6. Large sheet of paper; tape *(Expansion/Extension)*
7. Alphabet cards *(Expansion/Extension)*
8. Deck of cards *(Expansion/Extension)*

Presentation

1. Point to a world map and place a pushpin on the city/state where you live now and another pin where you are from originally. Introduce yourself to the group. Say *My name is . . . ; I'm from . . . ; I live in . . . ; I came here in . . .* Have learners introduce themselves and place pins on their respective countries on the map.

2. On the board, write the titles *Mr., Miss, Ms.,* and *Mrs.* Model the following sentences using your full name and preferred name. For example: *My name is Mrs. Barbara Robbins Smith. Please call me Barb/Barbara/Mrs. Smith.* Have learners follow the model with their own full names and preferred names. As a follow-up, ask learners to spell their names aloud for others to write on the board.

3. Practice questions and answers about languages and work. Model a question and answer, then ask a learner. After the learner answers, have him or her ask the next person in the chain. FOR EXAMPLE: *What languages do you speak? (I speak English and Chinese.) What did you do in your country? (I was a . . .)*

4. On the board, make a chart:

Name	Native Country	Job	Languages

   With a volunteer, model asking questions and recording the information on the chart. Model use of clarification questions. Ask *What's your name? (How do you spell it?) Where are you from? What did you do (in . . .)? (Could you repeat that?) What languages do you speak?*

   Give each learner a copy of the chart. Learners can interview four people and record the information on the chart. Encourage learners to ask for clarification as necessary. Walk around and listen. Make sure learners do not pass their charts around during the exercise, so you can assess learners' listening skills, pronunciation, and writing skills.

   As a group, review the results. Point to various learners and ask questions in the third person. Have others answer, using the information on their charts. FOR EXAMPLE: *What's his/her name? Where is he/she from? What languages does he/she speak? What did he/she do in . . . ?*

   ■ In a one-to-one teaching situation, have the learner interview some friends and neighbors. Then have the learner report his or her findings, using the third person.

5. On the board, write the following personal information:

Peter Liska	(current date in numbers)
329 Western Ave.	
Somerville, MA 02140	(617) 543-1297
194-33-6686	4/2/51

   Ask questions about the personal information. FOR EXAMPLE: *What's his name? What's Peter's address? What's his telephone number? What's his birthdate?*

   Distribute the personal information word cards and have learners tape them next to the corresponding information on the board. Ask learners for their personal information. *What's your address? What's your Social Security number?* and so on.

   Distribute copies of the personal information form and have learners fill them out with their own information.

6. On the board, write the following category headings: *People, Places, Clothing, Food.* Ask questions to elicit words that belong in the

PRELIMINARY LESSONS • 25

categories. FOR EXAMPLE: *What did you do in your native country?* (I was a student. I was a tailor.) *Where did you work?* (in an office) *Where did you study?* (in my house/at school) Write the content words under the appropriate heading. Then shuffle the sets of content word cards and give a set to each pair or small group. Have learners work together to arrange word cards by categories. Have volunteers copy the words under the headings on the board while others check their work. Have the pairs or groups add three additional words to the category lists.

Expansion/Extension

- Have learners say their names and something they like that begins with the same first letter as their name. Then ask learners to introduce themselves and all the learners preceding them in the activity. (FOR EXAMPLE: My name is Raymond. I like running. His name is Raymond. He likes running. My name is Stella. I like snow.) Learners should be encouraged to help those who cannot remember.

- Together make a list of ways to ask for clarification. Write them on large sheets of paper to hang in the room for reference. Some expressions to include might be *How do you spell that? Would you please repeat that? I'm sorry. I don't understand. Could you speak more slowly?*

- Have learners make a list of words that correspond with letters of the alphabet.

- Learners can practice spelling their names, using the words. (FOR EXAMPLE: My name is Danh. That's *D* as in *David*, *A* as in *apple*, *N* as in *Nancy*, *H* as in *hat*.)

- Learners can review letter names. Choose a topic, such as places, food, jobs, tools, sports, or clothing. Hold up various alphabet cards one at a time. Have learners identify the letter and say a word related to that topic. (FOR EXAMPLE: places—*B* bank, *T* Texas, *H* hospital; food—*P* potato, *E* egg, *L* lunch)

- Dictate spellings of other basic content words. Learners can write the words and then identify the appropriate category heading for the words. FOR EXAMPLE: *d-o-c-t-o-r* (Person); *a-p-p-l-e* (Food); *l-i-b-r-a-r-y* (Place).

- Have learners organize the content word cards into other categories and then have the rest of the group guess what the category heading should be. FOR EXAMPLE: *nurse, hospital, clinic, drugstore* (Health); *supermarket, banana, bread* (Shopping).

- Dictate telephone and Social Security numbers for learners to write. FOR EXAMPLE: *7-3-1, 5-5-2-2; 2-2-1, 4-6, 9-3-5-8.* Have learners identify which are telephone numbers and which are Social Security numbers.

- Practice numbers and basic arithmetic using a deck of cards. Give values to the picture cards. (ace = 15; jack, queen, king = 10) Learners can take two cards and add or multiply the numbers.

Preliminary Lesson B

Purpose: To introduce using a table of contents; to introduce self-evaluation of language needs

Teacher Preparation and Materials

1. Personal information word cards, used for Preliminary Lesson A
2. Index cards with the following: subjects— *My sister, My brother and I, My friend, The president,* and so on; verb phrases—*speak French, like to play soccer, visit neighbors, cooks dinner, goes shopping,* and so on; time expressions—*every day, yesterday, right now, last week, sometimes, every Saturday, two years ago, now,* and so on
3. Newspapers or magazines; scissors; folders *(Expansion/Extension)*

Presentation

1. Review personal information questions and answers. Have learners choose a word card and ask another learner the appropriate question.
2. Practice present, present continuous, and past tenses. On the board write three sentences, divided as follows:

My sister	works in an office	every day.
We	are studying English	right now.
Peng	worked in a hospital	two years ago.

Ask questions to emphasize the different verb

tenses, write the answers on the board, and circle or underline the verbs. FOR EXAMPLE: *What does my sister do? (She works in an office.) What are we doing now? (We are studying.) Where did Peng work? (He worked in a hospital.)*

Make three piles of word/phrase cards: one set of subjects (*My sister, My brother and I, My friend, The president,* etc.), one set of verb phrases (*speak French, like to play soccer, visit neighbors, cooks dinner, goes shopping,* etc.), and one set of time expressions (*every day, yesterday, right now, last week, sometimes, every Saturday, two years ago, now,* etc.). Demonstrate taking one card from each pile. Read the cards, then form a sentence with the words on the cards, using the correct verb tense. Then small groups or pairs of learners can draw cards from each pile and form sentences. Shuffle the piles of cards and have learners repeat the activity. Have learners write their sentences on the board.

3. Ask learners where or with whom they speak English. List the names of the places or people on the board. Be sure to include *job/work, school, clinic/doctor, stores, government offices.* For each of the places/people listed on the board, ask *Who do you talk to at work? at school? at the clinic? What do you talk about? Is it easy or difficult to talk to people there? What do you need to read or write there?* Write learners' responses on the board. Ask learners which places are the most important to them or where they need English the most. Ask which are less important to them.

4. Have learners turn to the table of contents in their books (pages 3–4). Give them time to look over the unit titles. Then ask *Which unit do you think is about work? Which unit is about stores? What page does the unit start on?* and so on. Give learners time to look through the book and share comments among themselves.

5. Have learners brainstorm goals for studying English. Use the following questions to guide the discussion: *Why do you want to study English? What do you want to be able to read or write? What do you want to be able to talk about in English? What is easy for you? reading? speaking? listening? What is difficult for you?* List learners' responses on the board. Have each learner choose two or three specific goals for their study of English from the list on the board. Have learners write their individual goals on the inside cover of their books or on separate sheets of paper. Encourage learners to review their goals periodically throughout the course and to assess their progress.

Expansion/Extension

- Use the subject, verb phrase, and time expression word cards to practice forming negative statements and interrogatives.
- Learners can look through newspapers and magazines for pictures, ads, or articles related to the Student Book units. Learners can cut them out, put them in folders, and make a file of supplementary materials to be used when studying the units.
- Learners can play a word game to review vocabulary for the categories on the board. Make a chart on the board for learners to copy on separate sheets of paper:

	L	E	A	R	N
School					
Work					
Health					
Shopping					

In pairs or small groups, have learners fill in words that they associate with the different categories, using the first letters *L,E,A,R,N.*

- Practice the present continuous tense, using the names of learners. Ask questions about people in the class and have others respond with the name of the correct person. FOR EXAMPLE: *Who's wearing a red blouse? (Anna's wearing a red blouse.) Who's looking at his book? (Gregor's looking at his book.)*
- Practice talking about past activities. Ask questions, such as *What did you do last weekend? Did you go anywhere yesterday? What did you do before class?*
- Have learners begin a daily writing journal. Give learners 5 to 10 minutes of class time to write about a topic of their choice. For learners that need more direction, write the beginnings of sentences on the board and have learners complete them. FOR EXAMPLE:

  I want to study English because . . .
  In America, it is easy/difficult for me to . . .
  In America, I like/don't like . . .
  In my native country, I like/don't like . . .

1 2 3 4 5 6 7 8 9 10 11 12 Summary
Getting a Job

Objectives

Functions
- Asking and answering questions
- Expressing ability
- Expressing likes and dislikes

Life Tasks
- Identifying personal goals
- Reading job notices
- Interviewing for a job
- Filling out forms

Structures
- Modal: *can*
- *Wh-* questions
- Past tense
- *Have you . . . ?*
- *Used to* + verb

Culture
- Ways of finding a job
- How to dress and act at an interview
- Equal opportunity employment

Vocabulary

Key words:

application	interview
bank teller	job
benefits	machine
cashier	manager
company	operator
computer	pay
cook	receptionist
delivery person	salary
driver	shift
experience	signature
hours	unemployed
housepainter	waiter
indoors	waitress

Related words:

apply	laid off
assistant	repaired
automated	résumé
availability	schedule
bilingual	sick days
business	supervisor
cash register	supplies
change	trainee
customers	training
employees	vacation
health plan	weekend

Looking for Work

Purpose: To introduce names of jobs and professions

Teacher Preparation and Materials
1. Pictures of people performing jobs and pictures of corresponding workplaces: cook, waiter/waitress—restaurant; cashier, delivery person—store; nurse, doctor—hospital; and so on
2. Audiotape for Level 2
3. Index cards with job titles: *cook, cashier, waiter/waitress, delivery person, factory worker, nurse, doctor, bank teller, mechanic, engineer,* and so on *(Expansion/Extension)*

Warm-up
1. Use pictures to review names of jobs and workplaces. Then hold up a picture and practice *Wh-* questions and answers. FOR EXAMPLE: *What is he? Where does she work? Who works in a restaurant?* Have learners practice asking *Wh-* questions.
2. Ask if learners have jobs. If so, find out what learners' jobs are, where they work, and how they found their jobs. Introduce *unemployed* or *not working* for those who do not work.
3. Have learners talk about past work experience. Ask if they worked in their native countries. What jobs did they have?

Presentation
1. Have learners turn to page 5. Identify the characters: Joon Lee, Kim Lee, Tony Martino, and Isabel Santos.
2. Ask questions about the picture to elicit known vocabulary. FOR EXAMPLE: *What do you see? Where are they?* Be sure to include in the discussion the occupations *cook, waitress, cashier*. Then give learners time to look at the pictures and share comments.
3. Review the present continuous tense by asking what the people in the picture are doing. Ask if everyone in the picture is working and elicit the word *unemployed* or appropriate phrases *(out of work, not working)*.

4. Read aloud the question at the bottom of the page. Tell learners to listen carefully to the conversation on the audiotape for the answer to this question. Play the audiotape and have learners summarize what they just heard. Replay the audiotape and ask specific questions. FOR EXAMPLE: *Who is talking? What are they talking about? Where is Joon looking to find a job?*

Expansion/Extension
- Put the job title cards in a pile face down. Have learners take turns picking cards and miming the jobs for others to guess.
- Discuss various places to look for job listings. Elicit names of places from learners. Make a list and have learners visit the locations and look for job postings. These locations might include local supermarkets, libraries, and employment and training offices.

More *Expansion/Extension* on page 40

What Do They Do?

Purpose: To introduce describing specific duties; to give practice with the simple present tense

Teacher Preparation and Materials
1. Map of the world
2. Pictures of job equipment: pots and pans, tray with dishes, computer (Expansion/Extension)
3. Copies of TRF Handout 1.3, *Job Description* (Expansion/Extension)

Warm-up
1. Make a chart on the board:

Name	Job	Duties
Tony	cook	make pizza
Isabel	cashier	use a cash register
I		

   Point to names and information and model sentences about jobs, using the simple present tense to describe job duties. FOR EXAMPLE: *His name is Tony. Tony is a cook. Tony makes pizza.* Point to the appropriate words on the chart as you say them. Model information about yourself. *I am a teacher. I teach English.* Once learners are familiar with the structures, point to various parts of the chart and have learners respond with complete sentences.

2. Use the same chart to practice questions and answers in the present tense. FOR EXAMPLE: *What is Tony's job? What does he do? What does Isabel do? Who makes pizza? Who uses a cash register? What is your job? What do you do?* Have learners answer in complete sentences. If necessary, give practice with pronunciation of the third-person singular *-s* at the end of the present tense verb.

Presentation
1. Have learners turn to page 6 and identify the characters. (Tony, Isabel, Kim, and Joon) Ask questions about the pictures to elicit known vocabulary. FOR EXAMPLE: *What is Tony doing? What is his job?*
2. Together, read about each of the characters. Help learners find the

What Do They Do?

Tony Martino is from Italy. He came to the United States 30 years ago. He makes pizzas and sandwiches.

- What do you call his job? **cook**
- What other things do you think he does? **Answers may vary.**

Isabel Santos is from El Salvador. She takes money from customers and makes change. She also uses a computer.

- What do you call her job? **cashier**
- What other things do you think she does? **Answers may vary.**

Kim Lee is from Korea. She serves meals to customers at the restaurant.

- What do you call her job? **waitress**
- What other things do you think she does? **Answers may vary.**

Joon Lee is Kim's husband. He is unemployed. He's looking for a job.

- Why do you think he is reading the newspaper? **Answers may vary.**

countries that are mentioned in the reading on the world map.

3. Ask questions about each of the characters, such as *Where is Tony from? How long ago did he come to the United States? What is his job? Who is a cashier? Who is married? What is Kim's job? Why do you think Joon wants to find a job right now?* Write key words on the board.

4. Together, read the questions following each paragraph and have learners answer them orally. They may also choose to write answers in their books.

Expansion/Extension
See **TRF HANDOUT 1.3**, *Job Description*

- Help learners write lists of job duties for their present and/or past jobs. Include job titles.
- Show pictures of equipment used in various jobs. Have learners identify the job(s) associated with each. (FOR EXAMPLE: hammer, nails, wood—carpenter, construction worker)

More *Expansion/Extension* on page 40

What Can You Do?

Purpose: To give practice with the modal *can;* to introduce discussion of abilities and skills

Teacher Preparation and Materials

1. Pictures of job equipment: machines, phone, computer, truck, and so on
2. Pictures illustrating action verbs: fix, paint, drive, and so on
3. Copies of TRF Handout 1.1, *Job Titles* (Expansion/Extension)

Warm-up

1. On the board write the names of the characters from the unit. Ask questions about their jobs and duties. FOR EXAMPLE: *Is Isabel a waitress or a cashier? Does she use a register or make pizza? Who is a cook? What does he do?*
2. Review learners' jobs and duties.
3. Show pictures of job equipment and pictures that illustrate corresponding action verbs. Model sentences about yourself and your abilities and skills. FOR EXAMPLE: *I can drive a car. I can use a computer. I can't fix machines. I can't drive a truck.* Have learners practice making statements about their own abilities and skills using *can* and *can't*.

Presentation

1. Have learners turn to page 7. Read the paragraphs aloud while learners follow along silently.
2. Ask questions about the characters. *Can Joon run machines? Can Isabel cook? Can Tony use computers? What can Joon do? What can Isabel do?*
3. Ask learners about their own abilities. List the responses on the board.
4. Have learners practice asking and answering *What can you do?* Ask them to use the abilities listed on the board as reference.
5. Have learners individually write things they can and can't do in the appropriate places on the chart. Then ask learners to interview others and to record responses on the chart. When they have finished, learners can report their findings to the class. They should use language like "Marie can type and speak French. She can't drive."
   ◖ In a one-to-one situation, have the learner first interview you, record the information, and then use that experience as a model for interviewing friends and family members. Discuss the completed chart during the next session.
6. Put learners in small groups and ask them to suggest appropriate jobs or job training for one another, based on skills and interests. Then learners can answer the questions in exercise B. ◖ In a one-to-one situation, you and the learner can discuss the same topics and make suggestions for each other.

Expansion/Extension

See **TRF HANDOUT 1.1**, *Job Titles*

More *Expansion/Extension* on page 40

Community Bulletin Board

Purpose: To introduce additional job titles and duties; to introduce Help Wanted ad abbreviations

Teacher Preparation and Materials

1. Pictures of jobs: housepainter, bank teller, machine operator, receptionist
2. Copies of Help Wanted ads
3. ▭ Audiotape for Level 2
4. Copies of TRF Handout 1.2, *Job Likes and Dislikes (Expansion/Extension)*
5. Copies of TRF Handout 1.4, *Work Wanted Notices (Expansion/Extension)*

Warm-up

1. On the board write several addresses. FOR EXAMPLE: *Mr. Thomas Ellis, 852 Endicott St., Apt. 17.* Have learners identify the abbreviations and what they stand for.
2. On the board write the days of the week. Ask learners for the abbreviations and write them next to the long forms.
3. Use pictures to review *housepainter, bank teller, machine operator,* and *receptionist.* If necessary, demonstrate the jobs by acting out the duties.
4. Distribute copies of Help Wanted ads. Point out the key words. (job title, workplace, and so on) Introduce the words *experience, pay,* and *benefits.* Ask questions to demonstrate the meaning of *experience.* Ask *Can you cook? Did you work as a cook?* Point out the difference between being able to do something and having done a particular type of work.
5. Make a list of different benefits, such as vacation, sick leave, and health insurance. Ask learners who work to describe their job benefits.

Presentation

1. Have learners turn to page 8. Ask them to identify the job in each ad, the address or phone number, and instructions about how to apply.

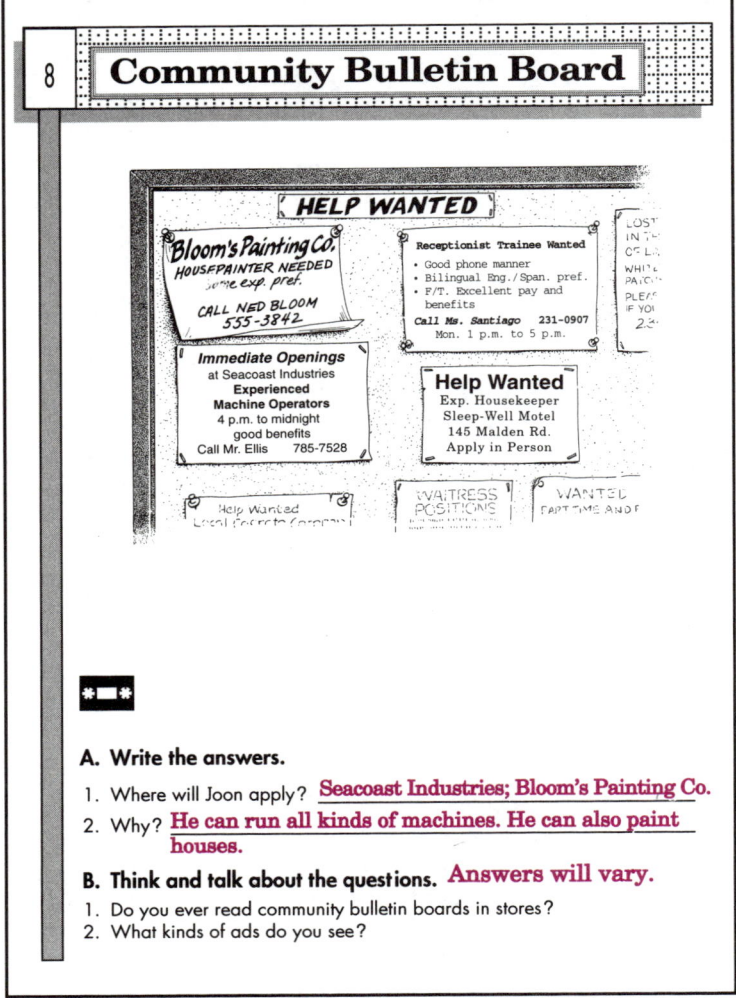

2. Together, read the ads aloud. Tell learners it is not necessary to understand every word. Help learners with any unfamiliar abbreviations or vocabulary. Ask what other information in the ads is important. (experience, hours, necessary skills)
3. Ask learners about the ads. FOR EXAMPLE: *Which ad looks interesting to you? Why? Which one do you think Joon might be interested in? Why?*
4. Read the questions in exercise A. Tell learners to listen carefully to the audiotape for the answer. ▭ Play the audiotape and have learners answer the questions in exercise A. ▭ Replay the audiotape so learners can check their work. Then ask specific questions. FOR EXAMPLE: *Where did Joon find the ads? Which jobs is he going to apply for?*
5. Have learners work with partners to answer the questions at the bottom of page 8.

Expansion/Extension on page 40

Joon's First Interview

Purpose: To give practice with the simple past tense; to introduce interviewing for a job

Teacher Preparation and Materials
1. Audiotape for Level 2
2. Copies of TRF Handout 1.6, *Recounting Past Work (Expansion/Extension)*

Warm-up
1. On the board make a chart to review the simple past tense. Describe any unfamiliar jobs. FOR EXAMPLE:

Name	Native Country	Job
Tomás	Mexico	mechanic
Lan	Vietnam	bank teller

   Point to names and use the past tense to model sentences about native countries, jobs, and job duties. Say *Tomás was a mechanic in Mexico. He fixed cars.* Continue with information about Lan and have learners repeat. Then point to various parts of the chart and have learners respond with the appropriate sentences.

2. Use the same chart to practice questions and answers in the past tense. Continue the chart to include information about learners. FOR EXAMPLE: *What was Tomás's job? What did he do? What did Lan do? What was your job? What did you do?* Ask learners to answer in complete sentences.

3. Talk about job interviews. Ask if anyone has had an interview. Have learners describe the jobs they applied for and what the interviews were like. Ask learners what kinds of questions are usually asked at job interviews. List their ideas on the board and discuss how to answer these questions.

Presentation
1. Have learners turn to page 9. Identify the character as Ned Bloom, the owner of a painting company. Ask questions about the picture to elicit known vocabulary. FOR EXAMPLE: *Where is this? Is it clean or messy?* Then give learners time to look at the picture and share comments among themselves.

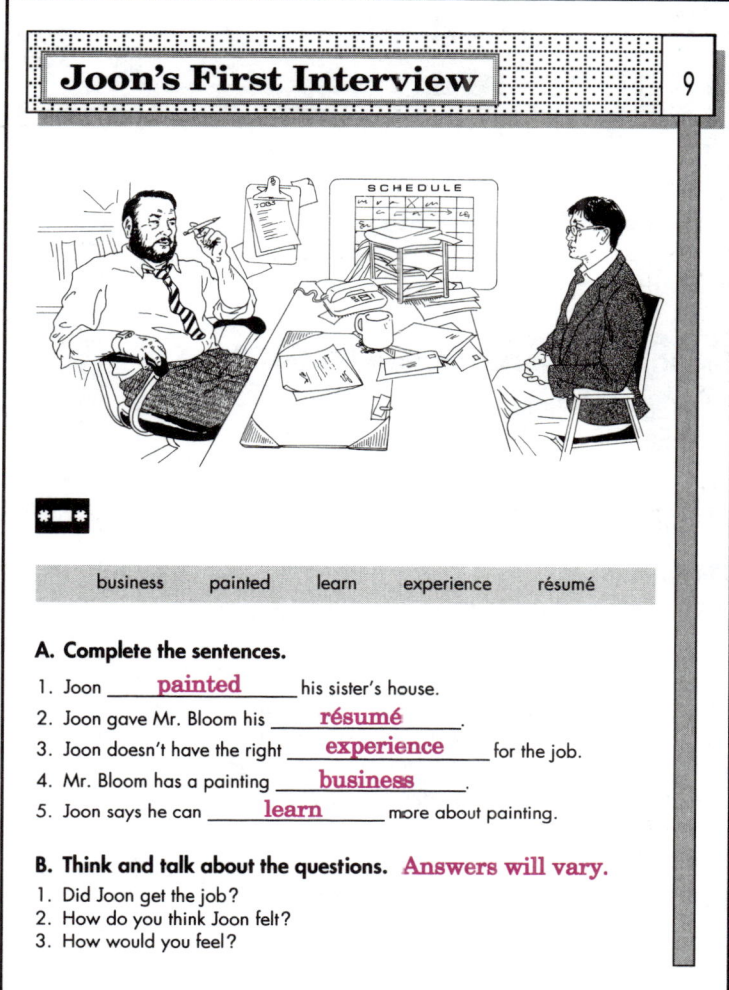

2. Read aloud the statements and words in exercise A. Tell learners to listen carefully to Joon's interview on the audiotape to help them complete the statements. Play the audiotape and have learners complete exercise A. Replay the audiotape so learners can check their work. Ask specific questions about the interview. FOR EXAMPLE: *What job is Joon applying for? Did he work as a painter? What did he paint?*

3. Follow up with discussion questions, such as *Do you think Joon really wants the job? Why or why not? Would you want the job? Why or why not?*

4. Have learners work in pairs to answer the questions in exercise B.

Expansion/Extension
See TRF HANDOUT 1.6, *Recounting Past Work*

- Have learners work in small groups to share experiences with job interviews. Tell each group to make a list of Do's and Don'ts for interviews. Discuss these ideas as a class.

More *Expansion/Extension* on page 41

Completing an Application

Purpose: To give practice in filling out forms; to introduce job application vocabulary

Teacher Preparation and Materials

1. Copies of job applications (Expansion/Extension)
2. Copies of TRF Handout 1.5, *Job Application* (Expansion/Extension)

Warm-up

1. Review personal information questions and common words found on applications. Write key words on the board. FOR EXAMPLE: *name, telephone number, Social Security number.* Ask random questions using the key words. FOR EXAMPLE: *What's your name? What's your Social Security number?* Point to the appropriate words to cue learners' responses.

2. Ask questions to elicit other information needed to complete an application. Ask a volunteer *What was your job in* (learner's native country)? *Where did you work? When did you work there?* If possible, elicit the name of the company, the job title, and years there. Write a simplified work experience chart on the board and fill in the volunteer's responses.

Company	Job	Years at Job
Regency Hotel	Cook	1984–1988

   Have learners write simple work experience charts about themselves.

3. Introduce *work shifts* and *work schedules.* FOR EXAMPLE: ask what time cooks usually work. (breakfast: 6 a.m.–2 p.m.; dinner: 4 p.m.–11 p.m.) Introduce standard shift times. (8 a.m.–4 p.m.; 4 p.m.–12 a.m.; 12 a.m.–8 a.m.) Have learners give advantages and disadvantages of working the various shifts.

4. Ask learners about their experiences with applications. Ask *Why do companies use applications? What types of questions are on them?*

Presentation

1. Have learners turn to page 10. Have them find the key words you listed on the board. Ask *Who filled out the application? Where is he applying for a job?*

2. Have learners use contextual clues to guess the meaning of other words. Ask what information follows the Availability section and how this might help learners understand the meaning of *availability.* Explain other words on the form as necessary.

3. Have learners fill out the form at the bottom of the page with their own work experience. If learners have not had jobs, ask if they have worked as volunteers, worked at home, or worked in refugee camps. Ask them to describe what they did, and to explain how this information may be included in the Work Experience section.

Expansion/Extension

See **TRF HANDOUT 1.5**, *Job Application*

More *Expansion/Extension* on page 41

Learning about the Company

Purpose: To give practice with the past tense; to introduce job-related vocabulary

Teacher Preparation and Materials
1. Pictures of workplaces such as restaurants, factories, hospitals, hotels, stores
2. Local yellow pages *(Expansion/Extension)*
3. Arrange for a small-business owner to visit the class. *(Expansion/Extension)*
4. Help Wanted ads *(Expansion/Extension)*

Warm-up
1. Review names of different types of workplaces. Show pictures and have learners identify the places. Write the names on the board as column headings (FOR EXAMPLE: Restaurants, Factories, Hospitals, Hotels, Stores). Ask learners for names of local companies that fit in the categories. Write their responses in the appropriate columns.

2. Choose a local business that most learners are familiar with and ask questions, such as *Where is it? What types of jobs are there? What does the company make/do? What kinds of machines do the workers use?*

3. Give learners practice in asking and answering questions, using the past and present tenses. Put the following chart on the board:

Joe's Fresh Fruit Market	
Opened 1960	Now
2 workers	10 workers
10 kinds of fruit	50 kinds of fruit/vegetables

Ask questions about the chart and have learners respond in complete sentences, using the appropriate tense. FOR EXAMPLE: *When did Joe's Fresh Fruit Market open? How many workers did the market have then? How many kinds of fruit did it have then? How many workers does it have now?*

Presentation
1. Have learners turn to page 11. Identify the character. (Joon)

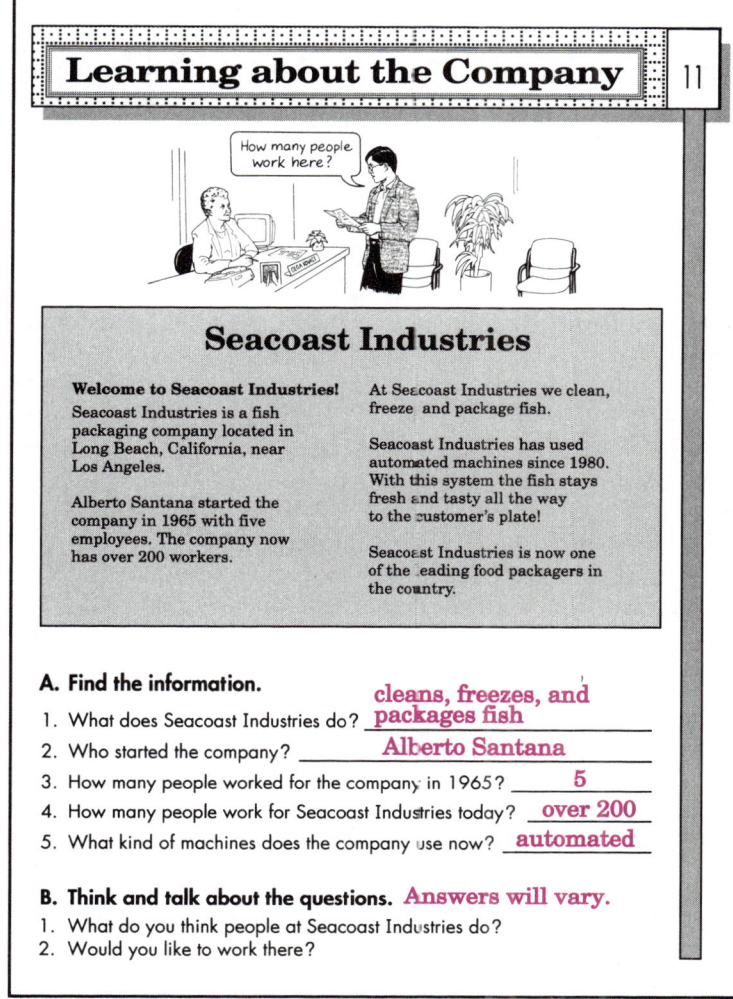

2. Ask questions about the picture to elicit known vocabulary. For example: *Where is Joon? What is the company's name? What do you think the company does?*

3. Read through the brochure with learners and have them circle key information (where the company is located, when it started, who started it, and what the company does). Tell learners that it is not necessary to understand every word in the brochure, but this key information will help them to learn a little about the company.

4. Have learners answer the questions in exercise A. Assist with any questions they have.

5. Put learners in small groups to answer the questions in exercise B.

Expansion/Extension
- Have learners work in groups to plan a business they would like to run. Have them choose the type of business, location, number of employees, equipment used, and the like. Have groups share their ideas with the class.

More *Expansion/Extension* on page 41

Joon's Second Interview

Purpose: To give practice with job interview questions and answers

Teacher Preparation and Materials
1. Audiotape for Level 2
2. Arrange for a guest interviewer to visit the class. *(Expansion/Extension)*

Warm-up
1. Use a chain drill to give learners practice with questions and answers about work experience. Provide examples, such as *Where did you work? When did you work there? What was your job?* In a one-to-one situation, take turns with the learner asking and answering similar questions.
2. Have learners look back at Joon's application on page 10. Have learners think of reasons why Joon might have left the two jobs he had in Korea. Introduce the phrase *laid off*. Ask learners to describe any experiences they have had with being laid off or to discuss any recent layoffs in local businesses.
3. Ask learners to think of other questions that an interviewer might ask Joon.

Presentation
1. Have learners turn to page 12. Ask questions about the picture to elicit known vocabulary. FOR EXAMPLE: *Where is this? How is it similar to the place where Joon had his first interview? How is it different?* Then give learners time to look at the picture and share comments among themselves.
2. Read aloud the sentences in exercise A. Tell learners to listen carefully to Joon's second interview on the audiotape to determine which sentences are true and which are false. Play the first part of the interview and tell learners to mark "True" or "False" for each sentence. Play the first part again for them to check their answers. Ask specific

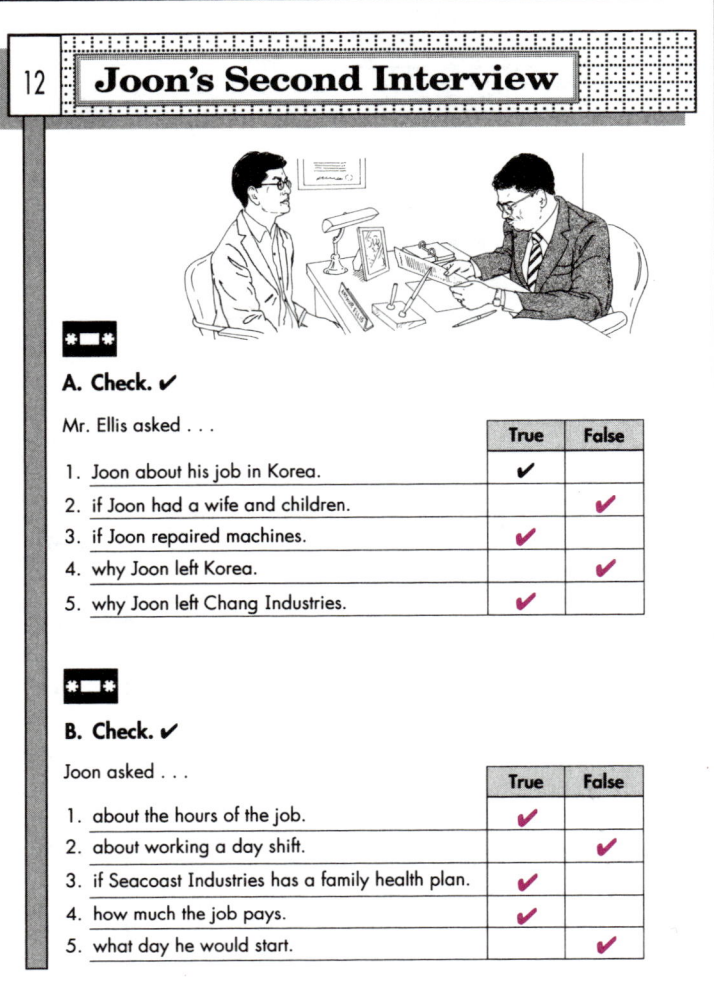

questions about the first part of the interview.
FOR EXAMPLE: *What did Joon operate in the factory? Did he repair machines? Did he work nights? Why did he leave his job?*

3. Listen to the second part of the interview and repeat the above procedure for exercise B. When learners have finished, list on the board topics that you might ask a potential employer about. (pay, benefits, different shifts available, overtime, job responsibilities, supervisor, etc.)

Expansion/Extension
- Play the audiotape again and have learners reword the sentences on page 12 into questions.
- Have learners work in pairs to role-play job interviews. Tell them to use the types of questions in Joon's recorded interview and the topics listed on the board. You may wish to model some questions with the class first. If possible, invite a guest interviewer to class to conduct mock job interviews.

More *Expansion/Extension* on page 41

Giving Answers

Purpose: To give practice in answering questions in an interview; to give practice with the past and present tenses

Teacher Preparation and Materials
1. Pictures of various workplaces, including an office
2. Blank index cards *(Expansion/Extension)*

Warm-up
1. Have learners practice personal questions and questions about work experiences in a chain drill. FOR EXAMPLE: *Where do you live now? When did you come to the United States? Where did you work? When did you work there? Why did you leave that job?* ◘ In a one-to-one situation, you and the learner take turns asking each other similar questions.
2. Show pictures of different workplaces and have learners identify the places. Introduce the structure *Have you ever . . . ?* Show a picture of or describe an office. Model the question and answer *Have you ever worked in an office? (Yes I have. No I haven't.)* Write this on the board for learners to use as a reference. Show pictures of different workplaces and ask similar questions. Have learners respond affirmatively or negatively according to their past work experiences.

Presentation
1. Have learners turn to page 13. Identify the characters as Mr. Ellis, from Seacoast Industries, and Emi Satoh, the woman he is interviewing.
2. Ask questions about the picture to elicit known vocabulary. FOR EXAMPLE: *Where is this? What is happening? What do you think they are saying?* Then give learners time to look at the picture and share comments among themselves.
3. Together, read aloud the questions and answers. Then have learners work in pairs, matching each question with an appropriate answer. When they are finished, partners can role-play the interview between Mr. Ellis and Emi Satoh.

Expansion/Extension
- Put learners in small groups to write several potential interview questions on separate index cards. Then have groups write answers to these questions on another set of cards. Groups can exchange sets of cards and practice matching the questions with the answers. Ask volunteers to role-play the interviews. ◘ In a one-to-one situation, write some interview questions and answers on index cards and have the learner match them. You may wish to have the learner prepare questions and answers too.
- Have learners work in pairs to write other questions and answers for the interview pictured on page 13.
- Develop a group LEA story about the woman in the interview. Include the information mentioned in the interview and ask learners to make up information to add to the story.

Asking Questions

Purpose: To give practice in asking questions in an interview

Teacher Preparation and Materials
1. Copies of the lists for the information-gap activity *(Expansion/Extension)*
2. Copies of TRF Handout 1.7, *Job Benefits* *(Expansion/Extension)*

Warm-up
1. Review the following terms: *vacation, sick time, salary, pay, hours*. On the board, show examples of each in a chart. Note for learners that the individual items on the chart do not necessarily go together.

Vacation	Sick Time
2 weeks/year	10 days/year
1 week/year	1 day/month

Hours	Salary/Pay
7 a.m.–3 p.m.	$4.50/hr.
8:30 a.m.–5 p.m.	$375/wk.

   Have learners add information to the chart based on their experiences.

2. On the board, write the question words *What? When? How much? How many?* Use the chart to review questions using these words. Point to and say *$4.50 an hour.* Then ask what question goes with it. Tell learners to respond with a complete question. Write questions on the board. Continue in this manner eliciting questions about the information on the chart.

Presentation
1. Have learners turn to page 14. Ask questions about the picture to elicit known vocabulary. FOR EXAMPLE: *What is happening? What questions do you think Mr. Ellis is asking?*
2. Read through the answers in exercise A. Read the question that has been written for number 1. Then have learners work with partners to write a question for each of the other answers. Suggest that they use the questions on the board as reference. When they are finished, ask

the pairs to role-play the interview with the questions they have written.

Expansion/Extension
See **TRF HANDOUT 1.7**, *Job Benefits*

- Have learners work in pairs. Distribute copies of the following lists for an information-gap activity:

A	B
1. vacation	3 p.m.–11 p.m.
2. salary	10 sick days a year
3. sick time	Mon., April 24, at 3:00 p.m.
4. hours	$325 a week
5. start date	2 weeks a year

  One learner in each pair gets list A and plays the role of a person interviewing for a job. The other learner in each pair gets list B and plays the role of interviewer. Learner A asks appropriate questions and records the information given by Learner B. Learner B records the key word(s) from the question next to the appropriate response. After the interview, have partners compare their lists.

Making the Connection

Purpose: To give practice in reading Help Wanted ads; to give practice with skills, functions, and vocabulary from Unit 1

Teacher Preparation and Materials
Copies of Help Wanted ads
(Expansion/Extension)

Warm-up
1. Have learners name several different kinds of jobs. Write their responses on the board. Then ask learners to look at the list and identify which jobs require a lot of experience and which require little experience. Have them also identify jobs that are done indoors/outdoors.

2. Write a sample Help Wanted ad on the board:

Help Wanted
Mechanic for a busy service station. Must have experience and own tools. Apply in person. Steve's Automotive, Lyndon Ave.

   Ask comprehension questions about the ad. *What kind of job is being advertised? Do you need experience? What else do you need? How do you apply?*

3. Review common abbreviations found in Help Wanted ads. Write some abbreviations on the board (FOR EXAMPLE: *Mon., exp.*) and have learners say the complete words.

4. Ask learners to describe training they have had for particular jobs. Explain that in many jobs, workers go through a training period to learn about the company policies or to learn how to use special equipment.

Presentation
1. Have learners turn to page 15. Read through the ads and have learners circle key information. Ask questions, such as *What jobs are listed? Which job offers training? Which jobs require experience?*

2. Read the directions for exercise A. Have learners work individually or with a partner to complete the chart.

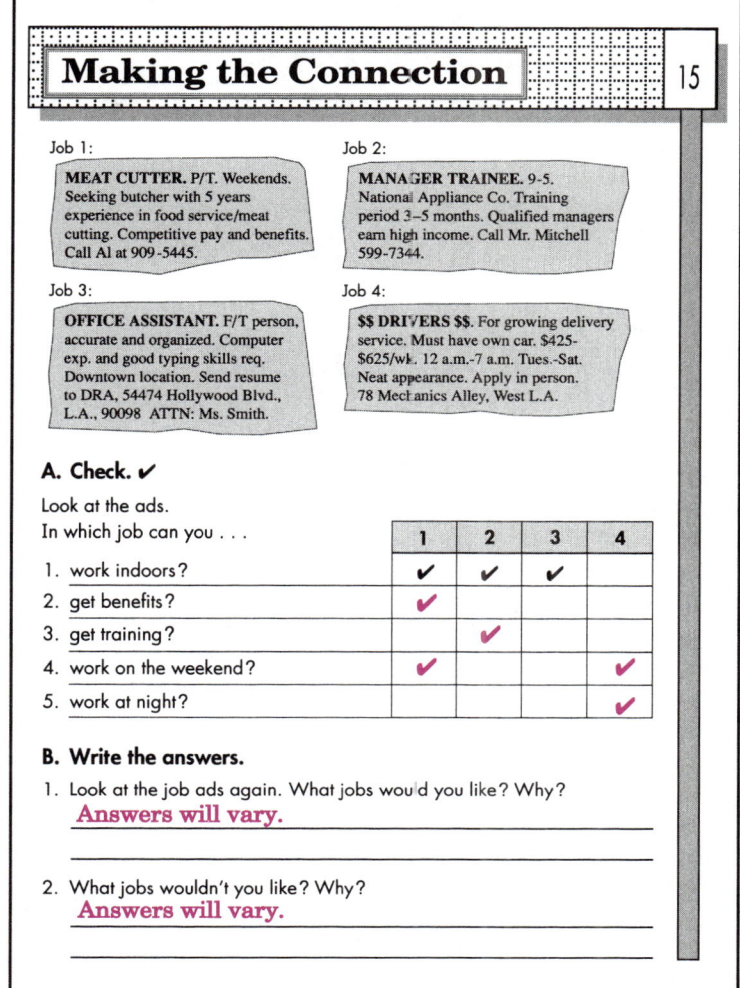

3. When they have finished, have learners discuss with their partners which jobs they might like. Have them give reasons for their choices. Then have learners write about their preferences in exercise B.

Expansion/Extension
- Distribute copies of Help Wanted ads and have learners find three ads for jobs they think might be interesting. Have learners rate the ads in order of preference. Ask volunteers to share their job choices and state reasons for these preferences.

- Have learners write a Help Wanted ad for a job they would like to have. Tell them to write the job title in big letters at the beginning of the ad. When they have finished, have the group alphabetize the ads and create their own Help Wanted page.

UNIT 1: Getting a Job
Expansion/Extension

Looking for Work
More *Expansion/Extension* for SB page 5

- Put the following chart on the board.

Name	Job(s) in Native Country	Job(s) in U.S.

  Have learners copy the chart, then interview each other about past and present jobs, and fill in the chart with the responses. When learners have finished, they can report their results back to the whole group. Summarize the data by tallying numbers of learners who held/hold similar jobs. ■ In a one-to-one situation, the learner can interview friends or family members and report the results during the next session.

- On the board, develop a Language Experience Approach (LEA) story about the picture and conversation on page 5. Learners can copy it into their notebooks.

- Assign the homework task of looking for Help Wanted ads in newspapers. Make a list of possible headings to look for in the newspaper or use the newspaper index to find the proper section. Some headings might be *Help Wanted, Employment, Classifieds*. During the next session ask learners to name some of the jobs they found in the ads.

What Do They Do?
More *Expansion/Extension* for SB page 6

- Ask learners to name different jobs and job duties. List them on the board. Have a volunteer think of a job. Other learners try to guess the job by asking *Yes/No* questions about its duties. (FOR EXAMPLE: Do you paint houses? Do you cook food? Do you serve meals?) Repeat the procedure with other volunteers.

- If appropriate, talk about job benefits such as health insurance, family leave, and paid vacations. Ask workers if their jobs offer any benefits and what they are. Have learners compare benefits in their native countries with those in the United States.

What Can You Do?
More *Expansion/Extension* for SB page 7

- Ask questions prompting learners to expand upon their abilities. FOR EXAMPLE: *Can you type?* (No, I can't, but I can use an adding machine. No, I can't, but I'm willing to learn.) *Can you take phone calls?* (Yes, I can. I can also work with numbers.)

- Have learners each tell one thing they would like to learn. Talk about how or where they can learn these things. Ask *Where can you get information about classes? Can you buy a book to study on your own? When can you study?*

- Ask learners to look at their lists of abilities and then to work with a partner, listing some jobs that use the various skills.

Community Bulletin Board
Expansion/Extension for SB page 8

See **TRF HANDOUT 1.2**, *Job Likes and Dislikes*
TRF HANDOUT 1.4, *Work Wanted Notices*

- Have learners rate the jobs on page 8 in order of preference. They put "1" next to the job they think is best, "2" next to their second choice, and so on. Compare results for all learners in a chart.

- Bring in newspapers and have learners look at the Help Wanted ads. Next they should select several different jobs they might be interested in and circle or underline the key words in each. (name of job, address or phone number to call, experience required, benefits, etc.) Learners can report to the class about the ads they found.

- Dictate days and times for learners to write in abbreviated form. FOR EXAMPLE: *(1) Please call Ed at 555-3345 on Friday after nine o'clock if interested. (2) Applications will be taken on Monday at ten o'clock.* Learners write "(1) Fri. 9:00; (2) Mon. 10:00."

- Have learners write a Help Wanted ad for a job they would like to have.

Joon's First Interview
More *Expansion/Extension* for SB page 9

- Discuss things to consider when deciding to take a job or not. (boss, type of work, hours, etc.)
- Review questions to ask for clarification. FOR EXAMPLE: *What did you say? Excuse me, would you mind repeating that?*
- Have learners practice pronunciation of past tense endings: /d/, /t/, /id/. Group regular verbs according to pronunciation used.

/d/	/t/	/id/
learned	cooked	painted
used	talked	needed
repaired	fixed	hated

Say other verbs from the unit and have learners choose the correct ending pronunciations.

Completing an Application
More *Expansion/Extension* for SB page 10

- Distribute copies of job applications. Have learners work in groups, comparing the types of information requested. Ask each group to make a list of synonyms used. Provide examples, such as *company—firm, employer; job—title, position*. Have the reporter in each group share the group's list with the class.
- Encourage learners to go to the personnel offices of local stores or businesses and to ask for job applications. They can practice filling in the applications.

Learning about the Company
More *Expansion/Extension* for SB page 11

- Write various categories of businesses on the board. (FOR EXAMPLE: *health-care businesses, department stores, supermarkets, manufacturers, restaurants, hotels*) Have learners work in groups, going through the local yellow pages for names of businesses that fit these categories. For each of the various categories, have the groups list types of jobs and equipment used.
- Invite a small-business owner to class to talk about his or her experiences with starting and operating a business.

Joon's Second Interview
More *Expansion/Extension* for SB page 12

- Develop LEA stories about learners' experiences with job interviews.
- Discuss questions that employers are not permitted to ask because they are considered discriminatory. These include questions about religion, political affiliation, marital status, children, and ethnic background. Talk about ways of handling these kinds of questions in an interview. Interviewees may choose to answer the questions, politely refuse to answer, or even threaten to report the incident. Discuss the possible outcomes from handling the situation each of these ways.
- Talk about various pay systems. Ask *What is the current minimum wage? What is the difference between hourly pay and a salaried position?* (paid a certain rate per hour versus paid a fixed amount per pay period) *How is overtime paid?* (for hours beyond 40 per week, one and a half times the regular hourly rate) *What types of jobs usually get paid tips or commissions?* (restaurant and sales jobs) *How are these usually figured?* (percentage of sales)
- Discuss health insurance plans. Ask how many workers in the class have health insurance plans through their employers. Have learners explain how their insurance plans work, who pays for them, and what they cover.

1 2 3 4 5 6 7 8 9 10 11 12 Summary
On the Job

Objectives

Functions
- Requesting assistance
- Following directions
- Understanding safety requirements
- Asking for clarification
- Making small talk
- Giving reasons and explanations

Life Tasks
- Performing on the job
- Using the telephone
- Talking to co-workers
- Understanding written communications in the workplace

Structures
- Positive and negative imperatives
- Sequence words
- Modal: *can*
- Present continuous tense
- Past tense

Culture
- Safety rules
- Written and unwritten company rules
- Relationships with co-workers and supervisors
- Small talk

Vocabulary

Key words:

absent	rear entrance
building	remove
caution	repairs
crew	rules
emergency exit	safety
factory	small talk
fired	supervisor
information	time card
machinery	time clock
memo	title
must	tools
office	total
packages	uniforms
pay period	visitors
personnel	weekly
problem	

Related words:

belt	punch in/out
boxing machine	push
co-workers	rack
(to) date	safety glasses
hard hat	sign
labeled	slot
lever	stack
load	stock
machine shop	switch
operate	turn on/off
operating	unlabeled

First Day on the Job

Purpose: To introduce job-site vocabulary; to give practice in requesting and giving assistance

Teacher Preparation and Materials

1. A sample floor plan with labels: office, telephone, employees' entrance, visitors' entrance, cafeteria, time clock, and bathrooms (drawn on the board)
2. Sample time card
3. Pictures of workers in uniforms (FOR EXAMPLE: doctor, nurse, police officer, mechanic, postal worker)

Warm-up

1. Tell learners to imagine that this is your first visit to the building where your class meets. You need directions and information. Ask questions such as *Where can I find the office? the supervisor? the entrance? the cafeteria? the telephone? the bathrooms? the ESL class?*
2. Read the floor-plan labels from the board with learners. Use the sample time card to explain what a time clock is. Then ask a volunteer to come to the front of the room and tell him or her *I'm at the employees' entrance. How do I get to the office?* After the volunteer has answered correctly, have other pairs of volunteers take turns asking for and giving directions from the floor plan.
3. Show learners pictures of workers in uniforms. Have learners describe what the people are wearing. Elicit/introduce the word *uniform*. Use the pictures to elicit the names of some jobs that require uniforms. Ask learners what kind of clothes they wear to work every day. Ask them to describe any uniforms or other special clothing they must wear to work.

Presentation

1. Have learners turn to page 16. Review the events of Unit 1, reminding the class that Joon just got a job at Seacoast Industries. Ask volunteers to tell what they remember about this company and about Joon's position.

First Day on the Job
What's going on?   **Answers may vary.**

2. Ask questions about the picture to elicit known vocabulary. FOR EXAMPLE: *What do you see? Where is Joon? Who do you think Joon is with? What are they doing?* Introduce Monroe Bonner, a worker at Seacoast Industries.
3. Read and discuss the question at the bottom of the page. Learners should understand that this is Joon's first day on the job. Have them talk about their own first days on the job or at school. Ask if learners found people to help them.
4. Have learners talk about some of the details in the scene. Point out the No Smoking and Personnel signs, asking learners what these signs mean. Ask *What is Monroe wearing? Why is he wearing a uniform? Why do people wear uniforms?*

Expansion/Extension

- Ask learners who have uniforms to bring them to class, to describe their jobs, and to explain why they need special clothing on the job.

More *Expansion/Extension* on page 54

UNIT 2 • 43

Before Starting Work

Purpose: To give practice in giving and receiving information, and in sequencing events

Teacher Preparation and Materials
None

Warm-up
1. Ask learners *Who answers the phone and greets visitors at a company?* (the receptionist)
2. On the board draw a semantic web with the word *Boss* in the middle. Ask learners to give different terms for *boss*. (*manager, supervisor, foreman, employer, owner, president,* etc.) Write the words on the board as part of the web. Discuss similarities/differences in the use of these terms.
3. Ask learners what usually happens on the first day of a job. Explain that new workers often fill out forms in the personnel office before starting a job. Depending on the job, they also get a uniform. Have volunteers describe what happened on the first day of their jobs. If possible, have volunteers describe the function of a personnel office.
4. Have learners watch you and remember what you do. Walk to your desk, sit down, open your book, and write something in it. Ask a volunteer to describe what you did. As the volunteer speaks, write on the board *First, I walked to my desk. Then, I sat down. Next, I opened my book. Finally, I wrote something in my book.* Read the sentences aloud with learners. Ask volunteers to do four things in a row and have others describe the sequence of actions using *first, then, next,* and *finally*.

Presentation
1. Have learners turn to page 17. Ask which characters they recognize. (Joon and Mr. Ellis) Have learners read the names of the other two characters and ask what jobs these characters have. (Olga Kovacs, receptionist; Ramón Fernández, supervisor)

2. Ask questions about the pictures to elicit known vocabulary and to practice the present continuous tense. FOR EXAMPLE: *Where is Joon at first? Who is he talking to? Then, where does he go? Who is Joon's supervisor?*
3. Read the questions at the bottom of the page. Put the class in small groups and ask them to discuss the answers to the questions. Afterward, have the reporter in each group share some of the group's ideas with the class. ◼ In a one-to-one situation, ask the learner to share his or her ideas about a first day at work.

Expansion/Extension
1. Divide the class into groups of four. Have members of each group take the parts of Joon, Olga, Mr. Ellis, and Mr. Fernández, and write a simple conversation, using the pictures as a guide. When they have finished, ask each group in turn to role-play its conversation in front of the class. ◼ In a one-to-one situation, choose any two of the characters and role-play a conversation between them with the learner.

More *Expansion/Extension* on page 54

Punching In

Purpose: To introduce on-the-job vocabulary; to give practice in filling out forms and in sequencing events

Teacher Preparation and Materials
1. Sample time cards
2. ▭ Audiotape for Level 2
3. Copies of TRF Handout 2.1, *Picture Strips* (Expansion/Extension)

Warm-up
1. Ask learners if they use time cards at work. If so, have a volunteer draw a sample time card on the board and explain how to use it. If not, distribute sample time cards or refer to the time card on page 18. Elicit/explain how and why companies use time cards.
2. On the board, write the title *Weekly Time Card*. Underneath in a column, write the headings that might be found on a time card, such as *Employee's Name, Job Title, Department (Dept.), Social Security Number, Pay Period Ending, Total Hours for Week, Signature*. Read through each category with learners and fill in the information about yourself. Then erase the information and repeat with one or two other volunteers.

Presentation
1. Have learners turn to page 18. Read aloud the title *Punching In*. Ask volunteers to explain when the term is used.
2. Ask *Where does the employee write information on the card? Where does the machine mark times and dates?* Ask questions about the time card to elicit known vocabulary. FOR EXAMPLE: *Whose card is this? What's his job? What's his Social Security number? When does he start work? When does he have dinner?*
3. Read the direction line and word choices at the bottom of the page. Tell learners to listen carefully to the audiotape for the order in which these steps should be done. ▭ Play the audiotape and then have learners write in the proper sequence

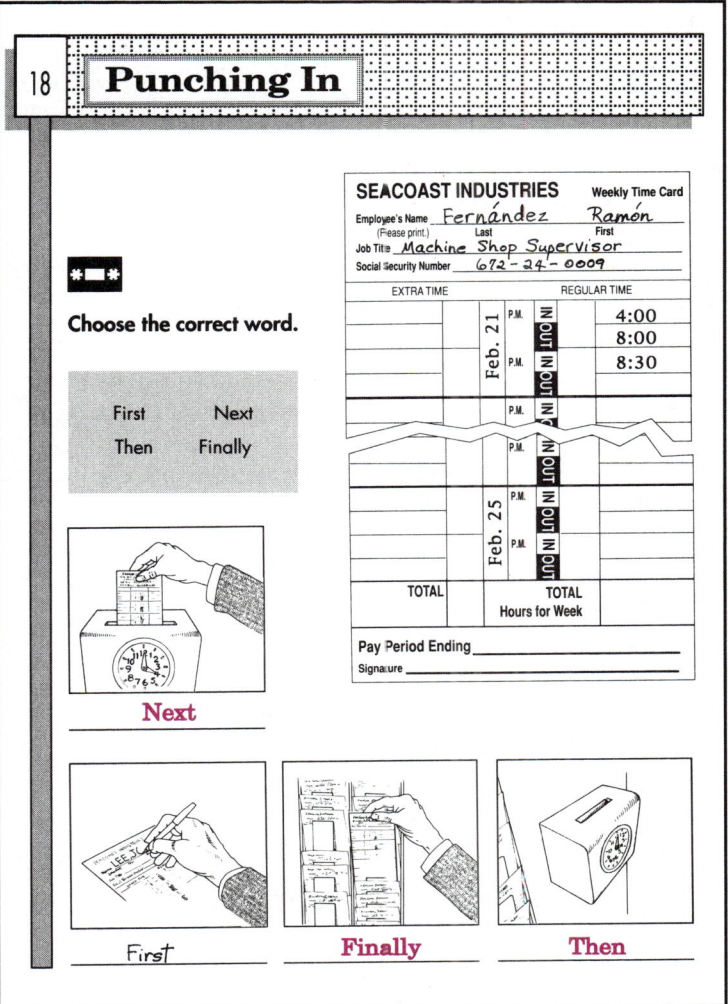

words. ▭ Replay the audiotape so learners can check their work and fill in missing information. When they are ready, ask volunteers to read the correct choices and to describe the pictures in sequence.

Expansion/Extension
See TRF HANDOUT 2.1, *Picture Strips*

- Distribute the sample time cards to learners. Have them fill out the cards for themselves. Then ask learners to exchange cards with a partner and to check that the information is properly placed on the cards.
- Ask a volunteer to come to the front of the class. Give a set of directions with four different actions in a row, such as *First, go to the board. Then, write your name on the board. Next, write your address. Finally, write your telephone number.* Ask other learner pairs to come to the front of the room to give and follow similar series of directions. Give them examples of actions, such as giving directions to move objects or furniture around the room or giving directions to write other personal information.

More *Expansion/Extension* on page 54

Rules at Work

Purpose: To introduce examples of information from an employee handbook; to introduce workplace rules

Teacher Preparation and Materials

1. Actual items or pictures of items on pages 19, 20, and 24: employee handbook, machinery, hard hat, safety glasses, tools
2. Copies of pages from a company or union handbook *(Expansion/Extension)*
3. Invite an industry employee, such as a foreman or a factory worker, to speak to the class. *(Expansion/Extension)*

Warm-up

1. Use pictures on pages 19, 20, and 24 or actual items to introduce new words: *employee handbook, tools, hard hat, safety glasses, machinery.* As you identify the different items, write the terms on the board. Ask learners where they would find items like these. Then have volunteers match pictures or items with the words on the board.
2. Ask volunteers for suggestions of things they must do every day at work or school. Ask *What can happen at work if you don't follow the rules?* (You can get hurt, get fired/lose your job, put other workers in danger.) Ask learners to name some school or class rules and to tell what will happen if they do not follow them.
3. Ask learners to identify different shifts at their workplace and to write the hours on the board, using *a.m.* and *p.m.*
4. Discuss with learners the importance of following safety rules. Have volunteers describe different safety rules from public places and workplaces. Ask them to explain why they think these rules should be followed. Draw a sign on the board that says *Caution* and ask learners where they might see a sign like this.

Presentation

1. Have learners turn to page 19. Ask *What is this page about? What are the two different categories on the handbook page?*

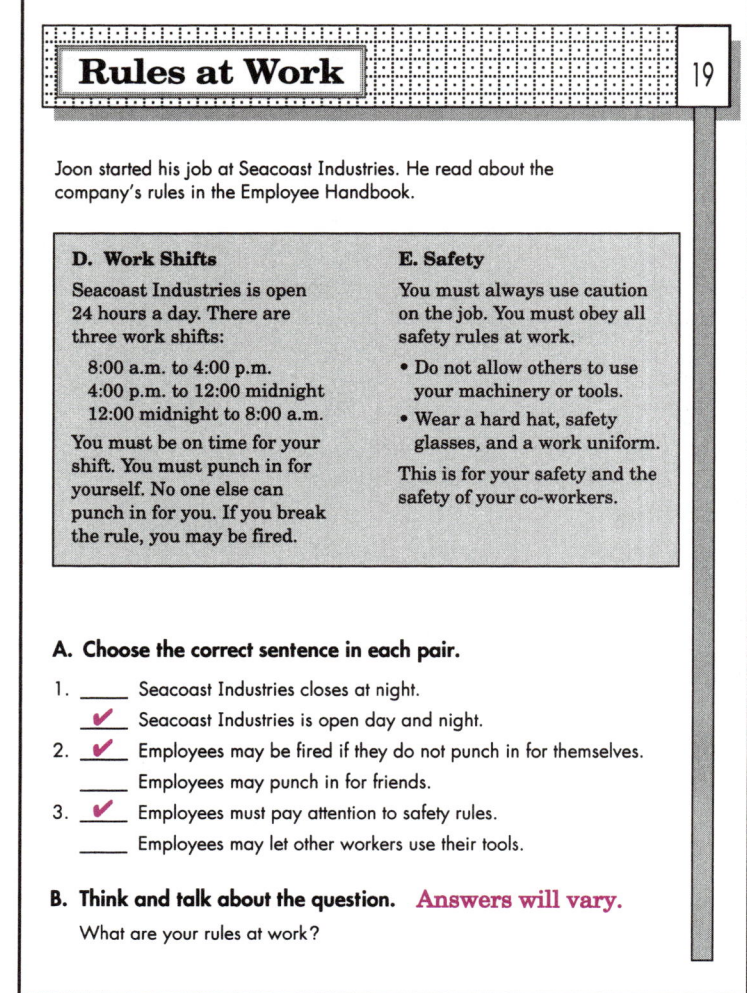

2. Have learners follow along silently as you read the page aloud or have them take turns reading in small groups. Allow advanced learners to read the page independently.
3. Direct learners to complete exercise A. Review the answers with them. Then put learners in small groups to discuss the question in exercise B. Ask the recorder in each group to write the group's responses. Then have the reporter in each group share some of the group's responses with the class. ◾ In a one-to-one situation, ask the learner to share his or her ideas with you.

Expansion/Extension

- Ask learners to bring in samples of handbooks and/or rules from their workplaces. Duplicate the examples and distribute them. Have learners work in small groups, reading and discussing them.
- Ask learners to think of other work-related rules they know. Have them work in pairs or small groups to make a list to share with the class. Discuss what learners think of these rules, what kinds of things can happen if they do not follow the rules, and if they have rules like these in their native countries.

Operating Machines

Purpose: To give practice in sequencing events and in following multistep directions; to give practice with positive and negative imperatives

Teacher Preparation and Materials
1. Address label; unlabeled mailing box
2. ▄▄ Audiotape for Level 2
3. Copies of TRF Handout 2.3, *Following Directions (Expansion/Extension)*

Warm-up
1. Use the pictures on page 20 to introduce terms such as *belt, switch, lever, load, packs, machine,* and *operating*. Show learners a mailing box. Tell them *This box is unlabeled.* Then attach the label and say *Now it's labeled. Joon's job is to operate the machine that puts labels on boxes.*
2. Use Total Physical Response (TPR) to practice imperatives. FOR EXAMPLE: *Remove your book from the desk. Put the book on the chair. Pretend to stack boxes on a shelf.* Point to a light switch and use imperatives to have a volunteer turn off and then turn on the light switch.

Presentation
1. Have learners turn to page 20. Ask questions about the picture to elicit known vocabulary. FOR EXAMPLE: *What's on the belt? How do you think the belt is operated? What is Joon doing? What is Ramón doing?* Ask learners to study the picture and then to describe what they think Joon's job is.
2. Read through the direction line and items in exercise A. Tell learners to listen carefully to the audiotape to find out how to operate the machine. ▄▄ Play the audiotape and have learners write the correct answers. ▄▄ Replay the audiotape so learners can check their work and fill in missing information. Ask specific questions. FOR EXAMPLE: *How does Joon start the machine? What does he do with unlabeled packs?*
3. Ask learners how Joon made sure he understood Ramón's directions. Tell them that repeating something in their own words is a very useful way to make sure they understand a set of directions.
4. Read the questions in exercise B. Then put the class in small groups to discuss the questions and to reach conclusions. Have the reporter in each group share some of the group's conclusions with the class. ▄ In a one-to-one situation, ask the learner to share and discuss his or her ideas with you.

Expansion/Extension
See **TRF HANDOUT 2.3,** *Following Directions*

- Put the class in pairs to create a set of directions on how to make or do something. This could be cooking rice, fixing a tire, or anything they are familiar with. Suggest that learners use the words *first, then, next,* and *finally*. Combine learner pairs to read their directions. Have listeners ask questions or repeat parts of the directions in their own words to ensure understanding.

More *Expansion/Extension* on page 54

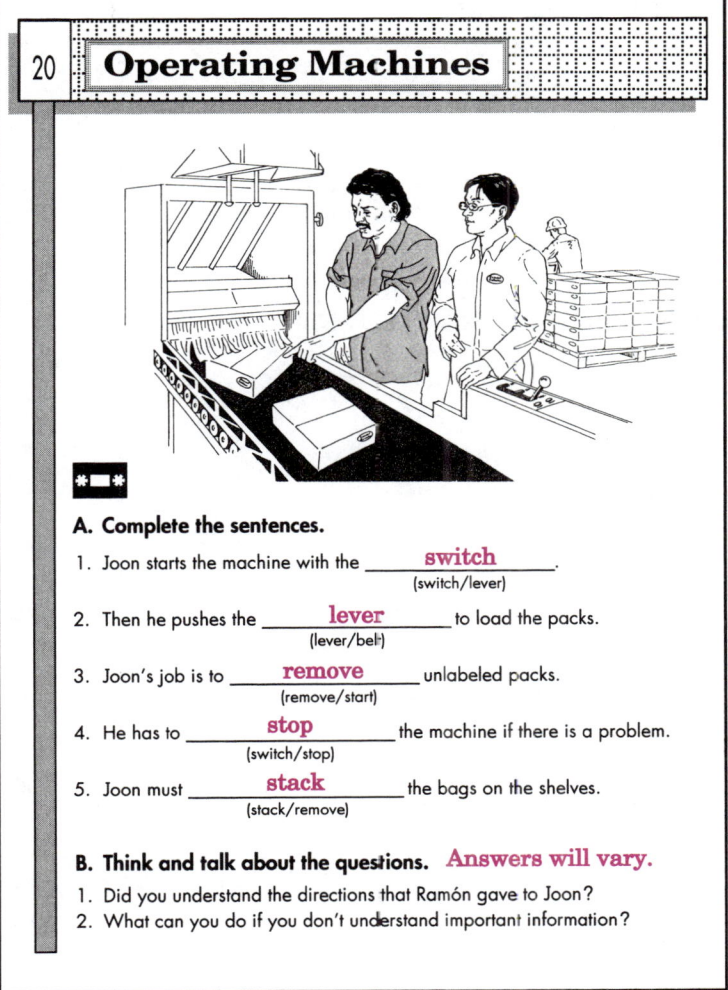

20 **Operating Machines**

A. Complete the sentences.
1. Joon starts the machine with the ___**switch**___. (switch/lever)
2. Then he pushes the ___**lever**___ to load the packs. (lever/belt)
3. Joon's job is to ___**remove**___ unlabeled packs. (remove/start)
4. He has to ___**stop**___ the machine if there is a problem. (switch/stop)
5. Joon must ___**stack**___ the bags on the shelves. (stack/remove)

B. Think and talk about the questions. **Answers will vary.**
1. Did you understand the directions that Ramón gave to Joon?
2. What can you do if you don't understand important information?

Calling In

Purpose: To give practice in using the telephone; to introduce how to give reasons/explanations for an absence from work; to give practice with *can/can't*

Teacher Preparation and Materials
Real or toy telephones

Warm-up
1. Ask learners to name different reasons for not going to work. Write the reasons on the board. Be sure to add explanations from page 21 if learners do not mention them.
2. Tell learners to listen as you model how to call in sick to work. Pick up the telephone and say *Hello, this is . . . . I have the flu. I won't be in today.* Have volunteers do this, using the reasons on the board.

Presentation
1. Have learners turn to page 21. Ask questions about the pictures to elicit known vocabulary. FOR EXAMPLE: *Who are the people in the first picture? Why are they on the phone? Why is the woman in her pajamas?*
2. Have learners look at the first picture in exercise A. Ask *What's the problem?* Tell learners to describe it in their own words, or to read the sentence aloud. Do the same for the second picture.
3. Have learners look at the first picture in exercise B. Ask *What's the problem?* Tell learners to describe it in their own words and then write the reason in their books. If necessary, write the reason on the board for learners to copy. Do the same for the second picture.
4. Pair the learners. Have them write a phone conversation based on one of the four problems pictured. Then ask learners to role-play their phone conversations in front of a small group or in front of the class. You may wish to have them use telephones.
5. Ask learners to think of two more reasons why someone might call in sick to work. Suggest that they think about their own

experiences. Tell learners to write these reasons in exercise C.

Expansion/Extension
- Have pairs of learners create a phone conversation based on the reasons in exercise C. Ask volunteers to role-play their conversations in front of the class. Set up the phones and position the "callers" at a distance, facing away from each other. Have them role-play their conversations in this way.
- Lead a discussion about attitudes toward missed work days in learners' native countries compared to attitudes in the United States. Ask questions, such as *What happened in your native country if you missed work or school? Did you have to call and give an excuse? What happens in the United States? What do you have to do?*

More *Expansion/Extension* on page 55

Absent from Work

Purpose: To give practice in using the telephone and in using polite conversation to give explanations; to give practice with *can/can't*

Teacher Preparation and Materials
1. Real or toy telephones
2. Audiotape for Level 2

Warm-up
1. Ask learners to listen as you pretend to make a phone call. Pick up the phone and say *Hello. Is this the school receptionist? Yes? This is . . . . Is the ESL supervisor available? She is? Good. I need to talk to her.* (pause) *Hello. This is . . . . Teresa Delgado, a student in my class, is absent today. She's sick. She can't take the ESL exam. Can she take it next week?* (pause) *Oh, good. Thanks. Bye.*

2. Ask comprehension questions. FOR EXAMPLE: *Who did I talk to first? Who did I want to talk to? Was that person available? How do you know? What was the problem? What do you think the supervisor said? How do you know?*

3. On the board, write the key words learners will be reading, such as *available* and *message*. Provide any necessary explanation.

Presentation
1. Have learners turn to page 22. Ask questions about the picture to elicit known vocabulary. FOR EXAMPLE: *Who's calling the office? Who's the receptionist? Why do you think Helen is calling?*

2. Tell learners to listen to the conversation on the audiotape to find out why Helen will not be in. Play the audiotape for learners, pointing out that three people take part in the conversation. Then have them answer the question in exercise A. Replay the audiotape so learners can check their work. Ask comprehension questions such as *Who answers the phone at Seacoast Industries? Who is sick? Why does Helen ask for Mr. Fernández?*

3. Have learners work in pairs to complete exercise B. Volunteers can use the phones to role-play their conversations in front of the class. Discuss the explanations presented in learners' conversations. Try to categorize the explanations. FOR EXAMPLE: *sickness, transportation problem, emergency*.

Expansion/Extension
- Put learners in pairs and ask them to imagine that it is the day after they called work to say they would not be in. Their problem is not solved. They cannot make it to work again, and they must call Olga. Ask what they will say and what they think Olga will say. Have them create new conversations to role-play in front of the class.

- Ask learners to look for "polite phrases" in the telephone conversation on page 22. Discuss and list other polite phrases that might be used for similar conversations. Allow learners to practice using these phrases. Then ask what they say when they answer the phone in their native language. Lead a discussion on the similarities and differences in telephone language.

UNIT 2 • 49

Small Talk

Purpose: To introduce making small talk; to give practice with the present continuous and the simple past tenses

Teacher Preparation and Materials
1. ▭ Audiotape for Level 2
2. Copies of TRF Handout 2.2, *Small Talk (Expansion/Extension)*
3. Copies of TRF Handout 2.6, *Question Formation (Expansion/Extension)*
4. Copies of TRF Handout 2.7, *Small Talk Review (Expansion/Extension)*

Warm-up
1. Elicit a conversation with a volunteer by asking questions, such as *What did you do last weekend? How are your children? What do you think about this weather?* Explain that conversations of this type are called *small talk,* and that small talk focuses on everyday things. Talk about when small talk is likely to occur. (free time at work or school, an unexpected meeting with an acquaintance, at parties or get-togethers, etc.)
2. On the board, write the words *game, runs, outs, pennant, pitching.* Ask learners what these words are about. Tell them that baseball and other sports are popular small-talk subjects in the United States. Ask if sports are popular small-talk subjects in learners' native countries. If so, have them tell what kinds of sports people discuss.
3. Have learners name other topics that would fit under the category of small talk. Lead a discussion about specific topics that people tend to talk about in the United States and in their native countries.

Presentation
1. Have learners turn to page 23. Ask questions about the pictures to elicit known vocabulary. FOR EXAMPLE: *What is Joon doing in the first picture? What sport are they playing in the second picture?* Have learners read the words that go with each picture. Be sure they understand

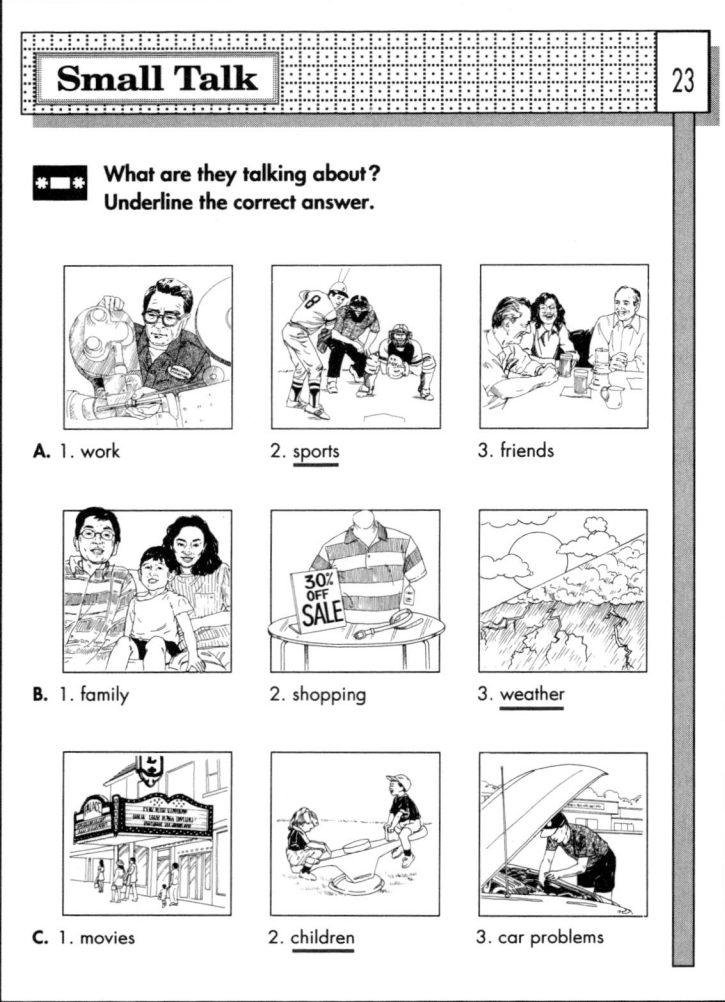

that each word names a small-talk topic that is illustrated in the picture above it.
2. Explain that learners will listen to three different conversations based on different small-talk topics. Tell them to listen carefully to the first conversation to determine the subject. ▭ Play the audiotape. Then have them draw a line under the subject in exercise A that corresponds to the conversation they heard. ▭ Replay the audiotape so learners can check their work.
3. Use this procedure with exercises B and C. After learners have listened to all three conversations, call on volunteers to give the correct answers.

Expansion/Extension
See **TRF HANDOUT 2.2,** *Small Talk*
TRF HANDOUT 2.6, *Question Formation*
TRF HANDOUT 2.7, *Small Talk Review*

More *Expansion/Extension* on page 55

50 • UNIT 2

Safety Signs at Work

Purpose: To introduce safety requirements and safety signs

Teacher Preparation and Materials

1. Copies of TRF Handout 2.4, *Safety Signs* (Expansion/Extension)
2. Copies of TRF Handout 2.5, *Warning Labels* (Expansion/Extension)

Warm-up

1. On the board, draw a sign and label it *Road under Construction*. Ask learners what they would do if they saw this sign while driving. Explain that this sign contains an important safety message. Drivers should know to slow down and watch for bumps, lane closings, equipment, and people in the road.
2. Ask learners to name safety signs they have seen outside, at school, or at work. Write their suggestions on the board and discuss the meanings of the signs. Ask learners why these signs are useful and how well people follow them. Compare safety signs in the United States with those in their native countries.

Presentation

1. Have learners turn to page 24. Ask questions about the picture to elicit known vocabulary. FOR EXAMPLE: *What is the man wearing? Why is he wearing it? What is the woman wearing and why? What looks dangerous in the picture?*
2. Read each of the messages in exercise A. Use the picture to help explain the meaning of each message. Tell learners they must find the correct sign in the picture and write the number of the matching warning message on the sign. You may want to do one as a class and then have learners work in pairs to complete the exercise. When they have finished, review the answers.
3. Have learners work in pairs to read the warning messages in exercise B and to decide how they could express each warning to a friend or co-worker.

FOR EXAMPLE: *Watch out! The floor is wet! Don't forget to wear your hard hat!* Ask volunteers to say their warning expressions. List the warnings on the board and have learners write one expression for each warning message in their books.

Expansion/Extension

See **TRF HANDOUT 2.4,** *Safety Signs*
TRF HANDOUT 2.5, *Warning Labels*

- Write these additional signs on the board: *Keep out! Flammable! Out of Order. Wet Paint.* Ask learners when and where they might see these signs. Have them draw situations for each.
- Take a tour of the school or neighborhood to look for similar signs or safety hazards. Learners should copy any signs they see and make notes about dangerous situations that should have signs but don't. They can make signs for these situations when they return to class.

More *Expansion/Extension* on page 55

Memo

Purpose: To give practice in reading and understanding work communications, and in making inferences; to give practice with *can/can't*

Teacher Preparation and Materials
Copies of simple memos from a workplace or a school *(Expansion/Extension)*

Warm-up
1. On the board, write the following:

   > MEMO
   > TO: All ESL Teachers
   > FROM: ESL Office
   > RE: Columbus Day holiday
   > Because of the holiday on Columbus Day, Monday, October 13, there will be no ESL classes.

2. Read the memo aloud with learners. Ask what a *memo* is, who this memo is written to, and what the subject is. Point out that the subject in a memo is often shown by *RE,* meaning "regarding." You may wish to point out that Columbus Day is officially October 12, but some holidays are celebrated on the Monday nearest the official date.

3. Ask learners *Is there a holiday on Monday, October 13? Are there ESL classes? Does the memo mention other holidays?* On the board, write *True, False,* and *Doesn't Say*. Below this, write:

   There is a holiday on October 13. _____
   There are ESL classes on October 13. _____
   There will be other holidays. _____

   Ask volunteers to write "True," "False," and "Doesn't Say" on the appropriate lines.

Presentation
1. Have learners turn to page 25. Give them a chance to skim through the memo. Review the parts of the memo, asking who it is written to, who it is from, and what the subject is.

2. Read the memo aloud while learners follow along silently, or have learners read the memo in pairs. Ask questions to check comprehension. FOR EXAMPLE: *What will the construction crew do? When will

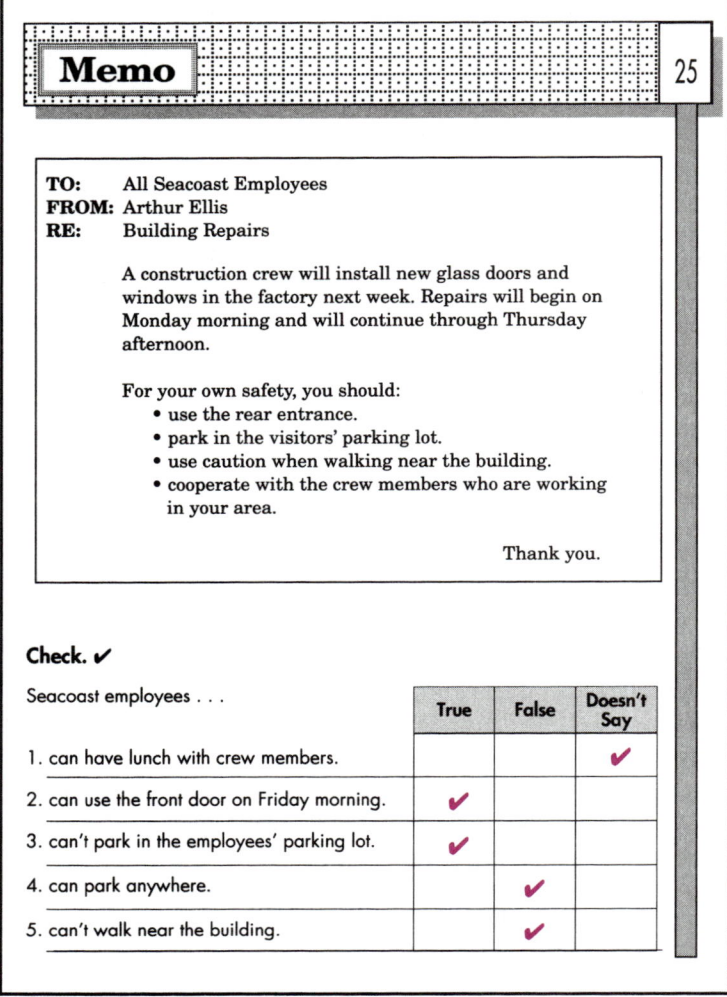

the repairs begin? When will they end? What should the employees do for their own safety?*

3. Have learners work with a partner to complete the chart at the bottom of the page. You may wish to do one or two items as a whole class to provide a model.

4. Ask volunteers to tell which column they checked for each statement. Have learners rewrite the false sentences to make them correct.

5. Ask learners why caution is needed at Seacoast Industries during the repairs. Lead a discussion about what kind of accidents might happen and why it is important for Seacoast to take the safety measures mentioned in the memo.

Expansion/Extension
- Distribute copies of simple memos from a workplace or a school. Put learners in small groups to read the memos and discuss their meanings.

More *Expansion/Extension* on page 55

Making the Connection

Purpose: To give practice with the simple past tense; to give practice in writing about a personal experience; to give practice with skills, functions, and vocabulary from Unit 2

Teacher Preparation and Materials
None

Warm-up
Ask learners *What did you learn about Joon in this unit? Where does he work? What does he do? What did he do on his first day? Do you think he's happy at Seacoast Industries? Why?* Write some of the learners' ideas on the board. Discuss any differences of opinion that they have.

Presentation
1. Have learners turn to page 26. Ask questions about the picture to elicit known vocabulary. FOR EXAMPLE: *Where is Joon now? What machine is he operating?*
2. Ask learners to read the paragraphs silently and to circle unknown words or phrases. Clarify vocabulary as necessary. Ask questions to check understanding.
3. Have learners look at the incomplete story at the bottom of the page. Tell them to use this framework to write a story about themselves. They can write about a job or work they do at home. (child care, home repair, etc.) Allow them to change words or sentences if they want to. You may wish first to have a volunteer tell his or her story while you write it on the board. Have learners use this as a model to write their own stories.
4. Ask learners to share their stories with a small group or with the entire class. ◼ In a one-to-one situation, write your own story as a model. Then have the learner write his or her story.

Expansion/Extension
- Ask learners what they would like to do in the future. Ask *Would you like to continue doing the same thing or make a change? How could you change?* Write some of their ideas for change on the board. Then tell them to add another paragraph to their story, beginning *In the future I would like to . . .*
- Ask learners what steps they should take to get a job/get a better job. They can use the words *first, then, next, finally*. Ask learners to write four steps and then have them share their ideas with the class.

UNIT 2: On the Job
Expansion/Extension

First Day on the Job
More *Expansion/Extension* for SB page 16

- Brainstorm with learners the names of other kinds of jobs where workers must wear uniforms or special clothing. Write the names of these jobs on the board. Ask learners why they think uniforms are required for these jobs.
- Ask learners if they can smoke at work or at school. If not, and if they are smokers, find out what they do. Have learners tell how they feel about no-smoking rules.
- Ask volunteers to draw on the board simple floor plans of their workplaces, and to label different areas, such as the office, time clock, and employees' entrance. Have pairs of volunteers role-play asking for and giving directions using the floor plans on the board. Ask if learners use time clocks at work. Have volunteers role-play asking for and giving assistance in using the time clock.

Before Starting Work
More *Expansion/Extension* for SB page 17

- Have pairs of learners interview each other about their first day on the job or at school. Each learner should take notes and present an oral report to the class.
- On the board, write job titles such as *supervisor, personnel officer, receptionist*. Put learners in small groups and tell them to think of as many job titles as they can. Set a time limit. When the time is up, have a member of each group read off the job titles while you write them on the board. Discuss the duties and responsibilities involved in the different jobs. Wherever possible, categorize the jobs by level, type, and so on.

Punching In
More *Expansion/Extension* for SB page 18

- On the board, write the headings *The United States* and *Native Countries*. Lead a discussion about differing cultural expectations regarding punctuality. Ask *Can we be late to work or school in the United States? Is there a difference between being late only once in a while or being late often? How late can we be? What do your bosses/teachers say if you're late?* Write learners' comments on the board under the heading *The United States*. Do the same with each learner's native country. Use this completed chart to compare and contrast attitudes about punctuality.

Rules at Work
More *Expansion/Extension* for SB page 19

- On the board, write the two headings *Safe Jobs* and *Dangerous Jobs*. Ask volunteers to name safe and dangerous jobs, and to write them under the appropriate headings. Ask questions such as *What makes these jobs safe/dangerous? What can workers do to make dangerous jobs safer?*
- Arrange for a guest speaker who is a foreman or factory worker. If possible, invite a speaker who is familiar with the needs of second-language learners. Ask the speaker to discuss different kinds of workplace rules and answer questions learners may have.

Operating Machines
More *Expansion/Extension* for SB page 20

- Ask learners if they have ever had any funny or difficult moments with machines. Have a volunteer tell his or her story while you write it on the board. Then ask learners to write their own story titled "My Most Difficult/Funniest Moment with Machines." Have volunteers read their stories to the class. ■ In a one-to-one situation, tell the learner your story and write it as a model. Then have the learner write a story.
- Divide the class into two teams. Appoint a scorekeeper to stand at the board and keep track of points for Teams A and B. Tell learners that they will make up stories using *first, then, next,*

and *finally*. Start off with a statement like *This is what I did yesterday. First, I went to work.* Point to a member of Team A to continue with "Then . . ." Point to a member of Team B to continue with "Next," and so on, alternating teams until the story is finished. Learners may wish to use *then* and *next* more than once. You may also wish to introduce other sequence expressions, such as *later* or *after that.* When the story is finished, have the next team member start a new story with "First, I . . ." Each team member who successfully completes a sentence scores a point for his or her team. A team member who cannot contribute anything loses the team's turn and scores no points. ■ In a one-to-one situation, start the story for the learner and then take turns adding sentences.

Calling In
More *Expansion/Extension* for SB page 21

- Have learners share their experiences with calling in sick to work/school. Ask them to describe the problem and what the boss/teacher said. Write one learner's experience on the board in story form as it is told to you. Then ask learners to write about their own experiences. When they have finished, have learners read their stories to partners or small groups. ■ In a one-to-one situation, tell the learner your story and write it as a model. Then ask the learner to write a personal story.

Small Talk
More *Expansion/Extension* for SB page 23

- Put learners in pairs to create a small-talk conversation based on one of the topics from the audiotape or on a topic of their choice. Allow them to choose who is taking part in the conversation and where it takes place. Ask volunteers to role-play their conversations in front of the class.
- On the board, write the headings *The United States* and the names of learners' native countries. Have learners name topics that are popular small-talk subjects in the United States.

(FOR EXAMPLE: family, weekend activities, weather, jobs, hobbies, movies or television shows.) Identify topics that are not appropriate in the United States. (FOR EXAMPLE: salaries, age, cost of possessions, religion, politics, physical problems, family problems.) Ask learners to name topics that are popular and topics that are not appropriate in their native countries. How do these compare with small-talk topics in the United States?
- Many idioms are used in small talk. ▭ Replay the audiotape and help learners recall some idioms from the conversations they hear. Write the idioms on the board. Ask learners to name other idioms, adding to the list and helping learners read them. Write these and read them with learners. Use the idioms on the board in sentences to illustrate them.

Safety Signs at Work
More *Expansion/Extension* for SB page 24

- Develop a class story or individual LEA stories based on the tour.
- Ask learners *Are you ever worried about unsafe conditions at work? What are they? What can you do about these conditions?* Write learners' comments on the board. Point out that the employer is responsible for safe conditions in the workplace. Learners should talk to their employers about unsafe conditions. Have them look back at the concerns on the board and discuss what employers should do about them.

Memo
More *Expansion/Extension* for SB page 25

- Ask learners if memos are used in business in their native countries. If not, ask how rules and needs are communicated to employees. Have learners compare different methods and decide which ones work best.
- Have learners write a memo to an employer about one of the unsafe conditions identified in *Expansion/Extension* for page 24 (Safety Signs at Work).

1 2 **3** 4 5 6 7 8 9 10 11 12 Summary
Making Choices about Money

Objectives

Functions
- Giving reasons and explanations
- Asking for and giving advice
- Dealing with numbers (budgets, costs)
- Comparing and contrasting

Life Tasks
- Shopping
- Budgeting
- Applying for credit
- Making choices about payment options
- Figuring costs

Structures
- Comparative adjectives
- Adverbs of frequency
- Negative questions
- *If/then* statements
- Modals: *can/can't* (possibility); *would, could, should*
- Intensifiers: *too, very*

Culture
- Alternative forms of payment: cash, credit cards, checks
- Advertising and sales
- Shopping in the United States

Vocabulary

Key words:

advantage	guarantee
bargain	income
budget	interest
cash	item
charge	miscellaneous
check	model
choice	money order
clerk	monthly
cost	owe
credit	paycheck
credit card	percent
disadvantage	price
discount	purchase
earnings	record
expenses	refund
expensive	repair
extra	return
features	(on) sale
fee	(federal/state) tax
groceries	utilities

Related words:

account	layaway
approved	mortgage
balance	(gross/net) pay
billed	policy
bring back	portable
checking	product
condition	references
customer service	(pay) stub
damages	terms
deductions	warranty
dependents	year-to-date
disapproved	

Payday

Purpose: To introduce comparing and contrasting

Teacher Preparation and Materials
1. Simulated or real paycheck
2. Utility bills and other kinds of bills

Warm-up
1. Show learners a simulated or real paycheck. Say *I got my paycheck today. What should I do with the money?* As learners name different options, write them on the board. If they do not mention paying bills, show learners different bills from utility companies and stores, and explain that part of your check goes to pay these bills.
2. Ask learners *How do you spend your money?* Request a variety of responses. Ask learners *Is it more important to pay bills or to buy new things? Why?*

Presentation
1. Have learners turn to page 27. Ask questions about the picture to elicit known vocabulary. FOR EXAMPLE: *Who is in the picture? What do you see? What is Joon thinking about? What does Monroe want to do with his paycheck? Where does Olga want to go? What does Kim want to do?* List learners' replies on the board.
2. Ask learners *What's going on?* Have volunteers describe the scene.
3. Ask learners to describe which character they are most similar to. You may wish to provide examples: *If you usually think about paying your bills, then you're like Joon. If you usually think about buying things for your children, then you're more like Kim.*
4. For those in the class who are not working, ask how they feel when they get money for their living expenses. Ask *What do you spend it on first? What would you like to do differently?*

Payday
What's going on?   Answers may vary.

Expansion/Extension
- Tell learners *Imagine that you are going to get a big raise in pay. What will you spend the extra money on?* On the board write *If I get a big raise, then I'll . . .* Have learners work in pairs, interviewing each other about their dreams. Ask volunteers to report on their partner's dreams.
- Tell learners *Imagine that Joon, Monroe, Olga, and Kim meet on a bus. They are talking about their paychecks. What are they going to buy?* Make up a conversation among the characters. Have learners work in groups of four, preparing and practicing their conversations. Then ask volunteer groups to role-play their conversations in front of the class. ■ In a one-to-one situation, you and the learner choose any two characters and create a similar conversation between them.
- Put learners in pairs. Ask them to imagine they just got their paychecks. Ask *What are you going to spend it on?* Have them prepare a conversation. Ask volunteers to role-play their conversations in front of the class.

Reading a Pay Stub

Purpose: To introduce information found on a paycheck stub; to introduce comparative adjectives; to give practice with adverbs of frequency and time

Teacher Preparation and Materials

1. A blank pay stub (copied from page 28 onto the board)
2. Wall calendar
3. Samples of various pay stubs from different companies
4. Copies of blank pay stubs *(Expansion/Extension)*

Warm-up

1. After you draw the blank pay stub on the board (as described above), ask a volunteer to come to the board and to fill in the information for you. The volunteer should ask you questions, such as *How do you spell your name? What's your Social Security number?* Make the amount of pay and other information similar to that on Joon's pay stub.
2. Review different categories and abbreviations on the pay stub that learners may have difficulty understanding. Elicit/explain the difference between *gross* and *net pay*, and answer any other questions learners have.
3. Ask learners *Is my gross pay more than my net pay? What is the biggest deduction I have?*
4. Tell learners how often you get paid. Point out that some companies pay weekly, every other week, or monthly. Use a wall calendar to demonstrate these time periods.
5. Show learners samples of pay stubs from different companies. If possible, have them compare these examples with their own pay stubs. **Note:** If learners bring in their own pay stubs, they may wish to cross out the pay amounts first.

Presentation

1. Have learners turn to page 28. Ask questions about the pay stub to elicit known vocabulary. FOR EXAMPLE: *Whose pay*

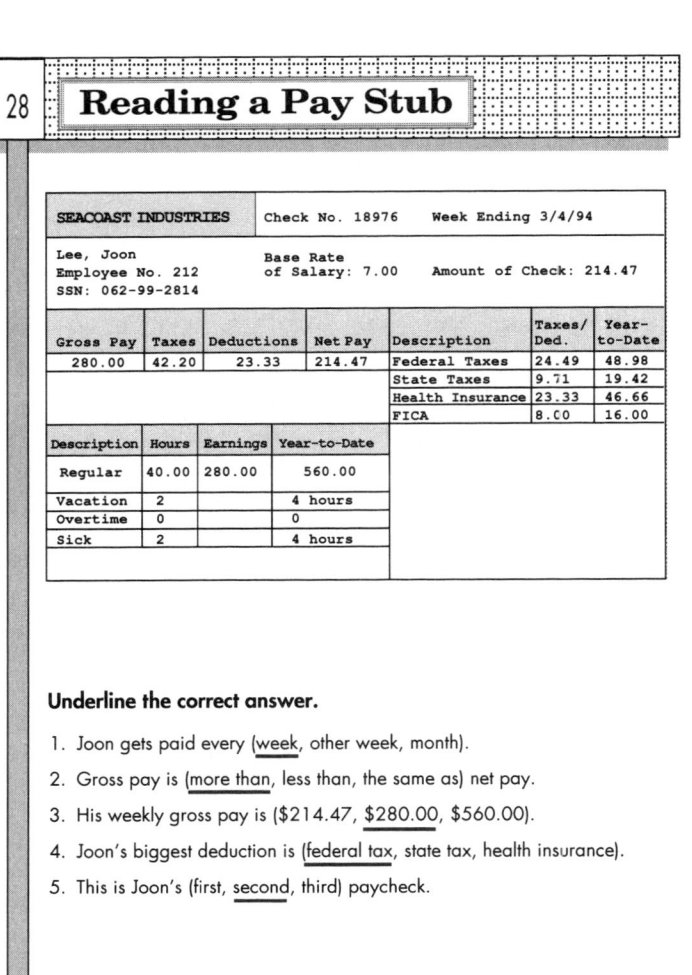

stub is this? How can you tell? How often is Joon paid? How do you know? What is his Social Security number? What is his gross pay?

2. Read the first statement in the exercise at the bottom of the page and help learners determine the correct answer. Tell them to underline the correct answer in their books. Then have learners work with a partner to complete numbers 2 through 5. Ask volunteers to read the completed sentences, explaining how they arrived at their responses.

Expansion/Extension

- Distribute copies of blank pay stubs, or erase the personal information from the model on the board and have learners copy the blank form. Tell them to fill out the form for themselves, making up figures if they prefer not to share this information. Have nonworkers make up figures. Ask learners to write sentences with choices about their pay stubs similar to those on page 28. They may exchange papers with a partner and complete each other's sentences.

More *Expansion/Extension* on page 68

The Lees' Budget

Purpose: To introduce budgeting; to give practice in figuring costs and in comparing and contrasting; to give practice with adverbs of frequency

Teacher Preparation and Materials
1. Copies of TRF Handout 3.4, *A Monthly Family Budget* (Expansion/Extension)
2. Copies of TRF Handout 3.6, *Frequency Game* (Expansion/Extension)

Warm-up
1. Use the pay stub on page 28 to introduce the term *take-home pay*. Ask learners what deductions were taken from Joon's gross pay and what the amount left after these deductions is called. Explain that another name for *net pay* is *take-home pay*. Have learners mention other possible deductions from a worker's pay. (life insurance, disability insurance, savings plans, stock plans, etc.)
2. Ask learners *What are some things you must pay for every day? every week? every month?* Write their answers on the board under the headings *Daily, Weekly,* and *Monthly*. Be sure to include *rent, utilities, food, transportation, phone,* and *dental/medical*. Group some responses as *miscellaneous expenses*. Explain the categories as necessary. Point out that some expenses, such as rent, are usually monthly and stay the same from month to month. Utilities are usually monthly but may vary according to use. Dental/medical expenses can change a lot from one month to the next. Learners should try to figure out an average for these kinds of expenses.
3. Work with a volunteer to figure out average monthly expenses for him or her. Itemize the expenses using the categories from activity #2 above and any other categories that arise.

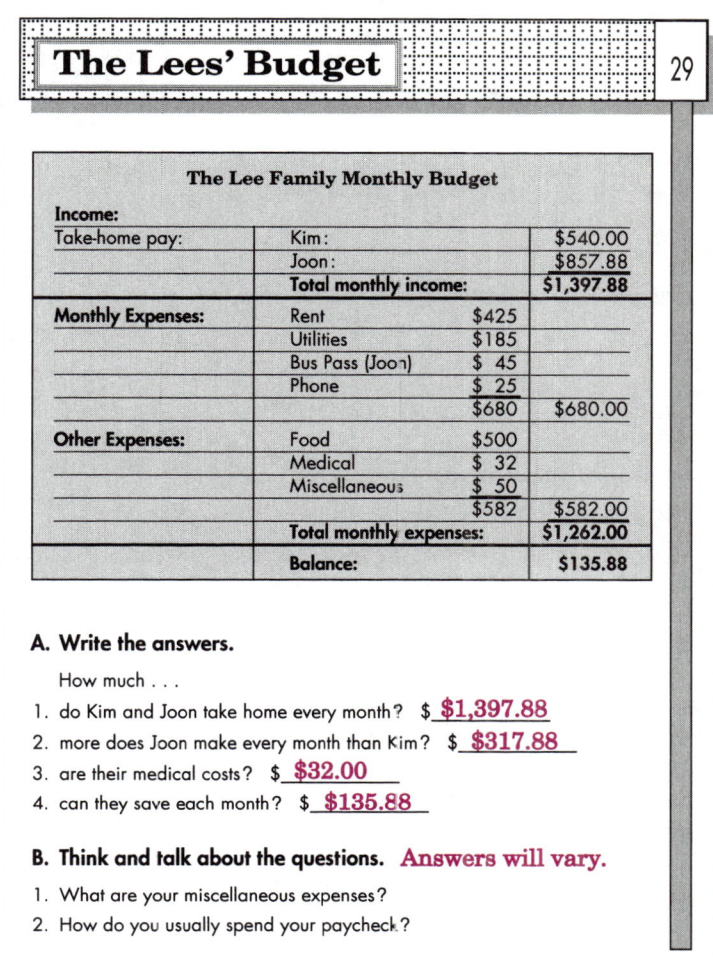

Presentation
1. Have learners turn to page 29. Ask questions about the budget sheet to elicit known vocabulary. FOR EXAMPLE: *What is Joon's take-home pay? What is Kim's? How much do they make together each month? What is this called on the budget? How much do they spend each month on food? What are their total monthly expenses? Do they have money left over at the end of the month? How much?*
2. Put learners in pairs and have them complete exercise A. Ask volunteers to share their answers with the class and to explain how they got the answers for questions 2 and 4.
3. Read aloud the questions in exercise B and have learners work with their partners to discuss their responses.

Expansion/Extension
See **TRF HANDOUT 3.4**, *A Monthly Family Budget*
TRF HANDOUT 3.6, *Frequency Game*

More *Expansion/Extension* on page 68

Need or Want?

Purpose: To give practice in giving reasons, in comparing and contrasting, and in figuring costs

Teacher Preparation and Materials
1. Pictures of various necessities and luxury items
2. Magazines/catalogs/fliers with pictures of necessities and luxury items; scissors *(Expansion/Extension)*

Warm-up
1. Tell the class *I just got my paycheck. I really need some new shoes. But I don't want to spend my money on shoes. I want to go to the movies!* On the board, write the headings *Need* and *Want*. Ask volunteers to name the things you need and want, and write them under the appropriate headings.
2. Show learners different pictures of necessities (food, housing) and luxury items (jewelry, stereo). Ask them *Do you really need this, or do you want it?* Discuss the ways in which these choices can depend on individual needs.

Presentation
1. Have learners turn to page 30. Ask questions about the picture to elicit known vocabulary. FOR EXAMPLE: *What does Joon want to buy for Kim? What do you think Kim is saying? Who might Kim be thinking about? What's the matter with the boy's jacket?* Learners should infer that the boy Kim is talking about is her son.
2. Read aloud the passage below the picture while learners follow along silently or put learners in pairs to take turns reading the passage aloud. Ask which item is a "need," which is a "want but don't need," and why. Have volunteers describe similar situations they have experienced with family members, when they had to wait to buy something they really wanted because there was something more important that they needed.

3. Have learners work in pairs, helping each other complete the lists at the bottom of the page. Ask volunteers to share their answers with the class and to write the items under the headings *Need* or *Want but Don't Need*. Use this information to compare and contrast individual needs and wants.

Expansion/Extension
- Ask learners to find pictures of one item they want but don't need and one item they need. In the following session, have learners take turns showing and describing their items to the class and explaining why the items are wants or needs.
- Put learners in small groups and distribute magazines, catalogs, or fliers. Have each group make a poster labeled "Wants" and a poster labeled "Needs," using pictures they cut out. Have the reporter in each group share the group's posters with the class.

More *Expansion/Extension* on page 68

Looking for a Bargain

Purpose: To give practice in giving reasons, in figuring costs, and in comparing and contrasting

Teacher Preparation and Materials

1. One or more everyday items, such as a hat, a purse, or a notebook
2. Copies of ads showing different models/styles of the same items *(Expansion/Extension)*
3. Copies of TRF Handout 3.2, *Match the Ad* *(Expansion/Extension)*
4. Copies of TRF Handout 3.5, *Garage Sale* *(Expansion/Extension)*

Warm-up

1. Show the class an item, such as a hat, and tell them *You have to buy this hat! It's a real bargain! It's usually $12. A great item—on sale for only $9.95! It's in great condition! Look at all these special features....* Continue in this manner, persuading them to buy your item. Then on the board write the words *bargain, on sale,* and *special features.* Ask volunteers to describe what they think a *bargain* is, based on your sales pitch.
2. Have volunteers present other "bargains" on sale, with many special features, using other items, such as a purse or a notebook.

Presentation

1. Have learners turn to page 31. Ask questions about the pictures to elicit known vocabulary. FOR EXAMPLE: *What's the first item? How much does it cost? How much does the other iron cost? Do they look the same? different?* Allow learners time to look at and compare the pictures.
2. Read aloud the description of each item while learners follow along silently. Clarify vocabulary as necessary. Ask learners to describe what they think the different features are and how they might be useful.

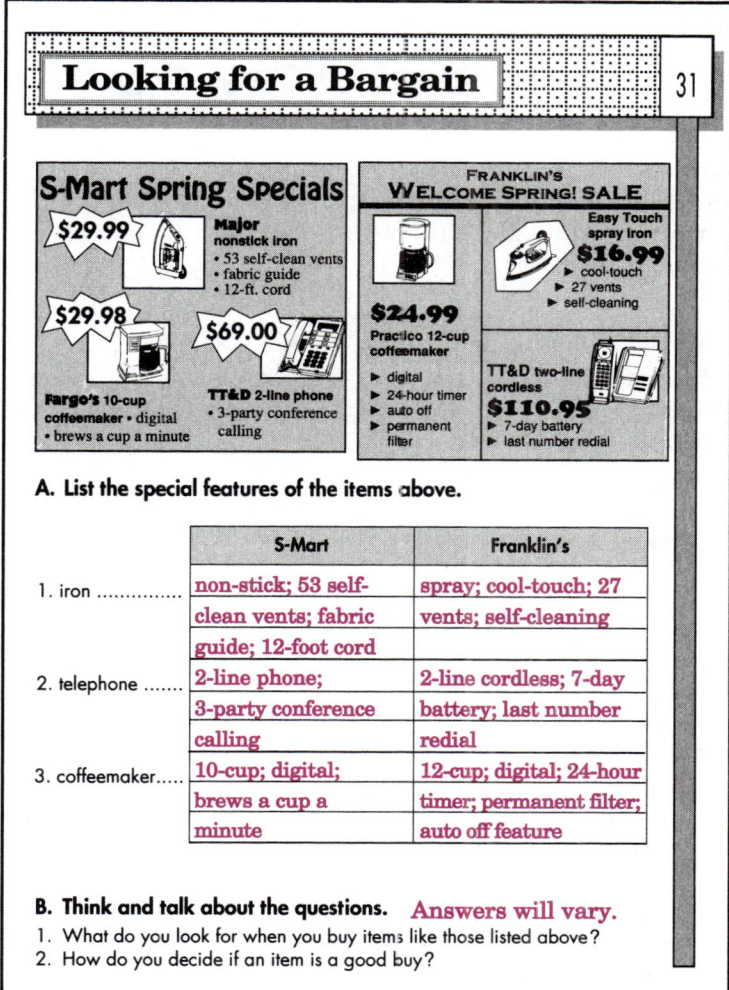

3. Read aloud the direction line and headings for exercise A. As a class, list the special features of the two irons. Then have learners work in pairs to complete the remaining two items. Have volunteers tell the class the correct answers.
4. Divide the class into three groups. Assign one group an iron, another group a telephone, and the last group a coffeemaker. Ask each group to talk about the features of the two models and decide which one they will buy. When they have finished, have the reporter in each group identify the chosen item and give the group's reasons. ■ In a one-to-one situation, discuss which iron, telephone, and coffeemaker you and the learner would select and why.
5. Put the class in small groups to discuss the questions at the bottom of the page. Have the reporter in each group share some of the group's conclusions with the class.

Expansion/Extension

See **TRF HANDOUT 3.2,** *Match the Ad*
TRF HANDOUT 3.5, *Garage Sale*

More *Expansion/Extension* on page 68

UNIT 3 • **61**

What's the Better Buy?

Purpose: To give practice in figuring costs, in giving reasons, and in comparing and contrasting; to introduce comparative adjectives

Teacher Preparation and Materials

1. Two radios or other items, one obviously more expensive, larger, and with more features than the other
2. Copies of fliers/catalogs/ads containing similar items with different features and prices *(Expansion/Extension)*
3. Pictures of different items, with prices removed *(Expansion/Extension)*
4. Copies of TRF Handout 3.3, *Cash Register Receipts (Expansion/Extension)*

Warm-up

1. Show the class two radios or other items as described in *Teacher Preparation and Materials* #1. Demonstrate the two items to the class, detailing the features and prices of each. Then ask questions, such as *Which item is larger? cheaper? Which has more features? Which is more expensive? less expensive?* On the board, write some of the comparative adjectives mentioned. (larger, cheaper, more expensive, etc.)
2. Point to other similar objects or people in the classroom and ask learners to compare these items/people, using words like those on the board. Choose a tall and a short person in the class and say *Compare the height of these two people.* Continue with other examples. Add the new comparative adjectives to the list on the board.
3. Introduce the use of *better/worse* in comparisons involving nouns. Say *One store sells a shirt for $15. The same shirt is on sale at a different store for $12. Which is the better buy?* Provide other nouns and ask learners to use them in comparisons. (FOR EXAMPLE: driver—a better/worse driver than me)

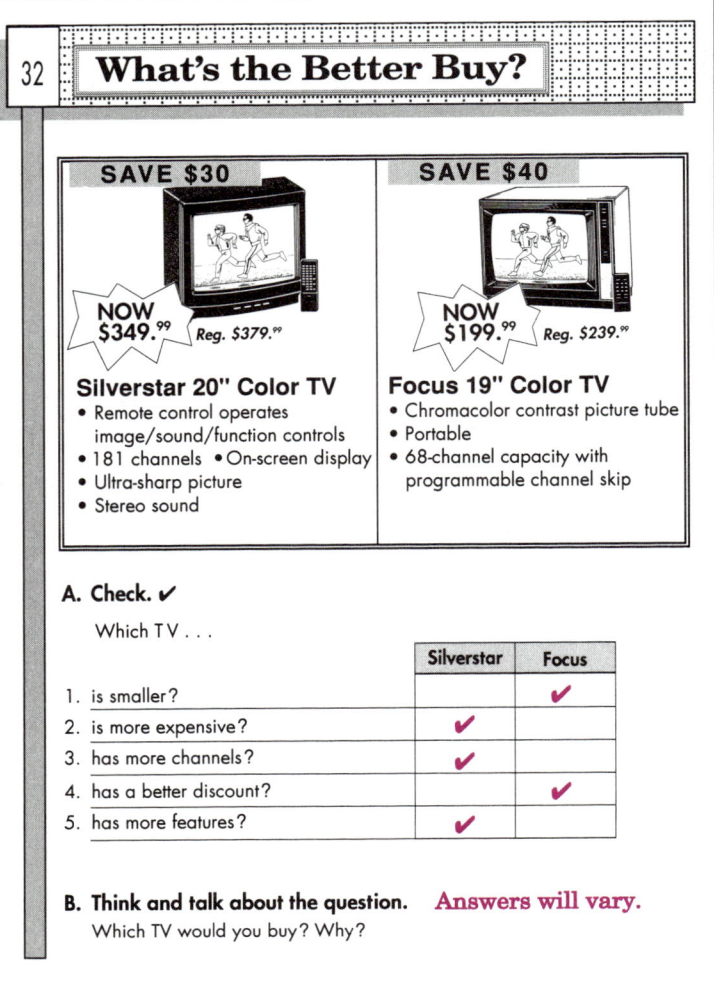

Presentation

1. Have learners turn to page 32. Ask questions about the pictures to elicit known vocabulary. FOR EXAMPLE: *What do you see in the pictures? Which TV looks larger/more expensive?*
2. Read the ads aloud while learners follow along silently or have them read the ads in pairs. Check comprehension by asking questions, such as *Which TV is portable? Which has a better price? Which TV has more channels?*
3. As a class answer the first question in exercise A. Then have learners complete the rest in pairs. Ask volunteers to give their answers and to explain why they chose those answers.
4. Put the class in small groups. Have them discuss what they like best about each TV. Each learner should tell which TV he or she would buy and explain why.

Expansion/Extension

See **TRF HANDOUT 3.3**, *Cash Register Receipts*

More *Expansion/Extension* on page 69

Talking to a Salesclerk

Purpose: To give practice in giving reasons, in giving advice, in figuring costs, and in comparing and contrasting; to give practice with *too/very*; to give practice in using negative questions

Teacher Preparation and Materials

1. An item for sale, such as a telephone or watch
2. ▭ Audiotape for Level 2
3. Copies of coupons, rebate offers, or ads for discounts *(Expansion/Extension)*
4. Arrange for a trip to a local discount or department store. *(Expansion/Extension)*
5. A list of small, inexpensive items needed for the class *(Expansion/Extension)*
6. Copies of TRF Handout 3.1, *Map of a Shopping Mall (Expansion/Extension)*

Warm-up

1. Display an item for sale, such as a telephone or watch. Pretend to be a salesclerk. Tell learners *Look at this special item on sale for today only. Today's price is only $39.99. That's 20% off the regular price of $50! Isn't that a great discount? Do you want to use cash, check, or charge?* Write some of the key words on the board, such as *model, item, 20% off, discount, cash, check, charge.* Clarify vocabulary as necessary.
2. Ask two volunteers to pretend to be salesclerks who are selling special items at a big discount. Play the part of a customer and react to one sales pitch in a positive way and to the other in a negative way. Give reasons for your different reactions. (FOR EXAMPLE: I already have the item, so I'm not interested.) Then have other volunteers take turns being the different salesclerks and the customer.

Presentation

1. Have learners turn to page 33. Ask questions about the pictures to elicit known vocabulary. FOR EXAMPLE: *What do*

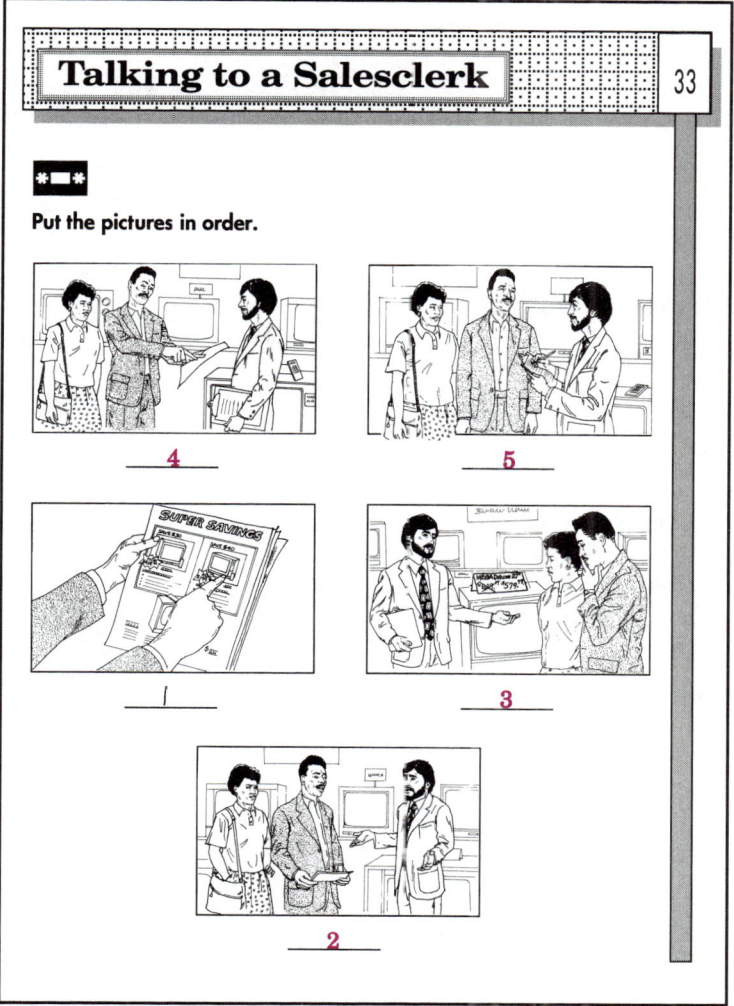

Monroe and Althea want to buy? What is the discount price? Why do you think Monroe doesn't want the TV the salesclerk suggested?

2. Ask learners to find the picture marked "1." Explain that the pictures are out of order. Ask learners to predict the correct order of the pictures. Write their suggestions on the board.
3. Tell learners to listen carefully to the conversation on the audiotape to determine the correct order of the pictures. ▭ Play the audiotape and then have learners number the pictures in the proper order. ▭ Replay the audiotape so learners can check their work. Finally, have volunteers give the correct sequence, saying the number and describing the action in the picture.
4. Ask learners to work with a partner to write a story describing Monroe's experience at the store.

Expansion/Extension

See **TRF HANDOUT 3.1,** *Map of a Shopping Mall*

More Expansion/Extension on page 69

UNIT 3 • 63

Ways to Pay

Purpose: To give practice in figuring costs, in budgeting, and in comparing and contrasting; to introduce the modal *may*

Teacher Preparation and Materials

1. Samples of cash, checks, money orders, and credit cards
2. Copies of food stamps and traveler's checks *(Expansion/Extension)*
3. Arrange for a trip to a bank or ask a guest speaker from a bank to visit the class. *(Expansion/Extension)*
4. Copies of TRF Handout 3.7, *Cash or Credit? (Expansion/Extension)*

Warm-up

1. Show learners samples (or copies) of cash, checks, money orders, and credit cards. Ask them to identify and to describe the use of each. Have learners describe their experiences using these different forms of payment. Discuss any problems they have had with cash, checks, money orders, or credit cards. Provide further clarification as necessary.

2. To introduce the concept of *advantages* and *disadvantages,* ask learners *What is good about owning a car? What are the advantages?* (get to work/school easily and when you want; don't have to rely on public transportation, and so on) On the board, write their comments under the heading *Advantages*. Then ask *What is bad about owning a car? What are the disadvantages of owning a car?* (creates many expenses like gas, insurance, repairs; adds to pollution, and so on.) Write their comments under *Disadvantages*.

Presentation

1. Have learners turn to page 34. Ask questions about the pictures to elicit known vocabulary. FOR EXAMPLE: *What is cash? What do you pay for with cash? What are the advantages of cash? the disadvantages?* Point out the + (plus) and – (minus) signs used as symbols for advantages and disadvantages.

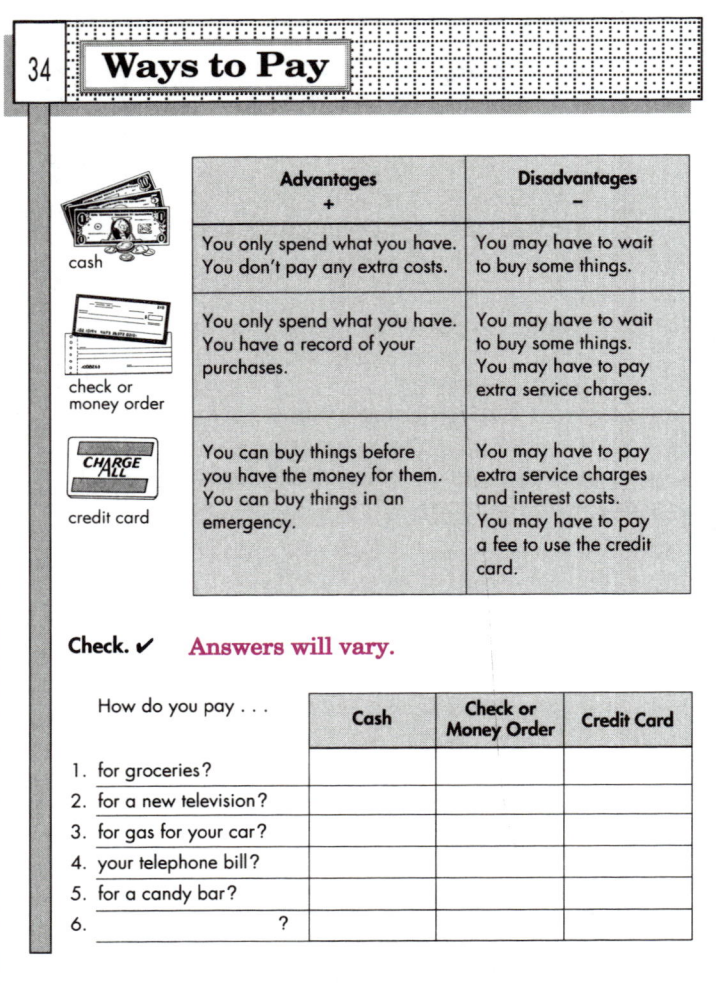

2. Put learners in pairs to read through the advantages and disadvantages of each payment option. Then have them complete the checklist on their own.

3. Ask volunteers to share their answers with the class. They can also explain why they chose these forms of payment.

4. Conduct a class survey of how people pay for each item on the list. Have learners raise their hands for each method they use and tally the totals on the board.
   ■ In a one-to-one situation, discuss and compare your shopping habits and payment methods with those of the learner.

Expansion/Extension

See TRF HANDOUT 3.7, *Cash or Credit?*

- Distribute copies of food stamps and traveler's checks. Provide any necessary explanation. If learners are somewhat familiar with these payment options, have them discuss in small groups how each is used. They can discuss the advantages and disadvantages of using food stamps and traveler's checks. Have the reporter in each group share some of the group's conclusions with the class.

More *Expansion/Extension* on page 69

Monroe's Choice

Purpose: To give practice in filling out credit card application forms and in giving and listening to advice; to introduce the modal *should*

Teacher Preparation and Materials

1. A blank credit card application (copied from page 35 onto the board)
2. 🔲 Audiotape for Level 2
3. Copies of blank credit card applications *(Expansion/Extension)*

Warm-up

1. On the board draw the credit card application as described above. Tell the class to imagine that you are Jan Smith. Have a volunteer come to the board and pretend to be Lee Jones from the customer service department. Have Lee Jones fill out the information on the application for Jan Smith, asking questions about your employer, and so on. Clarify vocabulary as necessary.
2. When the application is complete, ask Lee Jones if you can get the credit card. Ask if Lee will approve you for a credit card.
3. Erase the information and have other pairs of volunteers role-play a customer service representative and a person applying for a credit card.
4. Tell learners *I got my credit card last week and I lost it. What should I do?* Help the class conclude that you should call the store/company immediately. Ask what you should do if the card is stolen.

Presentation

1. Have learners turn to page 35. Ask questions about the form to elicit known vocabulary. FOR EXAMPLE: *Who is applying for a credit card? Who is Monroe's employer? Does Monroe own his home or rent? How many dependents does Monroe have?* Clarify vocabulary as necessary.
2. Allow learners time to read through the application and then ask additional comprehension questions, such as *Who is Monroe's nearest relative? Why do you think the store asks this question?* Ask learners who have applied for credit cards to name other information they had to provide.
3. Read aloud the questions at the bottom of the page. 🔲 Then have learners listen to the conversation on the audiotape to find the answers to these questions. Have them fill in the answers. 🔲 Replay the audiotape so learners can check their work and fill in missing information. Ask volunteers to read their answers aloud.

Expansion/Extension

- Distribute copies of other credit card applications. Have learners practice filling them out in pairs or small groups, assisting each other as necessary.
- Talk about the policy that many stores have of not accepting out-of-town or out-of-state checks. Have learners think of reasons for this policy.

Returns

Purpose: To give practice in giving reasons for returning an item to a store; to introduce *If/then* statements

Teacher Preparation and Materials
None

Warm-up

1. Ask learners if they have ever returned an item to the store where they bought it. Ask *What was wrong with it? What did the store do about it? Did the store give you any options of what to do with the damaged item?* Point out any of the four options on page 36 that learners do not mention. Have them describe situations when each of these actions might be appropriate. (exchange item—wrong size; refund money—paid cash for gift and person already has one, and so on)

2. Explain that most stores and manufacturers guarantee their products for a specified period of time. You may wish to point out that less expensive items usually carry shorter guarantees while more expensive items usually carry longer guarantees. Ask volunteers to describe guarantees for products they have purchased. Remind learners that guarantees do not usually cover any damage that was done (even by accident) by the purchaser.

Presentation

1. Have learners turn to page 36. Read the guarantee aloud while learners follow along silently. Ask questions about the form to elicit known vocabulary. FOR EXAMPLE: *How long is the guarantee for? What does it cover? What doesn't it cover? What is the charge for returned checks? What is the return policy?* Clarify vocabulary as necessary.

2. Put learners in pairs. Have them work together to fill out the chart at the bottom of the page. Complete the first couple of items orally with the class if necessary. Have volunteers give the correct answers aloud.

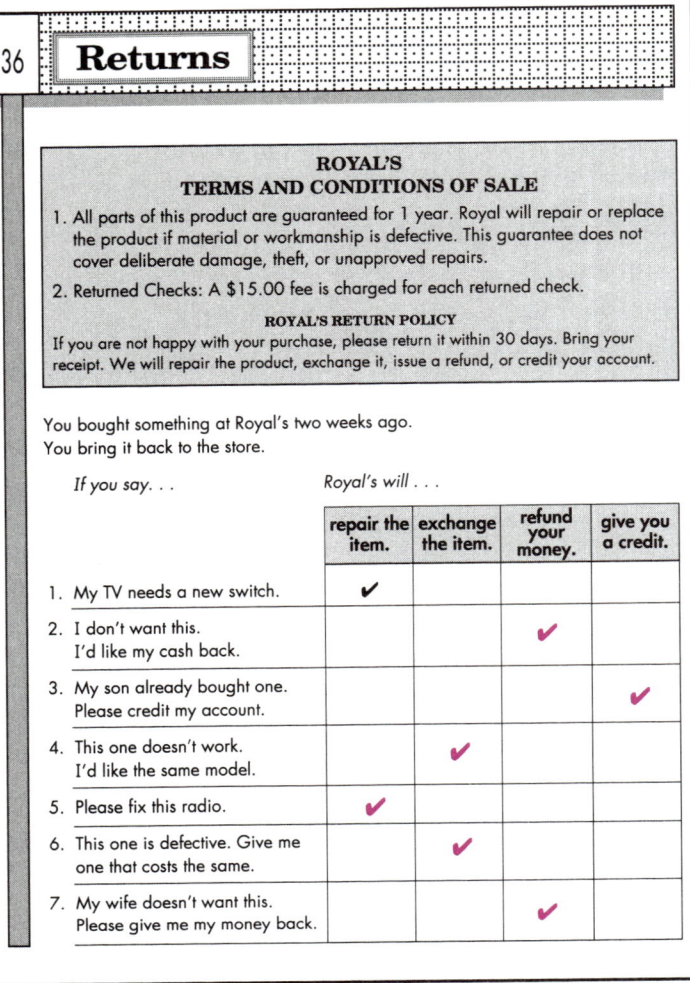

Expansion/Extension

- Call attention to the four choices at the top of the columns on page 36. Talk about which choice learners prefer and why. Divide learners into small groups and have them discuss the choices and offer their preferences.

- Ask each learner to bring in one item from home and to prepare a complaint about it. They should pretend that the item was purchased recently and is still covered by the manufacturer's or store's guarantee or warranty. Have them take turns showing their items to the class and complaining about the problems they have had. Have the rest of the class suggest one of the options on page 36 or other viable options they can think of.

- Put learners in pairs. Tell them *Pretend you are returning something to the store. What do you say? What does the salesclerk say? What reason do you give for the return?* Have partners write a conversation and role-play it in front of the class.

More *Expansion/Extension* on page 69

Making the Connection

Purpose: To give practice in figuring costs and payment options; to give practice with skills, functions, and vocabulary from Unit 3

Teacher Preparation and Materials
Blank index cards (Expansion/Extension)

Warm-up
1. Tell learners about a recent purchase you made, beginning *Last week I bought a bicycle at the Cycle Shop. The price was $70. I put it on layaway. I paid $30 that day. I still owe $40. When I pay the other $40, I can take the bike home.* Ask learners if they have ever put anything on layaway. Have them describe their purchases. If necessary, provide additional examples, such as *In October I found toys to buy for Christmas. I didn't have enough money to pay for them then, so I paid $20 and put them on layaway. I will pay $10 each week until the toys are paid off.*
2. Ask learners *What are the different ways you can pay for something?* (cash, check, money order, credit card) Ask volunteers to describe something they just bought, tell how they paid for it, and explain why they paid this way.

Presentation
1. Have learners turn to page 37. Read aloud the story about Kim while learners follow along silently, or have learners read the story in pairs. Ask questions to check comprehension. FOR EXAMPLE: *Why didn't Kim buy the bike that day? How much money did she put down on the bike? How much does she still owe? When can she bring the bike home?*
2. Read aloud the direction line and questions. If learners need a model, ask a volunteer to come to the front of the room to ask you the questions. Write your answers on the board. Then have learners complete the sentences individually. Have them read their paragraphs to the class or in small groups.

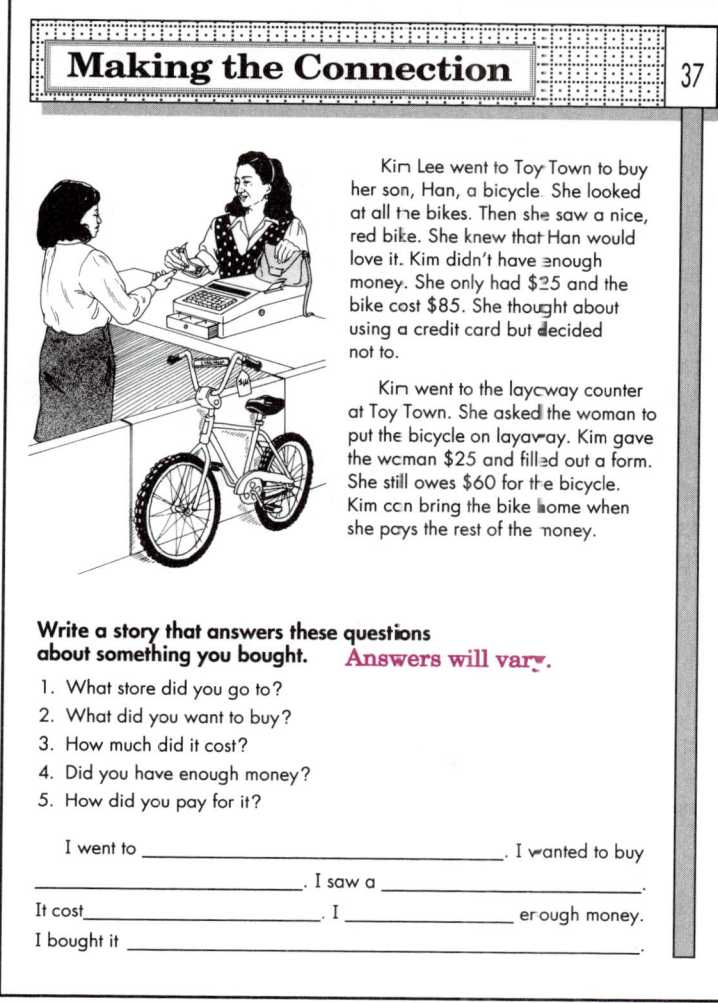

Expansion/Extension
- Put learners in pairs. Tell them *Imagine that you want to buy something and you put it on layaway. What do you say to the salesclerk? What does the salesclerk say to you? Write a conversation.* Have partners role-play their conversations in front of the class.
- Ask learners *Can you think of an item you would really like to buy? Where can you buy it? How much does it cost? How are you going to pay for it?* Have them bring in an ad or description of the item. During the next session, have volunteers show and/or describe their items to the class, answering the above questions.

UNIT 3: Making Choices about Money
Expansion/Extension

Reading a Pay Stub
More *Expansion/Extension* for SB page 28

- On the board write *Health Insurance*. Write as headings *The United States* and *Native Countries*. Lead a discussion, comparing and contrasting health insurance in the United States with coverage provided in other countries. Write learners' comments on the board under the appropriate headings.
- Repeat the above activity, comparing and contrasting Social Security benefits in the United States with similar benefits provided in learners' native countries.

The Lees' Budget
More *Expansion/Extension* for SB page 29

- Put learners in small groups. Ask them to name basic categories in a budget, such as housing, food, utilities, transportation, and miscellaneous, and then to write examples of each. When they have finished, have the reporter in each group share some of the group's conclusions with the class. On the board write their comments and ideas.
- Tell learners to use the Lee Family Monthly Budget as a model to create their own monthly budgets. They may wish to do this work at home where their personal information is readily available. Ask learners to bring in their budgets (but do not require them to share the details if they do not want to) and have volunteers name the categories they included. Allow them to add categories or make changes to their budgets as a result of the class discussion. Provide assistance for learners who request it.
- Remind learners that some expenses remain the same, while others change from one week or month to the next. On the board write the headings *Expenses That Don't Change* and *Expenses That Can Change*. Ask learners to write their examples in the appropriate column. Discuss why some expenses change during certain time periods. (FOR EXAMPLE: utility costs in different seasons)

- Ask learners to name expenses they have here in the United States that they did not have or that were very different in their native countries. (transportation, health insurance, housing, education, food costs, etc.) Discuss the problems these changes may cause. Lead a discussion on how learners can adjust to these changes.

Need or Want?
More *Expansion/Extension* for SB page 30

- Ask the class *What do you need to live in the United States? Did you need all these things in your native countries? Why or why not?* Lead a discussion on this topic, comparing necessities and luxuries in different countries. Have learners use this information to infer what they can about lifestyles in different countries.
- Put learners in pairs. Tell them *Imagine that your child, or younger brother or sister, wants to buy very expensive sports shoes. You don't have enough money for things like that. Explain why to him or her.* Have partners write a conversation between the adult and the child. Model the structure *You can/can't have those sneakers because . . .* Ask volunteers to role-play their conversations in front of the class.
  ■ In a one-to-one situation, have the learner choose one role, while you take the other. Write out and role-play the conversation.

Looking for a Bargain
More *Expansion/Extension* for SB page 31

- Distribute copies of ads for different models/styles of the same item, or ask learners to bring in ads. Have learners discuss the various choices in small groups and make decisions about the best purchases. You may suggest that they make lists of features like those on page 31.
- Set up an imaginary market. Ask each learner to bring in something to sell. Learners should take turns presenting their items for sale and persuading the rest of the class to buy them. Allow them to work in pairs if they wish.
- Ask learners to choose one item they must buy this week, such as food, an article of clothing, and so on. Suggest that they visit two or three different stores to find out the prices, sizes, and brand names for that item. Have learners share their discoveries with the class. Ask which product they would purchase and why. You may also wish to introduce the term *comparison shopping*.

What's the Better Buy?

More *Expansion/Extension* for SB page 32

- Ask if bargain hunting and sales are as important in learners' native countries as they are here. Lead a discussion. Have learners describe bargain hunting in their native countries.
- Distribute copies of ads with other items to compare. Often a store catalog or flier will have pictures of several different models of an item, with varying features and prices. Have learners work in pairs to compare and contrast the items, adapting the questions and chart on page 32.
- Play the game "The Price Is Right." Bring in pictures of different items and remove any prices included with the items. Have a panel of three volunteers sit at the front of the room and try to figure out the price of each item. The person who comes closest to the correct price, without going over, wins.

Talking to a Salesclerk

***Expansion/Extension* for SB page 33**

- Distribute copies of coupons, rebate offers, or ads for discounts. Put learners in small groups and have them discuss their experiences shopping with discount offers. Have them discuss which discount they prefer to use and what is good/bad about using these discounts. Have the reporter in each group share some of the group's conclusions with the class.
- If possible, take the class to a discount or department store. Beforehand, make a list of small, inexpensive items needed for the class. In the store, demonstrate how to ask for directions or information. Have volunteers do the same.
- During the next class, develop an LEA story about the visit to the store. You may wish to write this together as a class, or have learners write their stories individually. Ask volunteers to read their individual stories aloud. Note that each writer has a unique point of view of the same experience.

Ways to Pay

More *Expansion/Extension* for SB page 34

- Put the class in pairs. Tell them to write a conversation between a salesclerk and a customer. The salesclerk wants to persuade the customer to apply for a credit card and talks about its advantages. The customer does not want the credit card and talks about the disadvantages. If you wish, model this conversation with a volunteer for the whole class. Then have partners write out their own conversations. Ask volunteers to role-play their conversations in front of the class.
- On the board write the headings *The United States* and *Native Countries*. Put learners in small groups. Have them discuss how they paid for different items in their native countries and how that is different from the ways they pay for things in the United States. Ask what customs they think are better. Have the reporter in each group share some of the group's conclusions with the class.
- If possible, make an appointment at a local bank for a class visit (or invite a guest speaker from a bank). Tour the bank with the class and ask a representative to explain how to open savings and checking accounts.
- During the next class, write individual or group LEA stories about your visit to the bank, including the steps needed to open an account. If learners write individual stories, have volunteers share their stories with the class.

Returns

More *Expansion/Extension* for SB page 36

- Choose a purchase or a store policy/practice to complain about. Use LEA techniques to write a letter of complaint to the store. On the board write the proper heading, salutation, and so on. Have volunteers dictate the letter to you while you write it on the board. Read the final version aloud together. Then have learners copy it to keep as an example for the future.

1 2 3 **4** 5 6 7 8 9 10 11 12 Summary
Driving a Car

Objectives

Functions
- Expressing needs
- Expressing intention
- Following directions
- Reporting past events
- Describing problems

Life Tasks
- Getting a license
- Traffic tickets
- Reading graphs
- Completing forms

Structures
- Past tense
- Prepositions of place and direction
- Imperatives
- Conjunction: *but*
- Past continuous tense

Culture
- How and when to report accidents
- Traffic rules in the United States

Vocabulary

Key words:

accident	license
agent	manual
applying	notes
coverage	one way
crosswalk	park
drive	pulled over
driver	ramp
fine	road
form	route
get around	seat belt
handicapped	shape
height	sidewalk
injury	speed limit
injuries	speeding
insurance	ticket
intersection	traffic
learner's permit	

Key abbreviations:

DMV – Department of Motor Vehicles
DOB – date of birth
mph – miles per hour
M.I. – middle initial

Related words:

air bag	medical
antitheft device	not guilty
appointment	optional
automatic	ramp
compulsory	regulation
county courthouse	senior citizen
fill out	yield
judge	

Getting Around

Purpose: To give practice in stating needs and intentions; to introduce how to apply for a driver's license

Teacher Preparation and Materials

1. Pictures of cars or ads for new cars (*Expansion/Extension*)
2. Copies of TRF Handout 4.7, *Getting a Driver's License* (*Expansion/Extension*)

Warm-up

1. Ask learners *What is a driver's license? Why do people need them? Who has a license or who wants to apply for one? Who doesn't need a driver's license?* Discuss why you might not need a driver's license.
2. On the board, write the phrase *getting a license*. Have volunteers describe the requirements for getting a license. (must be a certain age, fill out an application, take a written test, take a driving test) Introduce the phrase *get around* and discuss how having a license can help a person get around.

Presentation

1. Have learners turn to page 38. Ask them to identify the characters, guessing who the teenage boy might be. Ask questions about the picture to elicit known vocabulary. FOR EXAMPLE: *What is Isabel thinking about? What is Johnny doing? What does he have on the table in front of him?*
2. Read aloud the questions at the bottom of the page. Have learners work in small groups to answer the questions. Have each group's reporter report to the class how the group members get around. Ask what they think is the best way to get around in their area and why.

Expansion/Extension

See **TRF HANDOUT 4.7**, *Getting a Driver's License*

- Ask learners with driver's licenses to describe what they had to do to get them. (If they moved here from other countries, they might have needed special papers or

documents.) Other learners may have international drivers' licenses. Ask volunteers to describe how they got their licenses in their native countries and then to compare that with the procedure in the United States.

- Put learners in small groups. Write the following questions on the board. *What are the advantages of having a license? Are there any disadvantages? What are they?* After discussing the questions, have the reporter in each group share some of the group's conclusions with the class.

- Show learners pictures of cars or ads for new cars. Ask *Do you need a new car? What kind of car do you need? Why? What kind of car do you want? Why do you want it?* Assign them the task of finding a picture of the kind of car they need and the kind of car they want. In the next session, have them take turns showing their pictures and describing what they need and want, and telling why.

More *Expansion/Extension* on page 82

Applying for a Learner's Permit

Purpose: To introduce the procedure for applying for a learner's permit; to give practice in following directions and in taking notes from a phone call

Teacher Preparation and Materials

1. Samples of passport, birth certificate, check or money order, application form for learner's permit, Social Security card, and library card or other document stating place of residence
2. Audiotape for Level 2
3. Driver's license manual from Department of Motor Vehicles for your state *(Expansion/Extension)*
4. Real or toy telephones *(Expansion/Extension)*

Warm-up

1. Ask learners if they have ever applied for a learner's permit. Have them name the documents they needed. (a check or money order; application form; passport, birth certificate, or other document proving age; Social Security number; a document showing place of residence in United States) Show learners any examples you have of these items.
2. Write on the board in the center of a semantic web *Proof of U.S. Residence*. Ask learners to name different documents that give this proof. (FOR EXAMPLE: an I-94 card, an Alien Resident card, a temporary amnesty card, an official letter from the Immigration and Naturalization Service) Complete the web with the names of these documents.
3. Ask learners *Where can you apply for a license?* (Department of Motor Vehicles, or DMV) Write the name on the board. (**Note:** The exact name of the agency may vary from state to state.)
4. Point to what you have written on the board. Explain that sometimes when learners give you information, you take notes on the board. Write the phrase *take notes*.

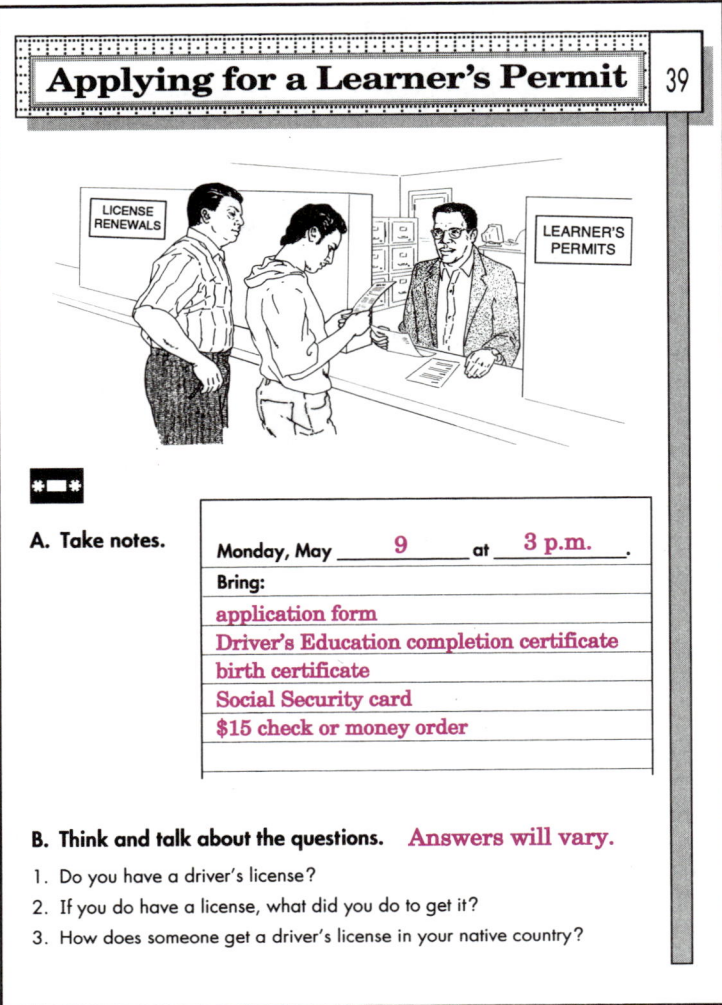

Presentation

1. Have learners turn to page 39. Ask questions about the picture to elicit known vocabulary. FOR EXAMPLE: *Who is in the picture? Where are Tony and Johnny? What are they applying for?*
2. Read aloud the direction line in exercise A and the outline for the note. Tell learners that Johnny wants to find out what he needs to apply for a learner's permit. Have them listen carefully to the conversation on the audiotape to find out the information. Play the audiotape and ask learners to complete the note. Replay the audiotape so learners can check their work and fill in missing information. Ask questions to elicit the correct answers. FOR EXAMPLE: *What time is Johnny's appointment? What are the three things he needs to bring with him?*
3. Put learners in pairs to answer the questions in exercise B. Ask volunteers to share their responses.

Expansion/Extension on page 82

Car Insurance

Purpose: To give practice in stating needs and in discussing options

Teacher Preparation and Materials

1. Information about compulsory and optional insurance coverage for your state
2. ▭ Audiotape for Level 2
3. Copies of car insurance applications and brochures *(Expansion/Extension)*
4. Arrange for an insurance agent to visit the class. *(Expansion/Extension)*
5. Copies of TRF Handout 4.6, *Sorry I Hit Your Car (Expansion/Extension)*

Warm-up

1. Ask learners *Who has a car? Do you have car insurance? What kinds of coverage do you have?* On the board write the headings *Must Have* and *Can/May Have*. Explain that *must have* means there is no choice; you are required to have it. *Can have* means that it is possible to have it, but you have a choice.
2. As learners describe their coverage, write under the appropriate heading what kinds of insurance a driver must have in your state (liability for medical injuries) and what kinds of insurance you can choose to have (collision). Explain that another word for *must have* is *compulsory*. Write this under the *must have* heading and say it aloud with the class. Repeat with *can have* and *optional*. Explain that when learners talk to insurance agents, they may hear the terms *compulsory* and *optional*.

Presentation

1. Have learners turn to page 40. Ask learners questions about the pictures to elicit known vocabulary. FOR EXAMPLE: *Who is Isabel talking to? What are Isabel and the insurance agent looking at? What must Isabel buy? What does it pay for? What can Isabel buy?* Read aloud the terms in the pamphlet and use the pictures to clarify any unfamiliar terms.

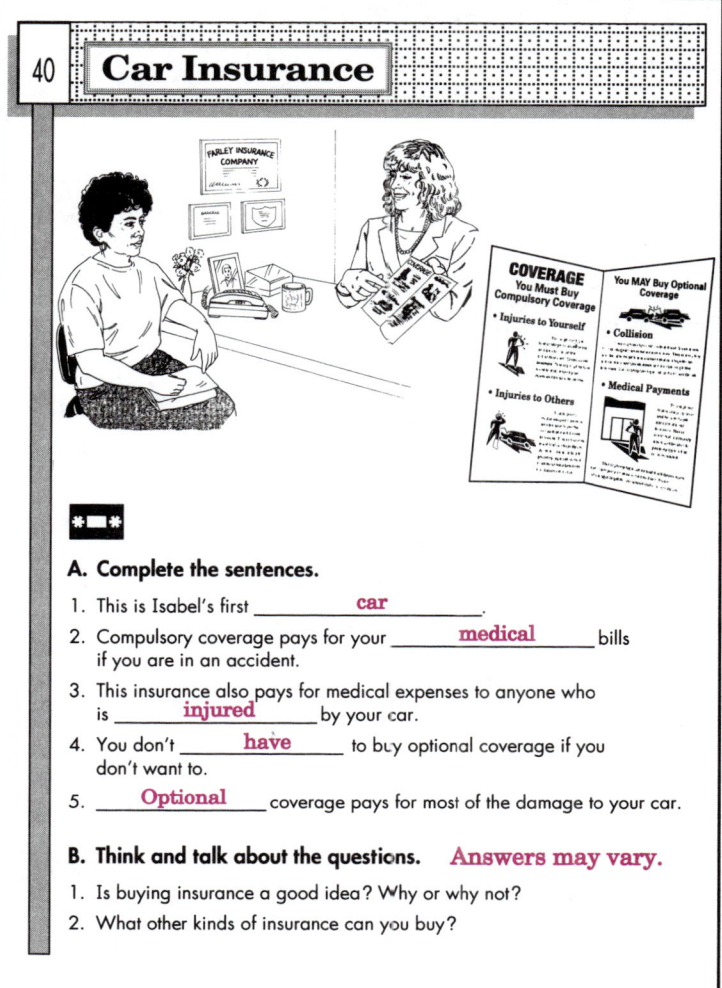

2. Read aloud the direction line and the statements in exercise A. Tell learners to listen carefully to the conversation on the audiotape to find out the missing information. ▭ Play the audiotape and then have learners complete each statement. ▭ Replay the audiotape so learners can check their work and fill in missing information.
3. Ask comprehension questions about the conversation. FOR EXAMPLE: *What does compulsory coverage pay for? What does optional coverage pay for?* Have volunteers give the correct answers for exercise A.
4. Put learners in small groups to discuss the questions in exercise B. Have the reporter in each group share some of the group's conclusions with the class.

Expansion/Extension

See **TRF HANDOUT 4.6**, *Sorry I Hit Your Car*

More *Expansion/Extension* on page 82

Reading a Graph

Purpose: To introduce information about insurance rates; to introduce reading a bar graph; to give practice in comparing and contrasting

Teacher Preparation and Materials
Pictures illustrating different kinds of seat belts, air bags, and antitheft devices, found in brochures from car dealers or auto magazines

Warm-up
1. Ask car owners *Does your car have seat belts? Are they automatic or do you fasten them? Does your car have an air bag? Does it have an antitheft device?* Show learners pictures illustrating seat belts, air bags, and antitheft devices. Explain that having these things can get you a discount on your car insurance. If necessary, review the meaning of *discounts*. Have learners guess why insurance companies give discounts for these features.

2. Tell learners you are going to make a graph that shows how many nationalities there are in the class. Start with your nationality. Make one square for yourself. Write your nationality under the square. Then ask what other nationalities there are. List the nationalities and the number of learners for each to one side of the graph. On the graph, make columns with the correct number of squares for each nationality. Write the nationalities under the appropriate columns. Tell learners *Nicaragua has five squares, so there are five Nicaraguans in the class.* Explain that this kind of graph is called a *bar graph*.
   ◼ In a one-to-one situation, make a bar graph showing the number of people with different nationalities that you and the learner know.

Presentation
1. Have learners turn to page 41. Ask questions about the graph to elicit known vocabulary. FOR EXAMPLE: *What is a senior citizen? What kind of discount is there for senior citizens? What do you need to get a 10% discount?*

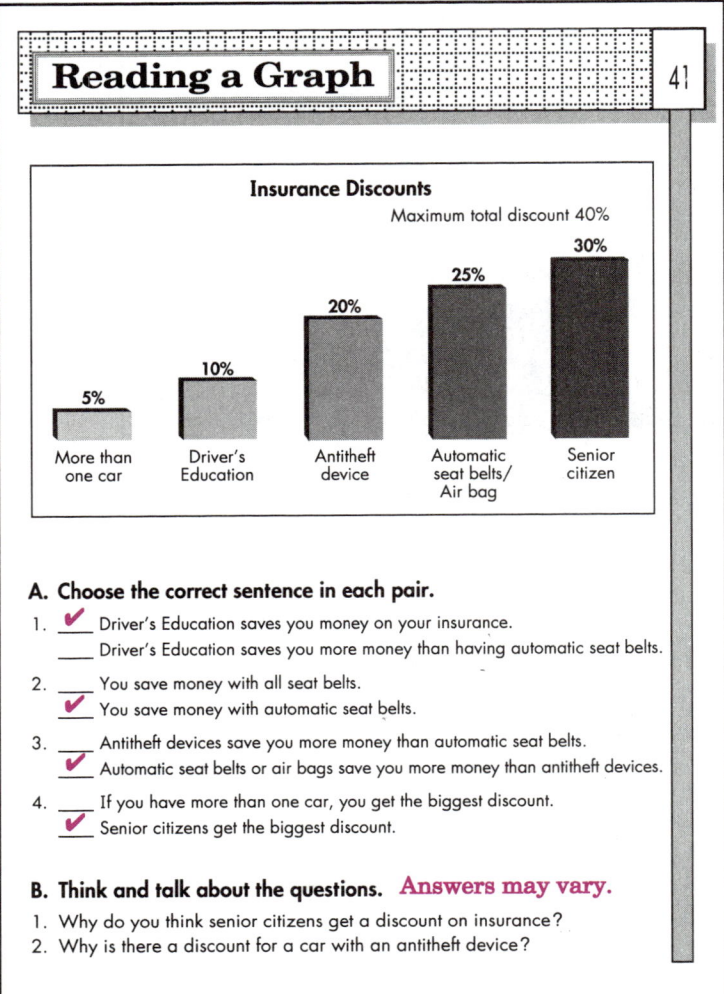

2. Have learners compare the discounts. Ask which one is the largest/smallest. Discuss how learners feel about the fairness of these discounts and why.

3. Point out the statement at the top of the graph about the maximum total discount. Ask volunteers to explain what this means and why an insurance company has this restriction.

4. Read aloud the direction line and sentences in exercise A while learners follow along silently. Explain that only one sentence in each pair is correct. Do number 1 together. Then divide the class into groups of three to complete the exercise. Have volunteers give their answers and reasons for the answers.

5. Have learners remain with their groups to discuss the questions in exercise B. Have the reporter in each group share some of the group's conclusions with the class.

Expansion/Extension on page 82

Reading a Driver's Manual

Purpose: To give practice in reading a driver's manual; to give practice with imperatives

Teacher Preparation and Materials

1. Sheets of colored construction paper; scissors; markers
2. Driver's license manual, used for page 39; copies of important pages from manual *(Expansion/Extension)*
3. Copies of TRF Handout 4.1, *Some Rules of the Road (Expansion/Extension)*
4. Copies of TRF Handout 4.2, *Driving Test (Expansion/Extension)*

Warm-up

1. Draw an octagon on the board. Tell learners *This is one shape for a traffic sign. Where have you seen this shape? What color is it? What word is usually written on it?* Write the word *STOP* in the center of the figure.

2. Ask learners to describe signs they have seen with different shapes and colors. Ask learners what each sign had written on it. Distribute sheets of construction paper and scissors and ask pairs of volunteers to cut out and create the signs they described. Have pairs take turns showing their signs to the class while others identify the signs.

3. Tell learners that they are going to read a page from a driver's manual. Explain that the manual prepares a person for the driver's license test. Even someone who never plans to take the test should still know the rules. The rules affect bicyclists and pedestrians, too. Note that rules vary from country to country and from one state to another (and occasionally even within a state). Whenever they move to a new state, drivers should obtain a copy of the manual from their new state.

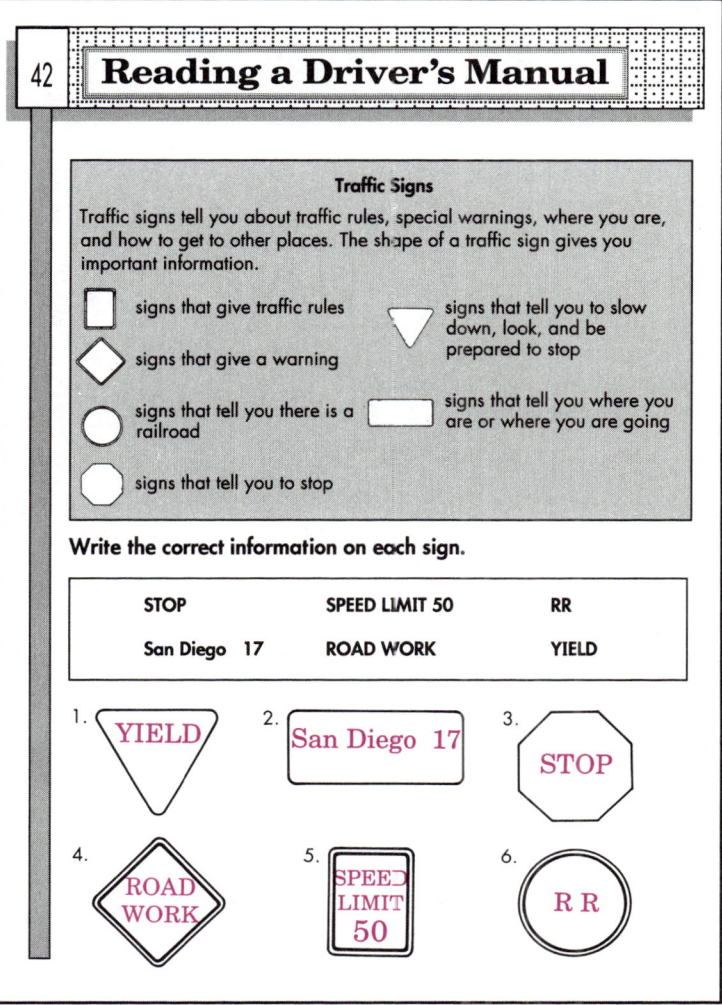

Presentation

1. Have learners turn to page 42. Ask questions about the signs to elicit known vocabulary. FOR EXAMPLE: *What shape is a railroad crossing sign? What do diamond-shaped signs tell you?*

2. Read the page aloud or have learners take turns reading in pairs. Clarify vocabulary as necessary. Show learners how to write *Yield* in number 1. Have them complete the rest of the exercise independently. Have volunteers give the correct answers to the class, explaining why they chose those answers.

Expansion/Extension

See **TRF HANDOUT 4.1,** *Some Rules of the Road*
TRF HANDOUT 4.2, *Driving Test*

- Tell learners to observe traffic signs for the next week. They should record the messages found on signs, as well as the shapes of the signs. Have volunteers draw and write on the board the signs they observed.

More *Expansion/Extension* on page 83

No Parking

Purpose: To give practice in reading a driver's manual; to introduce parking regulations

Teacher Preparation and Materials

1. A simple diagram of a street, including a crosswalk, fire hydrant, bus stop, and sidewalk (drawn on the board)
2. Copies of TRF Handout 4.3, *Where Can I Park? (Expansion/Extension)*

Warm-up

1. On the board, draw a simple diagram of a street, as described above. If necessary, explain the use of these features. Point to the different areas on the diagram and ask questions, such as *Do you think a car should park in a crosswalk? Should a car park right next to a fire hydrant? Why?* Point out how parking rules can affect pedestrians or people who use public transportation.
2. If possible, take the class outside to look for places where parking is prohibited. Point out any parking signs and ask learners why the signs are placed in these locations.

Presentation

1. Have learners turn to page 43. Ask questions about the pictures to elicit known vocabulary. FOR EXAMPLE: *Why shouldn't you park in front of a handicapped ramp? Where is the car parked in the first picture?*
2. Read the regulations aloud while learners follow along silently. Ask what can happen if you break the rules. (You can get a ticket.) Have learners think of other reasons why following parking rules is important. (to be polite to other people, for safety, to allow room for cars to pass, fire engines to reach buildings, and so on)
3. Read the directions for the exercise. Do the first item with the class. Then have learners complete the exercise independently. Ask them to share their answers with the class and say sentences that describe what is happening in each picture.

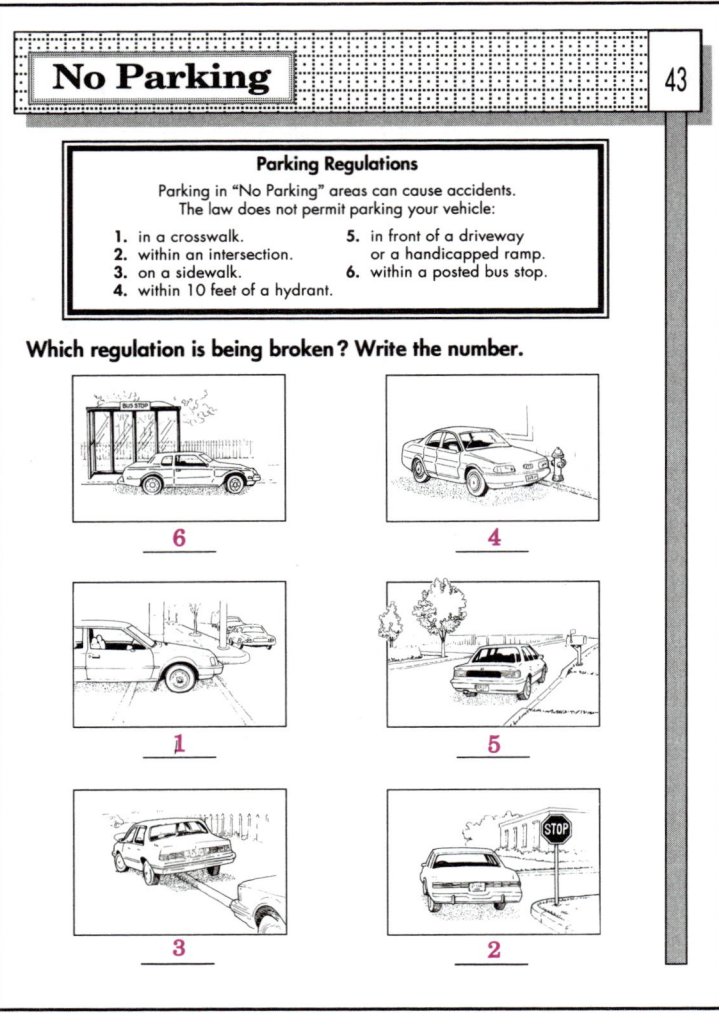

Expansion/Extension

See TRF Handout 4.3, *Where Can I Park?*

- Ask learners to think of other parking rules or parking signs they have seen. (FOR EXAMPLE: No Parking, Loading Zone) Put learners in small groups to brainstorm a list of parking rules. Have the reporter in each group share some of the group's conclusions with the class. Discuss the importance of these rules.
- Ask learners to observe parking signs in their neighborhoods for the next day or two. Have them copy the messages on the signs to share with the class.
- Ask if anyone in the class has ever gotten a parking ticket. Have them tell what happened and how much the ticket was for. Ask volunteers to share their experiences.
- Tell learners to think about parking rules in their native countries. Ask *Are the rules the same as in the United States? different? How? Are there more or fewer problems with parking? Why?* Put learners in small groups to discuss the answers to these questions.

More *Expansion/Extension* on page 83

Applying for a License

Purpose: To give practice in filling out a driver's license application

Teacher Preparation and Materials

1. A blank driver's license application (copied from page 44 onto the board)
2. Copies of a driver's license application form from your state DMV *(Expansion/Extension)*
3. Tape measure or yardstick *(Expansion/Extension)*
4. Bathroom scale *(Expansion/Extension)*
5. Arrange for a trip to a DMV or for a DMV representative to visit the class. *(Expansion/Extension)*

Warm-up

On the board, draw the blank license application, as described above. Call on a volunteer and fill out the application with the information he or she gives you. Clarify any unknown vocabulary. Discuss why this information is necessary.

Presentation

1. Have learners turn to page 44. Ask questions about the picture to elicit known vocabulary. FOR EXAMPLE: *What is Johnny doing? What form is he filling out?*
2. Read the direction line below the picture. Have learners fill out the forms individually. When they are finished, they can exchange forms with partners to check each other's answers.

Expansion/Extension

- Distribute copies of driver's license applications from your state. Have learners work in pairs, helping each other fill out the forms. Ask them to compare the information found on the state form to the information found on the application in the book. They should determine which questions are included on one form and not on the other and then discuss why particular information is/is not requested.

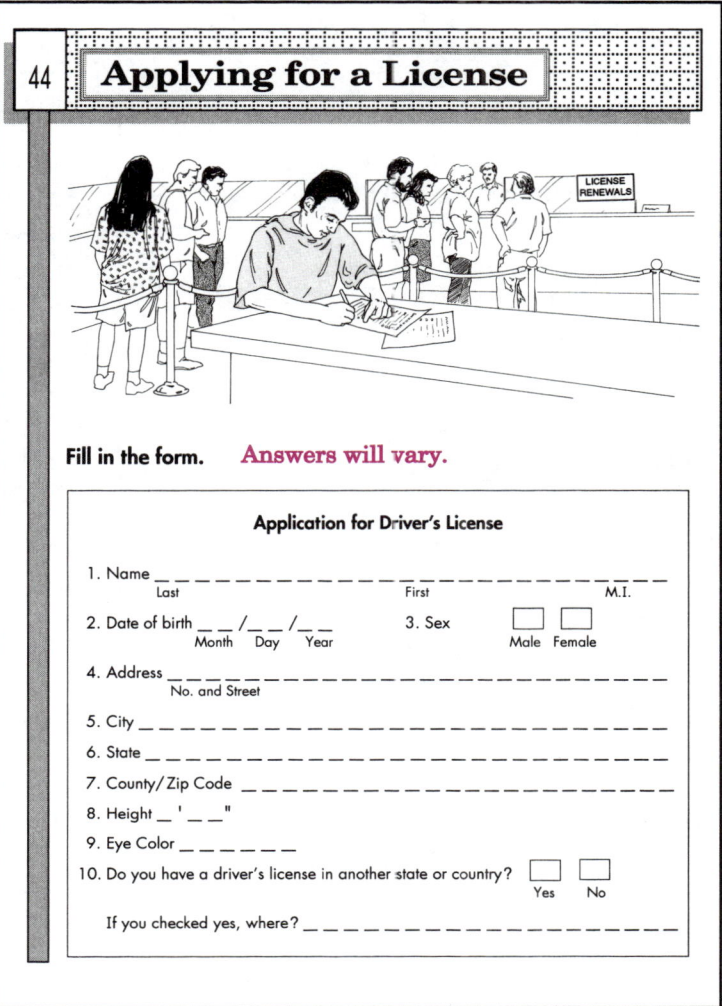

- Learners may not know their height in feet and inches. Bring in tape measures or yardsticks and have learners work in pairs to measure and record each other's height measurements. Ask learners to name other situations where people might have to know this information. (health insurance applications, etc.) If appropriate, and if learners are interested, bring in a scale for learners to weigh themselves in pounds. Teach the metric equivalent. (2.2 pounds = 1 kilogram)
- If possible, visit a DMV with your class or ask a representative to visit the class. Point out the different steps, such as application, payment of fees, license renewal, written test, road test, vision testing, photographing. Explain each step. If possible, have a DMV clerk give the group a tour and explain the procedure.
- Develop group or individual LEA stories about the visit to the DMV.

More *Expansion/Extension* on page 83

Taking the Road Test

Purpose: To give practice in following directions; to introduce instructions given during a road test

Teacher Preparation and Materials

1. A simple street map covering six to eight blocks in the neighborhood, with landmarks and signs (modeled from page 45 and drawn on the board)
2. 🔲 Audiotape for Level 2
3. Colored pens/pencils for tracing routes (optional)
4. Copies of a local map (*Expansion/Extension*)
5. Copies of TRF Handout 4.5, *How Do I Get to the Library?* (*Expansion/Extension*)
6. Copies of TRF Handout 4.4, *How Far Is It to San Diego?* (*Expansion/Extension*)

Warm-up

1. On the board, draw the map as described above. Ask a volunteer to come to the board. Give a series of directions on how to go from one place to another, while the volunteer traces the route on the map. Repeat with one or two more volunteers. Then have volunteers give you, or each other, directions.
2. Tell learners they will often need to know how to follow directions. Ask them to name some situations where following directions is important. Point out that one such situation is during a road test for a driver's license. Have learners who have taken a road test share their experiences with the class. ⬤ In a one-to-one situation, discuss your experience with the learner, and have the learner do the same, if appropriate.

Presentation

1. Have learners turn to page 45. Ask questions about the map to elicit known vocabulary. FOR EXAMPLE: *What street is the DMV on? Where is Carter School? Where do you think the road test will take Johnny?*
2. Read aloud the direction line for exercise A. Tell learners to listen carefully to

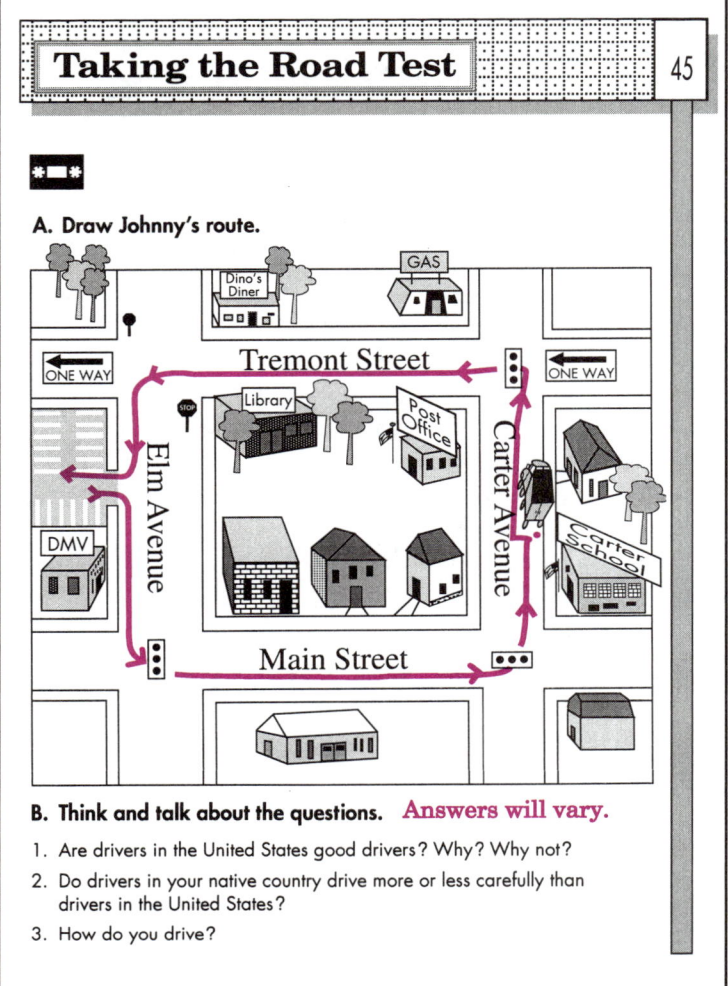

the conversation on the audiotape to find the route Johnny took on his road test. Give them colored pens/pencils, if available. 🔲 Play the audiotape and ask them to trace the route on the map as they listen to the examiner give directions. If necessary, show learners how to trace the route in your book. 🔲 Replay the audiotape so learners can check their routes and fill in missing information. 🔲 Play the audiotape a third time if learners are still unsure of their work.

3. Have learners compare their routes with a partner and note any differences. If necessary, copy the map and the correct route onto the board.

Expansion/Extension

See TRF HANDOUT 4.5, *How Do I Get to the Library?*
TRF HANDOUT 4.4, *How Far Is It to San Diego?*

- Distribute copies of a local map. Choose a starting and finishing point, and give learners directions to trace a route between these two points. Then have them continue in pairs, giving each other directions between two points on the map.

More *Expansion/Extension* on page 83

Getting Pulled Over

Purpose: To introduce talking to a police officer; to give practice with the past continuous tense, with the use of imperatives, and with *should have*

Teacher Preparation and Materials

1. ▭ Audiotape for Level 2
2. Slips of paper; a box or bag *(Expansion/Extension)*
3. Arrange for a police officer to visit the class. *(Expansion/Extension)*

Warm-up

1. Ask learners to describe times when they or someone they know was pulled over by a police officer. Have them tell what the problem was and what the officer said and did. If no one mentions it, describe a situation similar to the one on page 46.
2. Ask learners who have received tickets *What was it for? How much did you have to pay? What happened? Did the experience encourage you to follow traffic rules more closely?*

Presentation

1. Have learners turn to page 46. Ask questions about the pictures to elicit known vocabulary. FOR EXAMPLE: *Who's driving? Who got his license? What is the police officer doing?*
2. Tell learners that when the pictures are in the correct order, they tell a story about getting pulled over by a police officer. Ask learners to predict the correct order of the pictures and write the appropriate numbers in the boxes.
3. Tell learners to listen carefully to the audiotape to see if they numbered the boxes correctly. ▭ Play the audiotape and have learners check their sequencing. ▭ Replay the audiotape if necessary.
4. Read the direction line for exercise B. ▭ Have learners listen to the audiotape again and think about what they can write to describe what happened in each picture.
5. Pair learners and have them help each other write sentences about the pictures. ▭ Then play the audiotape one more time for them to check their work. Ask volunteers to share their stories with the class or in small groups.
6. Put learners in small groups to discuss the questions in exercise C.

Expansion/Extension

- Put learners in pairs. Tell them to pretend that one is a police officer and the other is a driver who has been pulled over for speeding. They should make up a conversation between the two. Have volunteers role-play their conversations in front of the class. Discuss what is appropriate and inappropriate to say in a situation like this. Ask learners what they might have done in their native countries in similar situations. Compare and contrast what is appropriate or inappropriate behavior in a situation like this in different cultures.

More *Expansion/Extension* on page 83

---

46 Getting Pulled Over

A. Put these pictures in order. Write the numbers.

[Pictures numbered 6, 4, 1, 2, 3, 5]

B. Write sentences about the pictures. *Answers may vary.*

1. _____
2. _____
3. _____
4. _____
5. _____
6. _____

C. Think and talk about the questions. *Answers will vary.*

1. Why do you think Johnny was angry?
2. Why do you think Tony drove home from the Department of Motor Vehicles?
3. What should Tony do about his speeding ticket?
4. Have you ever received a speeding ticket?

UNIT 4 • 79

A Speeding Ticket

Purpose: To introduce information found on a traffic/speeding ticket

Teacher Preparation and Materials

1. Form showing the basic parts of a speeding ticket: name, address, location, time of day and date of violation, road conditions, type of road, kind of offense, and total amount due (copied from page 47 onto the board)
2. Copies of a blank traffic ticket from the local police department *(Expansion/Extension)*

Warm-up

1. Review with learners why a driver might get a speeding ticket. Ask *What is the normal speed limit in a city? on a highway? What might happen if I drive faster than that limit?* Review with learners Tony's story from page 46. Explain that the terms *speeding ticket* and *traffic ticket* are sometimes used to mean the same thing.
2. On the board, copy the basic parts of the speeding ticket, as described above. Tell learners *Imagine that I got a traffic (or speeding) ticket yesterday. . . .* Invent a scenario and fill in the information as you read each section of the ticket aloud. Clarify vocabulary as necessary. Ask comprehension questions about the completed ticket, such as *What did I do wrong? How much do I have to pay?*

Presentation

1. Have learners turn to page 47. Ask questions about the ticket to elicit known vocabulary. FOR EXAMPLE: *Who got the ticket? Where did the violation happen? When did it happen? What is the total amount due?*
2. Read aloud the exercise below the ticket. Complete the first item together. Then have learners work in pairs to complete the exercise. Have volunteers share their answers with the class. Ask learners to rewrite the false statements to make them true.

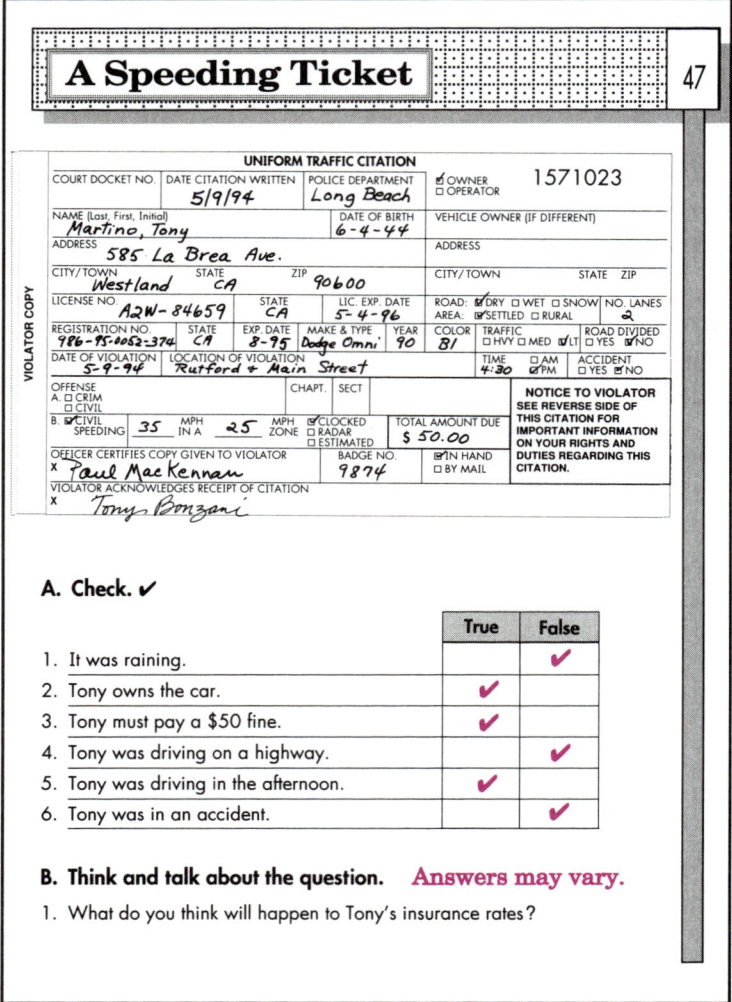

Expansion/Extension

- Have learners look at the ticket again. Ask *Why do you think all the information is important, such as conditions and time of day?* Lead a discussion about when and why accidents happen more frequently.
- On the board write *Ticket* as the center of a semantic web. Have volunteers add to the web with other words for *ticket*, other related words and phrases, and other situations where tickets are used. (movie theater, train or bus, sporting event, etc.)
- Ask *What else can happen when you get a ticket?* (You can get a fine, be put in jail, lose your license, have to take driver's education classes, go to court, etc.) Have learners describe times when they got a ticket unfairly. Ask what they did. If a majority of learners have had the experience of getting a ticket, have them develop LEA stories about their experiences. They may wish to read their stories in small groups.

More *Expansion/Extension* on page 83

Making the Connection

Purpose: To give practice in writing a note; to give practice with skills, functions, and vocabulary from Unit 4

Teacher Preparation and Materials
1. Pictures of dented/damaged cars
2. Real or toy telephones
   (Expansion/Extension)

Warm-up
1. Show the class pictures of dented/damaged cars or refer them to the picture of the dented car on page 48. Ask learners what is wrong with the cars and how the damage might have happened. Assist with vocabulary as necessary. (dented, damaged, fender, bumper, bumped into, etc.) Talk about the procedure that should be followed when a person is involved in a minor accident. (FOR EXAMPLE: Get the other person's name, address, license plate number, license and registration numbers, insurance company and insurance policy number. Note details of the accident. Contact your insurance company. Fill out accident reports.)
2. Tell the class *Imagine that I bumped into a parked car and dented it. I'm going to leave a note for the driver.* On the board compose a brief note similar to the one on page 48 and read it aloud with the class. Discuss why it is important to leave a note like this.

Presentation
1. Have learners turn to page 48. Ask questions about the pictures to elicit known vocabulary. FOR EXAMPLE: *What happened to the parked car? What did the driver put on the parked car?*
2. Have learners take turns reading the story in pairs. Next read the directions aloud to the class. Ask learners to write their notes independently and then have volunteers read their notes aloud to the class.

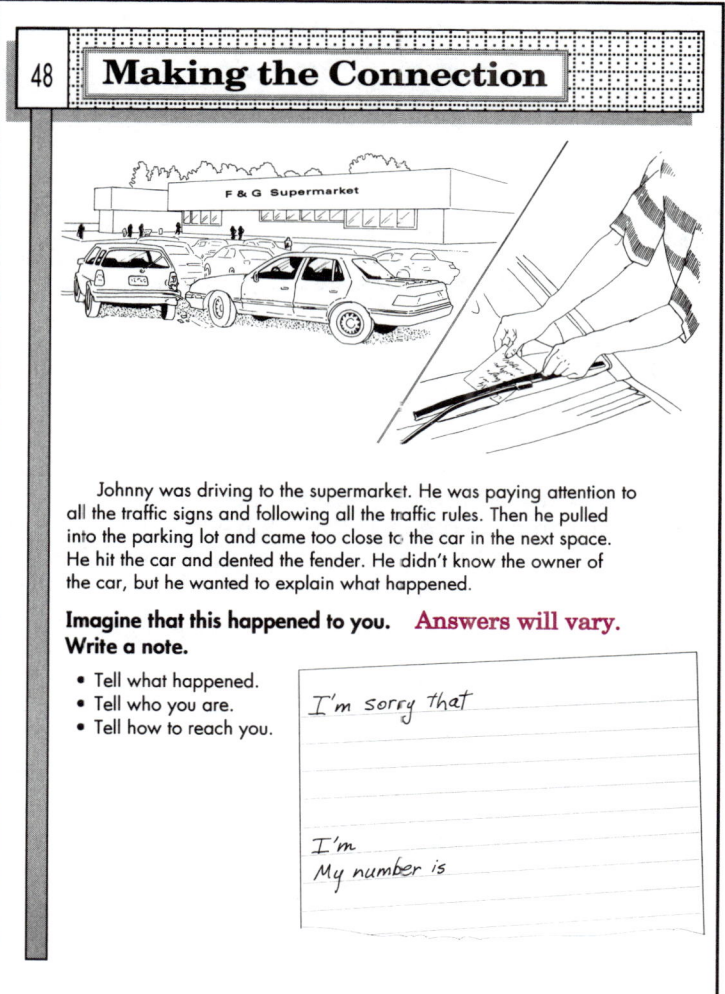

3. Discuss with learners how they think Johnny feels and how they think the owner of the parked car will react after reading Johnny's note.

Expansion/Extension
- Pair learners and ask them to change the ending of the story. (FOR EXAMPLE: Johnny didn't wait. He drove away fast.) Have volunteers read their new endings aloud.
- Put learners in pairs. Tell them *Imagine that one of you is Johnny and the other is the owner of the parked car. The owner has just called Johnny on the phone. What does the owner say? What does Johnny say?* Ask learners to write a conversation between Johnny and the car owner. Have volunteers role-play their conversations in front of the class. If possible, supply them with phones to use.

UNIT 4: Driving a Car
Expansion/Extension

Getting Around
More *Expansion/Extension* for SB page 38

- Tell learners *Johnny's dad is going to help him learn to drive. Did you ever teach someone to drive? Did someone teach you? What happened?* Ask a volunteer to describe the experience while you write the description on the board in story form. ■ In a one-to-one situation, tell and write your own story as a model. Then have learners write individual LEA stories about what happened when someone taught them how to do something or when they taught someone how to do something. It could be driving a car, riding a bike, or cooking a meal. Have learners read their stories aloud to a small group.

Applying for a Learner's Permit
***Expansion/Extension* for SB page 39**

- Show a driver's license manual for your state. Talk about the differences between a learner's permit and a driver's license. Identify ways that people learn to drive after getting their permits and have learners suggest advantages and disadvantages of each.

- Brainstorm with learners acceptable documents for proof of age. Write their suggestions on the board. Ask when else learners might need proof of their ages.

- Tell learners that the application and permit test are usually available in several languages. A volunteer can call the DMV, find out which languages they are available in, and then report back to the class. Discuss the advantages and disadvantages of taking the test in a language other than English.

- Put learners in pairs. Tell them to pretend that one is the DMV clerk and the other is the applicant. Have them make up a conversation about applying for a learner's permit. They can use the conversation on the audiotape as a model. Ask one or two pairs of volunteers to role-play their conversations in front of the class.

Car Insurance
More *Expansion/Extension* for SB page 40

- Distribute copies of car insurance applications and brochures to learners. Put learners in pairs and have them review the information. Answer any questions they have. Then have them individually fill out the application forms.

- Invite an insurance agent to visit your class and to discuss different kinds of automobile insurance that are available. Have learners ask questions. Encourage learners to ask why people need different types of insurance. After the agent has left, review the information that was discussed and answer any additional questions.

Reading a Graph
***Expansion/Extension* for SB page 41**

- Put learners in pairs. Ask them to discuss and to list the advantages and disadvantages of having seat belts and air bags. Have volunteers share their lists with the class.

- Have learners create another bar graph on how many learners use each method of transportation. (car, bus, subway, train, taxi, bike, etc.) Appoint a leader to gather the information from the class and a recorder to write the information on the board. A third volunteer can create the bar graph. ■ In a one-to-one situation, graph something familiar to the learner. FOR EXAMPLE: Graph how many of each type of relative he or she has—sisters, brothers, daughters, sons, aunts, uncles, nieces, nephews.

- Ask learners *Do you know of any families in the United States who own more than one car? How many do they own? Were there as many cars in your native country? Do you think it's good or bad to have so many cars?* Put learners in small groups to discuss whether it is good or bad and why. (FOR EXAMPLE: some good points—easier to travel and visit friends, easier to go shopping; some bad points—more pollution, more accidents, more traffic jams, less exercise) Have the reporter in each group share some of the group's conclusions with the class.

Reading a Driver's Manual
More *Expansion/Extension* for SB page 42

- Bring in a manual from your state DMV and distribute copies of important pages. Have learners read and discuss the rules in small groups. Ask them to talk about why these rules exist and why it is important for both drivers and pedestrians to understand and follow the rules.

No Parking
More *Expansion/Extension* for SB page 43

- Discuss special parking provisions, such as for the handicapped. Introduce the handicapped symbol and talk about where this symbol is found. (parking lots, on car license plates, on entrance doors and rest room doors) Ask learners why it is important for handicapped people to have special parking privileges and why it is necessary for others to follow handicapped parking restrictions.

Applying for a License
More *Expansion/Extension* for SB page 44

- Put learners in small groups. On the board write *DOB = date of birth, M.I. = middle initial,* and *DMV = Department of Motor Vehicles.* Explain that *DOB, M.I.,* and *DMV* are *abbreviations,* or short forms for longer words. Ask learners if they can think of other abbreviations and write their suggestions on the board.
- Tell learners you are going to have a contest to see which group can list the most abbreviations (and be able to explain them) within five minutes. They cannot include the ones on the board. When the time limit is up, have the group reporters come to the front of the class with their lists and take turns reading them aloud. The group with the longest, correct list wins. ■ In a one-to-one situation, brainstorm a list with the learner.

Taking the Road Test
More *Expansion/Extension* for SB page 45

- Ask if learners took road tests in their native countries. If so, have them describe what they were like and how they were different from road tests in the United States. Appoint a volunteer to lead a class discussion.
- Ask learners to describe anything funny, scary, or strange that happened to them while taking a road test.

Getting Pulled Over
More *Expansion/Extension* for SB page 46

- Ask learners to think of different problems that could cause a driver to get a ticket. (speeding, going through a red light, parking at a bus stop, and so on) Ask them to each write the problem on a slip of paper. Collect the strips in a box and shuffle them. Have each learner pick one and give an excuse or reason for the poor driving. (FOR EXAMPLE: My wife is about to have a baby, so I was driving a bit fast.) You may want to model one or two responses first. ■ In a one-to-one situation, both you and the learner should contribute several problems to the box. Take turns choosing a problem and giving an excuse or reason.
- Invite a police officer to talk to your class about traffic rules. Have learners ask questions. Afterward, provide any additional clarification.
- Put learners in small groups. Have them make up lists of traffic rules that affect bicyclists and pedestrians. Have the reporter in each group share some of the group's conclusions with the class.

A Speeding Ticket
More *Expansion/Extension* for SB page 47

- Discuss the possible consequences of disobeying traffic rules. (FOR EXAMPLE: losing your license, increase in your insurance rates) Ask volunteers to describe fines and other punishments given in their native countries for disobeying traffic rules. Learners can, in small groups, share their experiences with traffic violations.

1 2 3 4 **5** 6 7 8 9 10 11 12 Summary
Having a Good Time

Objectives

Functions
- Expressing preferences and pleasure
- Describing events and objects
- Comparing and contrasting
- Accepting and declining invitations

Life Tasks
- Choosing leisure-time activities
- Participating in sports
- Planning for recreation
- Getting information

Structures
- Tag questions
- Demonstratives: *these/those*
- *While* clauses
- Descriptive adjectives
- Future tense: *going to*
- Past tense

Culture
- Vacations and recreational activities
- U.S. holidays
- Leisure in the United States and in native countries
- Seasons

Vocabulary

Key words:

activity	how about
baseball	invite/invitation
basketball game	movies
beautiful	noisy
busy	picnic
concert	rides
cookout	short
daily	skinny
dancing	soccer
date	sounds good
delicious	special
describe	spring
fall	summer
fat	swimming
fishing	tall
free (time)	ugly
handsome	vacation
having a good time	weekend
holiday	winter

Related words:

aquarium	kite flying
boating	marine (animal)
bowling	outing
company	parade
exhibits	pool
festival	skiing
fireworks	sleeping bag
fishing pole	slide
football	talent show
get together	volleyball

Plans for the 4th of July

Purpose: To introduce U.S. holidays; to give practice in expressing preferences and in describing events; to introduce using the future tense: *going to*

Teacher Preparation and Materials
1. Pictures or photos of Fourth of July celebrations
2. Wall calendar *(Expansion/Extension)*
3. Copies of TRF Handout 5.1, *What Do You Like to Do? (Expansion/Extension)*

Warm-up
1. Have learners tell you what they know about the Fourth of July, such as when and why it is celebrated. Note that the Fourth of July is also called *Independence Day*. Ask if anyone has celebrated this holiday and how. Write key words and ideas on the board. Show pictures or photos of Fourth of July celebrations and ask learners to describe them.
2. Put the class in small groups. Model a chain drill, asking the first member of one group *What do you like to do for fun?* Have learners continue in their small groups. They can repeat the activity, using variations such as "What do you like to do on the Fourth of July? on weekends? at night? when it's hot outside?" Write the variations on the board. ◼ In a one-to-one situation, use the above questions to prompt a discussion with the learner.
3. Ask the class *What are you going to do this weekend?* Write some of their responses on the board. Go over the answers, saying *I'm/He's/She's/They're going to . . .* Explain that *going to* is a way to talk about the future. ◼ In a one-to-one situation, talk about plans for yourself, the learner, and members of the learner's family.

Plans for the 4th of July
What are they going to do?
What do you like to do on holidays?

Answers will vary.

Presentation
1. Have learners turn to page 49. Ask them to identify the characters they know. (Tony, Kim, Johnny, Joon, Han, and Isabel) Ask questions about the pictures to elicit known vocabulary. FOR EXAMPLE: *What holiday are Tony and Kim talking about? What are Tony and Johnny going to do? What are Kim and her family going to do? What is Isabel doing? What is she going to do?*
2. Read the questions at the bottom of the page. Have learners discuss the answers in small groups. Have the reporter in each group share with the class what the group members like to do on holidays.

Expansion/Extension
See TRF HANDOUT 5.1, *What Do You Like to Do?*

- Display a wall calendar and have volunteers find the date(s) for different holidays they celebrate.

More *Expansion/Extension* on page 96

Things to Do

Purpose: To give practice in expressing preferences and pleasure, in describing events, and in comparing and contrasting

Teacher Preparation and Materials
1. Copies of the entertainment section from your local newspaper
2. Arrange a class excursion (to a movie, festival, museum, or baseball game). *(Expansion/Extension)*

Warm-up
1. Tell learners that you are going to act out different things to do. Ask them to guess what the activities are. (FOR EXAMPLE: dancing, eating, playing basketball) Have volunteers act out other things to do while the rest of the class guesses what they are. Write the words for the activities on the board.
2. Ask learners *Do you like to go to the movies? to concerts? to parades? to watch fireworks? Why do you like them?* Clarify vocabulary as necessary.
3. Distribute copies of the entertainment section and ask learners if they ever read this part of the newspaper. Review the kind of information that can be found on these pages. (FOR EXAMPLE: activities, descriptions, locations, times, costs) Allow learners to look at the different activities. Answer any questions they have.

Presentation
1. Have learners turn to page 50. Ask questions about the newspaper page to elicit known vocabulary. FOR EXAMPLE: *Where is the listing for the basketball game? What time does the concert begin?*
2. Read the listings aloud while learners follow along silently. Clarify vocabulary as necessary. Point out that learners do not need to understand every word when they read these listings. They only have to understand the information they need, such as the time, place, and cost of an event.
3. Read the story aloud while learners follow along silently. Go over one or two items in

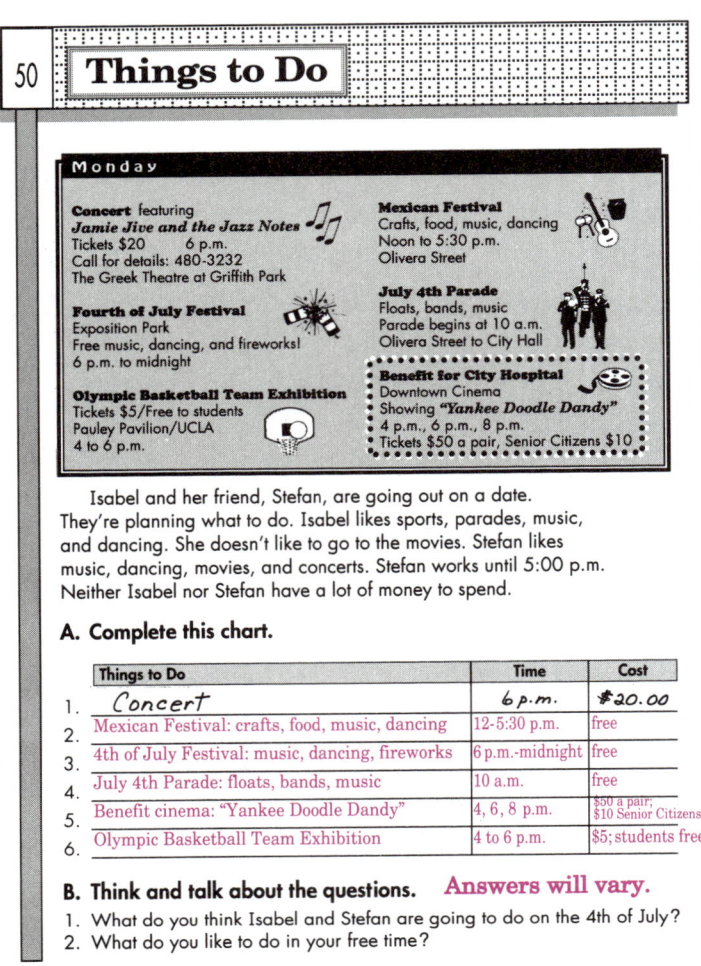

exercise A with the class orally. Then put learners in pairs to complete the chart. Have them check their answers in small groups.
4. Read aloud the questions in exercise B. In the same small groups, have learners answer the questions. Have the reporter in each group share some of the group's answers with the class.

Expansion/Extension
- Put learners in pairs. Have them rewrite the story on page 50, substituting their names and likes and dislikes for Isabel's and Stefan's. Do a model on the board with a pair of volunteers, if necessary. Then have the pairs decide on an activity to do together, based on their preferences. They can share their stories and choices in small groups. ◼ In a one-to-one situation, have the learner substitute his or her name for one character and your name for the other. Then decide on a suitable event to attend together.

More *Expansion/Extension* on page 96

Inviting Friends

Purpose: To introduce the skills of inviting, accepting, and declining

Teacher Preparation and Materials
1. Real or toy telephones
2. Audiotape for Level 2
3. A simple party invitation *(Expansion/Extension)*

Warm-up
1. Model phrasing for an oral invitation. (FOR EXAMPLE: *Would you like to go . . . ?*) Ask a volunteer to talk on the phone with you. Pick up one of the phones (or pretend to pick up a phone) and call him or her. Invite the volunteer to an event. Next have another volunteer call and invite you somewhere. Expand on the conversation, saying *Yes, Maybe,* or *No, I can't, but how about . . . ,* and offering alternatives. Then ask other pairs of volunteers to do the same. Have them vary the choice of events and their answers.
2. Ask learners to make a list of people who are likely to invite them places. (friends, co-workers, neighbors, family members, fellow students, and so on) Have learners describe their experiences with accepting and declining invitations.

Presentation
1. Have learners turn to page 51. Ask them to identify the characters they know. (Isabel, Olga, Monroe, and Joon) Ask questions about the picture to elicit known vocabulary. *Who is Olga talking to? Where does she want to go? Where does Monroe want to go?*
2. Tell learners to listen carefully to the conversation on the audiotape between Olga and Isabel to find out what they are saying. Play the audiotape and then ask comprehension questions, such as *What does Olga want to do? Can Isabel go with Olga? Where is Isabel going? What plans do Olga and Isabel make?*

3. Tell learners to look at the picture of Monroe and Joon. Ask a volunteer to pretend to be Monroe and suggest what Monroe might be saying. Ask another volunteer to take the part of Joon and suggest what Joon might be saying.
4. Put learners in pairs. Have them take the parts of Monroe and Joon, and write a conversation in their books. Ask volunteers to role-play their conversations in front of the class.

Expansion/Extension
- Write a simple invitation on the board (or bring in a real one), beginning with *You are cordially invited . . .* and concluding with *RSVP regrets only.* Discuss with learners how to read and respond to such an invitation. Then have them work in pairs to write similar invitations, such as an invitation to a birthday party.

More *Expansion/Extension* on page 96

The Company Picnic

Purpose: To introduce using *while* clauses; to give practice in describing events, and in comparing and contrasting

Teacher Preparation and Materials
Pictures of picnics

Warm-up

1. Display pictures of picnics and ask learners what is going on, where the event takes place, and so on. If necessary, explain what a picnic is.
2. Ask learners if they have ever gone on a picnic. If so, have them describe it.
3. Ask if the companies or factories where learners work ever have picnics or parties for the employees. If so, have them discuss what they do at the parties or picnics and where the events take place. Ask learners if they had company picnics or parties in their native countries and what they were like.
4. Perform two simple actions at the same time, such as opening the door and waving good-bye. Tell learners *While I opened the door, I waved good-bye.* Explain that when we talk about two things that happen at the same time, we often use *while*. Ask volunteers to perform two other actions at the same time. Describe the actions, using *while*, and write the sentences on the board for learners to use as reference.

Presentation

1. Have learners turn to page 52. Ask questions about the picture to elicit known vocabulary. FOR EXAMPLE: *Where are the people? What are they looking at? Who is giving the picnic? What is there to do? When is lunch?*
2. Ask volunteers to take turns reading the items on the announcement board. Then read the story aloud while learners follow along silently. Ask them simple comprehension questions, such as *What did Han and Jody do? Who ate lunch together? Who played soccer while others were in the talent show?*

3. Put learners in small groups. Have them read and discuss the questions at the bottom of the page. Have the reporter in each group share some of the group's answers with the class.

Expansion/Extension

- Put the class in small groups. Model a chain drill. Ask the first member of one group *What do you like to eat at a picnic?* That learner should answer, then turn to the next learner and ask the same question, and so on. If learners have never been on a picnic, ask *What would you like . . . ?* Provide additional questions, such as *What do you like to wear? do? play? Where do you like to go? Who do you like to go with?* ● In a one-to-one situation, use the above questions as the basis for a discussion with the learner.

More *Expansion/Extension* on page 96

Your Kind of Fun

Purpose: To give practice in comparing and contrasting, and in expressing preferences

Teacher Preparation and Materials

1. The Venn diagram (copied from page 53 onto the board)
2. Copies of the Venn diagram (Expansion/Extension)
3. Copies of TRF Handout 5.6, *I Want to See My Favorite Program (Expansion/Extension)*

Warm-up

1. Ask two volunteers to come to the front of the class. Write their names as the headings of two columns. Ask one volunteer *What do you like to do in your free time?* List the answers under the learner's name. Repeat with the other learner. Have them mention things they like to do at different times of the day, on the weekends, on sunny/rainy days, during different times of the year, and so on. Continue until a few of the same activities appear in both columns.
2. Ask the rest of the class *What activities do both of them like?* Have a volunteer draw circles around activities found in both lists.
3. On the board draw a Venn diagram as described above. In the center of the diagram, write the names of the circled items from the list. Write the names of the other items in the outer circles, labeling each with the appropriate learner's name.

Presentation

1. Have learners turn to page 53. Ask them to identify the characters they know. (Joon and Monroe) Ask questions about the pictures to elicit known vocabulary. FOR EXAMPLE: *What are Monroe and Joon talking about? What activities do you see?*
2. Put learners in pairs. They can read the question and write their own names on the blanks. Then ask learners to fill in the diagram, asking and answering each other's questions. Give a few examples with volunteers at the front of the class,

asking *Do you like swimming?* The learner should respond, "Yes, I do. Do you?" Then you say *Yes*. Explain that when both answers are yes, they should write the name of the activity in the intersection of the two circles. If only one answers yes, they should write that activity in the outer part of the circle for the appropriate learner. If both answer no, they should cross out the name of that activity. Ask learners to add other activities they like. ◼ In a one-to-one situation, complete the diagram with the learner.

3. Have volunteers copy their Venn diagrams onto the board. Discuss the similarities and differences between the diagrams.

Expansion/Extension

See **TRF HANDOUT 5.6,** *I Want to See My Favorite Program*

More *Expansion/Extension* on page 97

UNIT 5 • 89

Going Away for the Weekend

Purpose: To give practice in using the future tense: *going to;* to give practice in describing events

Teacher Preparation and Materials

1. 📼 Audiotape for Level 2
2. Copies of travel brochures or ads from the travel section of your local newspaper (*Expansion/Extension*)
3. Copies of TRF Handout 5.4, *Visit New York City* (*Expansion/Extension*)
4. Copies of TRF Handout 5.5, *What Movie Do You Want to See?* (*Expansion/Extension*)

Warm-up

1. Ask *Are any of you going away for the weekend? Where are you going? What are you going to do? What do you need to bring?* Make a list on the board. If none of the learners are going away for the weekend, pretend that you are. Tell learners where you are going and ask what you should bring. Write their suggestions on the board.
2. Ask learners if they have ever gone to a beach or to a lake. Ask *What did you do? Did you go swimming or fishing? Did you have a good time?*
3. Ask learners if they usually stay with someone they know or if they stay in motels/hotels when they go away. Discuss the advantages and disadvantages of staying in hotels versus staying with someone they know.

Presentation

1. Have learners turn to page 54. Ask questions about the picture to elicit known vocabulary. FOR EXAMPLE: *What is Johnny doing? Who do you think he is talking to?* Have learners guess Johnny's relationship to the woman on the other end of the phone. Then identify her as his Aunt Tessa.

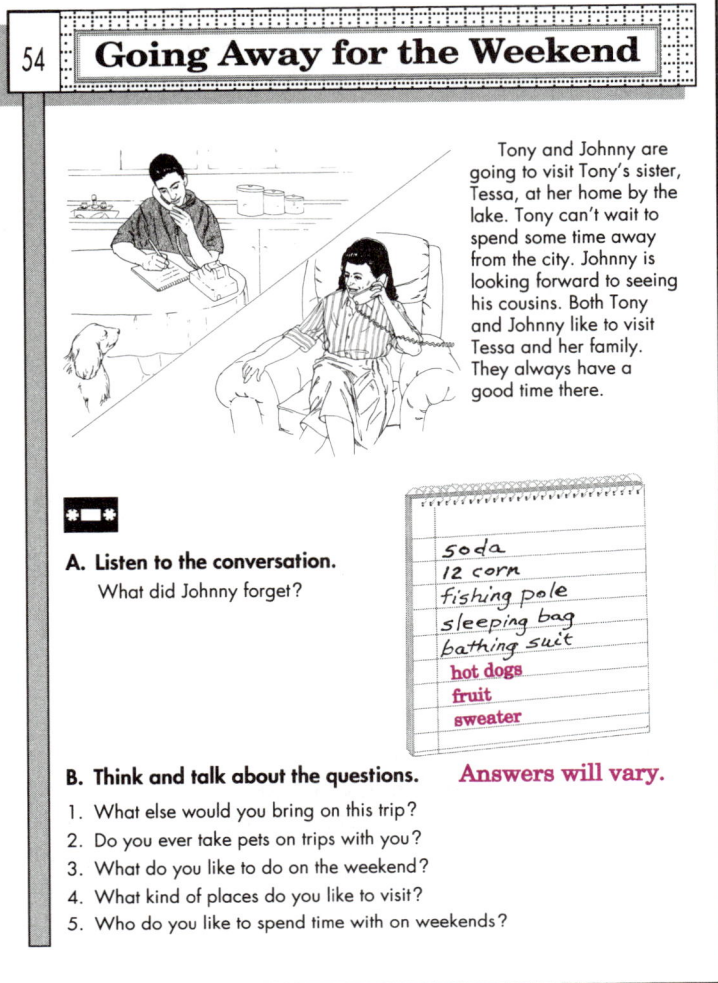

2. Put learners in pairs and have them read the story. Clarify vocabulary as necessary. Then tell them to look at the notepad and identify the purpose of the notes.
3. Tell learners to listen carefully to the conversation on the audiotape to determine the items that are missing from Johnny's list. 📼 Play the audiotape and then have learners complete Johnny's list. 📼 Replay the audiotape so learners can check their work and fill in missing information. Ask volunteers to name the things missing from the list.
4. Ask simple comprehension questions, such as *When are Tony and Johnny leaving for the lake? What are they going to do on Saturday? What does Tessa mean by "The fish are really biting"?* Clarify meaning as necessary.
5. Put learners in pairs to interview each other about the questions in exercise B. Have volunteers report the responses to the class.

Expansion/Extension on page 97

A Special Outing

Purpose: To give practice in describing events and in expressing preferences; to introduce reading vacation brochures

Teacher Preparation and Materials

1. Brochures from theme parks, zoos, and other attractions
2. Copies of TRF Handout 5.7, *Visit the San Diego Zoo (Expansion/Extension)*

Warm-up

1. Display pictures or brochures from different theme parks, zoos, or other attractions. Ask learners *What kinds of things can you do at these places? Who might like the different places? Why? What would you wear if you visited these places?*
2. Ask learners if they have ever visited a theme park, such as Disney World, or a zoo. Have volunteers describe their experiences, including what they did and saw. Ask if they would like to go back again. Discuss why or why not. Have a learner who has been to a water park tell what it was like.

Presentation

1. Have learners turn to page 55. Ask questions about the brochure to elicit known vocabulary. FOR EXAMPLE: *What can you see at Waters of the World? What can you do there? Who might enjoy this place?*
2. Read the brochure aloud while learners follow along silently. Point out that they do not have to understand every word. Clarify vocabulary as necessary.
3. Put learners in pairs. Read aloud the directions to exercise A. Have partners work together to answer the questions. Then group pairs of learners together to share and discuss their answers to exercise A.
4. Read the direction line and questions in exercise B. Suggest that learners stay in their groups and continue the discussion with the answers to these questions.

Expansion/Extension

See **TRF HANDOUT 5.7**, *Visit the San Diego Zoo*

- Ask learners to imagine that they are going to Waters of the World with their families or with a group of friends. Have them list the people who would be going and then figure out how much it will cost.
- Pair learners and ask them to bring in brochures or pictures of a theme park, water park, or zoo. They can get brochures from a local travel agency or bring in magazines from the library. Ask each pair of learners to select an attraction and to present interesting facts about the place.
- Put the class in small groups. Have each group look through the collection of brochures, select one place, and then plan a trip there. They should decide how much money they will need and what exhibits they will visit. Ask volunteers to describe their plans to the class.

More *Expansion/Extension* on page 97

Seasons

Purpose: To give practice in comparing and contrasting, and in expressing preferences

Teacher Preparation and Materials

1. Wall calendar
2. Map of the United States (or use map on Student Book pages 126–127)
3. Pictures of representative seasonal scenes
4. Copies of TRF Handout 5.2, *Let's Go on a Trip!* (Expansion/Extension)

Warm-up

1. Ask a volunteer to point out the present date on a wall calendar. Have another volunteer name what season of the year it is. Ask *What months are in this season? What are the names of the other seasons?* Have volunteers show on the calendar which months are in each season.
2. On the board, write the words *spring, summer, fall,* and *winter.* Display pictures showing representative seasonal scenes. Ask learners to describe the weather in your area during each season. Display a map of the United States and have a volunteer point to your location. Indicate other places around the country. Elicit or provide descriptions of the four seasons in different parts of the United States and in other countries.
3. Ask learners what they like to do in the spring, summer, fall, and winter. List their answers on the board under the appropriate season. Ask why they like to do those activities at that time.

Presentation

1. Have learners turn to page 56. Ask questions about the pictures to elicit known vocabulary. FOR EXAMPLE: *What is the young man doing? What is the weather like?*
2. Have volunteers take the parts of the characters and read the sentences aloud.
3. Put learners in pairs to ask and answer the questions in exercise A. Then tell them to find four different people to interview with the same questions.

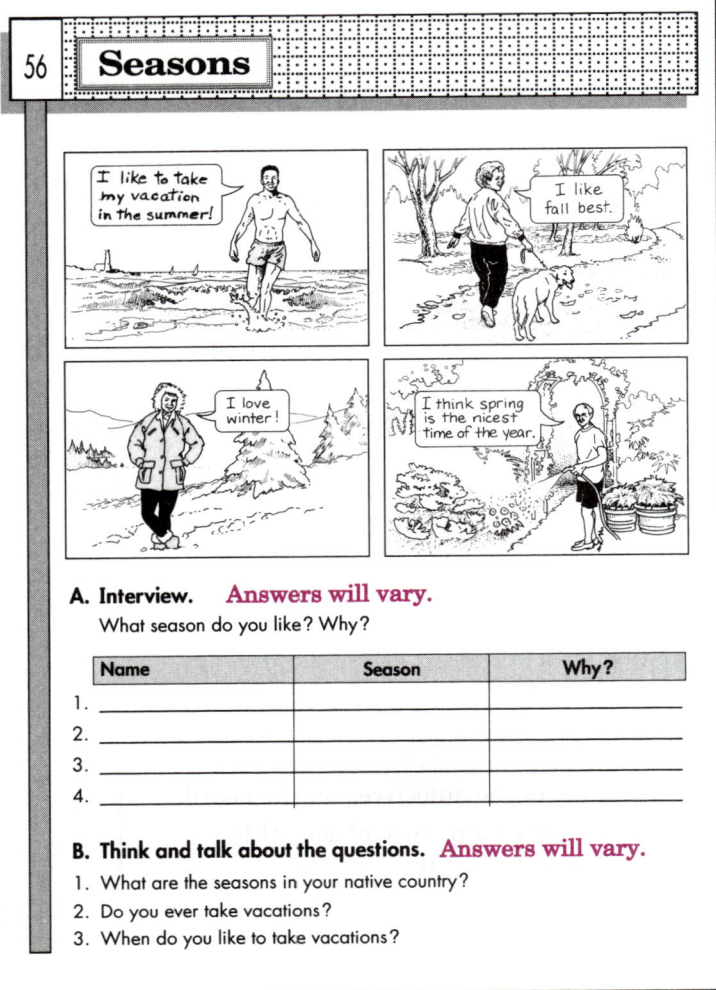

In exercise A, learners should write the names of the people interviewed, the seasons these people prefer, and the reasons for their choices. Ask volunteers to present the results of their interviews to the class. ◼ In a one-to-one situation, have the learner interview four people outside of the classroom. During the next session, go over the learner's results.

4. Put learners in small groups to discuss the questions in exercise B.

Expansion/Extension

See **TRF Handout 5.2,** *Let's Go on a Trip!*

- Group learners by favorite season. Have each group make a poster, mural, or collage about its season. Have them display and describe their work to the class. Display the posters in a prominent place.

More *Expansion/Extension* on page 97

Pictures from Vacation

Purpose: To give practice in describing people, events, and objects

Teacher Preparation and Materials

1. Pictures from a vacation you took
2. Pictures that demonstrate the adjectives *short, tall, fat, thin, pretty, ugly, dirty, clean, quiet, noisy, calm, wet,* and so on
3. Pictures of people with different features and clothing *(Expansion/Extension)*
4. Copies of TRF Handout 5.3, *Dream Vacation (Expansion/Extension)*

Warm-up

1. Bring in pictures from a vacation you took. Ask learners to comment on and describe the people and places they see. Write some of the adjectives on the board.
2. Display or draw a picture of something that is tall (a person or a building, for example). Elicit a description. (It's tall.) Write the word *tall* on the board. Then ask *What's the opposite of tall?* Write *short* opposite *tall*. Repeat with other pictures and opposites. FOR EXAMPLE: *dirty* and *clean; beautiful/handsome/pretty* and *ugly; calm/quiet* and *noisy*.

Presentation

1. Have learners turn to page 57. Ask questions about the pictures to elicit known vocabulary. FOR EXAMPLE: *What is Johnny doing? Does the lake look pretty? How does the food look?* Suggest that learners use the words on the board in their answers.
2. Read through the descriptions of the pictures. Then ask simple comprehension questions, such as *Is Aunt Tessa pretty? Is her husband short? What is Aunt Tessa's dog like? Were the children quiet?* Add to the list on the board any new adjectives mentioned. Ask learners for other words that mean the same or almost the same as these adjectives. Write their suggestions on the board next to the appropriate synonyms.

3. Put learners in pairs to write descriptions for the pictures in exercise A. Ask volunteers to read their answers aloud.
4. Have partners follow the directions in exercise B. Have them note any adjectives they use that are not listed on the board. Have them add these adjectives to the list.

Expansion/Extension

See **TRF HANDOUT 5.3,** *Dream Vacation*

- Explain how to play the following guessing game. Describe someone in class. Learners look around and try to think of who it is. When they have guessed correctly, continue describing other learners. (Avoid any features they may find embarrassing.) Use the pictures of people for additional practice in describing and identifying people. ◼ In a one-to-one situation, display the pictures of people with different features and clothing. Take turns describing a person and identifying the appropriate picture.

More *Expansion/Extension* on page 97

A Holiday Weekend

Purpose: To give practice in describing events and objects, and in comparing and contrasting

Teacher Preparation and Materials
Wall calendar *(Expansion/Extension)*

Warm-up
1. Ask learners to name some holidays and ask if they get time off from work or school on these different days. Talk about the concept of a *holiday weekend*.
2. On the board, draw a semantic web with the phrase *Holiday Weekend* in the center. Ask learners to add to the web with names of related activities, foods, events, descriptions of weather, and so on.
3. Have volunteers describe a recent holiday weekend, including what they did and where they went.

Presentation
1. Have learners turn to page 58. Ask questions about the picture to elicit known vocabulary. FOR EXAMPLE: *Who do you see? What are Isabel and Stefan doing? Where are the Lees?*
2. Have a volunteer read the words in the box. Then read the directions aloud and complete the first example with the class. Allow them to finish the rest of the exercise individually or in pairs. Ask volunteers to read the completed sentences aloud.
3. Put learners in pairs to write some sentences about how they think Isabel, Stefan, and the Lees felt the next day. Have volunteers read their sentences aloud to the class.

Expansion/Extension
- Put the class in small groups to brainstorm a list of activities for a holiday weekend. Ask them to name the time of year and typical weather for the holiday. Have the reporter in each group share some of the group's conclusions with the class.

- Ask learners to bring in pictures of holidays that are celebrated in their native countries or in the United States. Put learners in small groups. Have them show and describe the pictures to each other.
- Plan an International Holiday Festival. Have learners bring in costumes, food, music, and art objects used during the celebration of a particular holiday in their native countries. Ask them to make banners with the names of the holidays in their native languages and in English. Invite other classes to participate, if possible. On the day of the festival, assign one table for each holiday. Have learners hang their banners on the tables and display special items. Visitors can walk among the tables, sampling food and asking about artwork and costumes. ◼ In a one-to-one situation, investigate the possibility of attending a festival that is important in the learner's native culture.

Making the Connection

Purpose: To give practice with tag questions; to give practice with skills, functions, and vocabulary from Unit 5

Teacher Preparation and Materials
None

Warm-up
Ask a volunteer to help you write a letter on the board. Tell the volunteer *Pretend you want to write to a friend in English. You want to write about last weekend or something exciting that you did recently. Who are you going to write to? What do you want to say?* As the learner dictates to you, write the letter on the board. Read it aloud with the class, pointing out the date and the greeting and closing used in most personal letters in English.

Presentation
1. Have learners turn to page 59. Ask questions about the letter to elicit known vocabulary. For example: *Who wrote the letter? What day did he write it? Who is the letter to?*
2. Read the letter aloud while the class follows along silently. Ask simple comprehension questions, such as *What is Johnny writing about? Did he have a good time? Is he going back? When? What other news does he have? Is he going to see Gerry soon? When?*
3. Tell learners to think of different people they could write to. Discuss what they would like to write about. Elicit responses from different volunteers. Then have them write their letters to a relative or friend, using the outline on page 59 and the letter on the board as a model. Ask volunteers to read their letters aloud.

Expansion/Extension
- Ask learners to write letters to one of their former ESL teachers. They might write about something that happened recently or about a vacation they took. Have pairs of learners help each other with their letters. Ask learners to mail them and to report back on any responses they get.
- If appropriate, have the class write a letter to a former classmate. They can tell the classmate about things that have happened since he or she left. If possible, supply the classmate's address and mail the letter. Ask learners to report back on any responses they get.
- If any of the learners go on vacation or out of town, ask them to send postcards back to the class. Write the proper address on the board for them to copy and keep for future use.

UNIT 5: Having a Good Time
Expansion/Extension

Plans for the 4th of July
More *Expansion/Extension* for SB page 49

- Have volunteers describe holidays in their native countries. Do a model LEA story on the board by having a volunteer dictate a holiday story or description to you. Then ask learners to each choose a holiday in his or her native country and to write individual stories about it. Ask them to read their stories aloud in small groups.

- Conduct a class survey on favorite and least favorite holidays. On the board, write the names of the holidays named in the survey. Ask *Is the Fourth of July your favorite holiday?* Ask learners to raise their hands if their answer is yes. Continue with other holidays. Have a volunteer make a bar graph based on the survey, determining the class's favorite and least favorite holidays. ■ In a one-to-one situation, compare answers for the learner and yourself, but do not make a bar graph.

Things to Do
More *Expansion/Extension* for SB page 50

- Distribute copies of the entertainment section of your local newspaper. Have learners work in small groups to choose activities to do together. Ask volunteers to share their choices with the class, giving reasons for the decisions.

- Together, plan a field trip with the class (to a movie, festival, museum, or baseball game). Choose a time when all are able to attend. Plan transportation and expenses.

- After the field trip, have the class write individual stories about the experience. You may want to write a class LEA story on the board as a model. Ask volunteers to share their stories with the class.

Inviting Friends
More *Expansion/Extension* for SB page 51

- Discuss different ways of inviting people, and saying yes and no to invitations. Have learners help you construct a chart on the board, such as the following:

Inviting	Saying Yes	Saying No
Would you like to...?	Thanks, I'd like to....	Sorry, but I'm....
Can you come over on...?	Yes, thanks. I'm free on....	Thanks, but I'm busy on....

Generate additional items for the chart. Then have pairs of learners practice inviting each other in person or by using the phones. They should use a variety of questions, responses, and events.

- Tell learners to pretend that you are Isabel. It is the day you are supposed to go to dinner and you are sick. You must call Olga and tell her you cannot make it, but you would like to plan dinner for another time. Model this conversation for learners. Then put them in pairs and have them create conversations beginning with "Sorry, I can't go. I . . ." (have a sick child, have to work, have an emergency, have car trouble) "Can we . . . ?" (reschedule, postpone, make another date) Have volunteers role-play their conversations in front of the class.

The Company Picnic
More *Expansion/Extension* for SB page 52

- Plan a class picnic for learners and their families. On the board, list suggestions for picnic places in the area and kinds of food to serve. Put the class in small groups. Have each group take charge of one of the following details: place, date, and time; invitations; food; activities; and transportation. Have each small group present their plans to the class. Elicit suggestions to improve the plans.

- After the picnic is over, have learners write individual stories (or develop LEA stories) about the event. Have volunteers share their stories with small groups.

- Ask learners to compare picnics in their native countries with those in the United States. Ask *How are they the same? How are they different?* Write their comments on the board under the headings *Same* and *Different*.

Your Kind of Fun

More *Expansion/Extension* for SB page 53

- Distribute copies of the Venn diagram. Have learners choose new partners and repeat the exercise to find out if they have more or less in common with their new partners. ◘ In a one-to-one situation, have the learner fill out the diagram with a friend or family member. You may wish to vary this activity by using a more focused topic, such as kinds of music preferred or kinds of food preferred.

- On the board, list the activities from around the Venn diagram on page 53. Take a class survey, asking *Do you like baseball?* If the answer is yes, learners should raise their hands. Count the number of hands and write it on the board under the activity name. Determine which were the most favorite and least favorite activities. ◘ In a one-to-one situation, use the above questions as the basis for a discussion with the learner.

- Have a volunteer make a bar graph for the class, based on the information in the class survey.

Going Away for the Weekend

***Expansion/Extension* for SB page 54**

See TRF HANDOUT 5.4, *Visit New York City*
TRF HANDOUT 5.5, *What Movie Do You Want to See?*

- Put the class in small groups to list different places in the area where people go on the weekends. Suggest that they also make a list of things to bring to the different places. Have the reporter in each group share some of the group's ideas with the class.

- Distribute travel brochures or pages of ads from the travel section of your local newspaper. Have learners work in small groups to read the ads and discuss the advantages and disadvantages of each place advertised. Ask them to decide on and then to tell the class about the best offer and their reasons for choosing it.

A Special Outing

More *Expansion/Extension* for SB page 55

- Ask learners to use their imagination and to pretend they have free tickets to visit any place they want. Put them in pairs to discuss where they will go and what they will do and see.

- Have learners write individual stories about a special place they visited. If necessary, first interview a volunteer and write a model LEA story on the board. Ask them to read their stories aloud in small groups.

- Divide the class into two teams: Team A and Team B. Explain how to play the game called "I went to the park and saw a/an ____." The first player on Team A repeats the sentence and fills in the blank with a word that begins with the letter *a*. Then a player on Team B repeats what was said and adds a word that starts with the next letter of the alphabet. Continue playing alternating turns between teams. Score one point for each correct answer. ◘ In a one-to-one situation, play the game, alternating turns with the learner.

Seasons

More *Expansion/Extension* for SB page 56

- Ask learners to write stories about their favorite seasons in their native countries. Have them describe what the seasons are like, why they like them, and what they like to do during those seasons. Ask volunteers to read their stories aloud to the class. If they have any pictures, have them show the pictures to the class.

- Have learners play charades, acting out activities that can be done during different seasons. The rest of the class identifies the activity and tells during which season it can be done.

Pictures from Vacation

More *Expansion/Extension* for SB page 57

- Have learners take turns describing some object in the classroom. The rest of the class must guess what it is.

- Ask learners to bring in pictures of their families and/or pictures from vacations they have taken. They can show and comment on the pictures in small groups. They can also write captions or short descriptions.

1 2 3 4 5 **6** 7 8 9 10 11 12 Summary
Discovering Patterns

Objectives

- To help learners discover grammatical patterns already used in context
- To teach and give practice with those patterns

The structures covered are:

- past tense
- irregular past tense
- past continuous tense
- comparative adjectives
- modals: *can, could, would, should*

Learners will require frequent practice with and reinforcement of these structures before complete mastery can be expected.

About the Structures

• Verbs: Past Tense

This page concentrates on the regular past tense forms of verbs, including examples of verbs ending in a consonant that doubles before adding *-ed* and verbs ending in *y* that changes to *i* before adding *-ed*. Learners may have problems pronouncing the final /d/, /t/, and /id/ sounds.

• Verbs: Irregular Past Tense

The chart presents some common verbs that are irregular in the past tense. Frequent practice in different contexts should lead to memorization of these irregular forms.

• Verbs: Past Continuous Tense

This page introduces the forms of the past continuous tense and then compares the use of the past continuous with the past tense. Many ESL learners tend to overuse the past continuous, so it is important to give practice in distinguishing the two tenses and in demonstrating appropriate use in context.

• Adjectives: Comparative

The chart presents some common comparative adjectives that take different forms: forms with the *-er* ending, irregular forms, and forms using the words *more* and *less*. Learners identify comparative adjectives in context and practice their formation.

• Modals: *Can, Could, Would, Should*

The meanings and use of these modals are taught directly. Both affirmative and negative forms are taught and practiced. Extensive oral practice may be necessary for learners having difficulty with pronunciation of some initial consonants and with negative forms.

Verbs: Past Tense

Purpose: To give practice with the formation and use of the regular past tense

Teacher Preparation and Materials
Pictures that can be used to suggest a story in the past tense *(Expansion/Extension)*

Warm-up
1. Ask learners questions that will elicit answers with regular past tense forms. FOR EXAMPLE: *Did you walk to school today?* (Yes, I walked to school today.) *What time did our class finish yesterday?* (It finished at two o'clock.) *What time did it start?* (It started at nine.) *What did you study last night?*
2. Have learners answer questions about the characters, using regular past tense forms. FOR EXAMPLE: *What country did Joon and Kim Lee move from?* (They moved from Korea.) *Whose house did Joon paint?* (He painted his sister's house.)

Presentation
1. Have learners turn to page 60 and look at the chart. Point out the "Past Tense" column, explaining that these forms are used to talk about what happened in the past. (You may want to describe the past tense as the "yesterday" or "before" tense.) Tell learners that in English many, but not all, verbs add *-ed* for the past tense. Explain the irregular spellings if learners ask about them. (**Note:** To help learners hear the three different sounds of the *-ed* endings, it may be necessary to emphasize their pronunciation.)
2. Read through the sample sentences. Point out the structure *did/didn't* + simple form. Give additional practice, asking and answering questions such as *Did you work yesterday?* (No, I didn't work yesterday.) *Did your children study yesterday?* Have learners ask you similar questions.

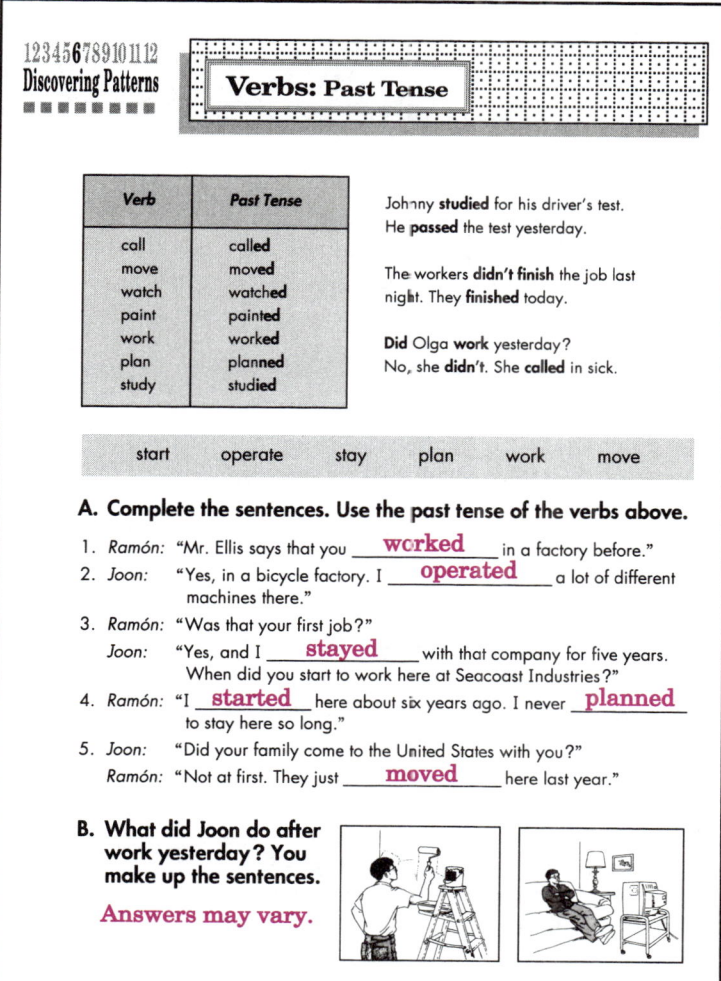

3. Read through the "Past Tense" column in the chart. Tell learners to complete the conversations in exercise A with the past tense of the appropriate verb. Ask two volunteers to read the completed conversation aloud.
4. Have learners work in pairs to complete exercise B orally. Ask volunteers to share their answers with the class.
5. Ask questions about the conversation that require the use of past tense verbs in the answers. FOR EXAMPLE: *Where did Joon work?* (He worked in a bicycle factory.)

Expansion/Extension
- Conduct a chain drill in which learners ask and answer questions, such as *What did you do after work/class yesterday? last week?*

UNIT 6 • 99

Verbs: Irregular Past Tense

Purpose: To give practice with the formation and use of the irregular past tense

Teacher Preparation and Materials

1. Index cards with words: *I, you, he, she, it, we, they*
2. Copies of a weekly calendar or enough small notebooks for each learner to keep a daily log *(Expansion/Extension)*

Warm-up

1. Ask learners *Where were you yesterday?* After they have given several answers, write the question and some of the answers on the board. Point out that *was* and *were* are irregular past forms of the verb *be*. Use the personal pronoun cards to conduct a substitution drill, showing the *I* card and saying *I was at home.* Show the *we* card and have a volunteer say the sentence, using the correct past tense form: "We were at home." Continue with other pronoun cards. Then repeat the drill, using questions and negative statements.
2. Ask learners if they know any other irregular verbs (that don't add *-ed* to form the past tense). As learners name verb forms, write them on the board. Include verbs from the chart on page 61.
3. Conduct a chain drill, using the verbs on the board. Have learners ask and answer questions, such as *What did you do yesterday?* Tell them to answer with complete sentences.

Presentation

1. Have learners turn to page 61 and look at the chart at the top of the page. Point out that some of the shortest and most common verbs have irregular forms in the past tense. Read through the simple forms and the past tense forms. Then name a simple form and have learners call out the correct past tense form.

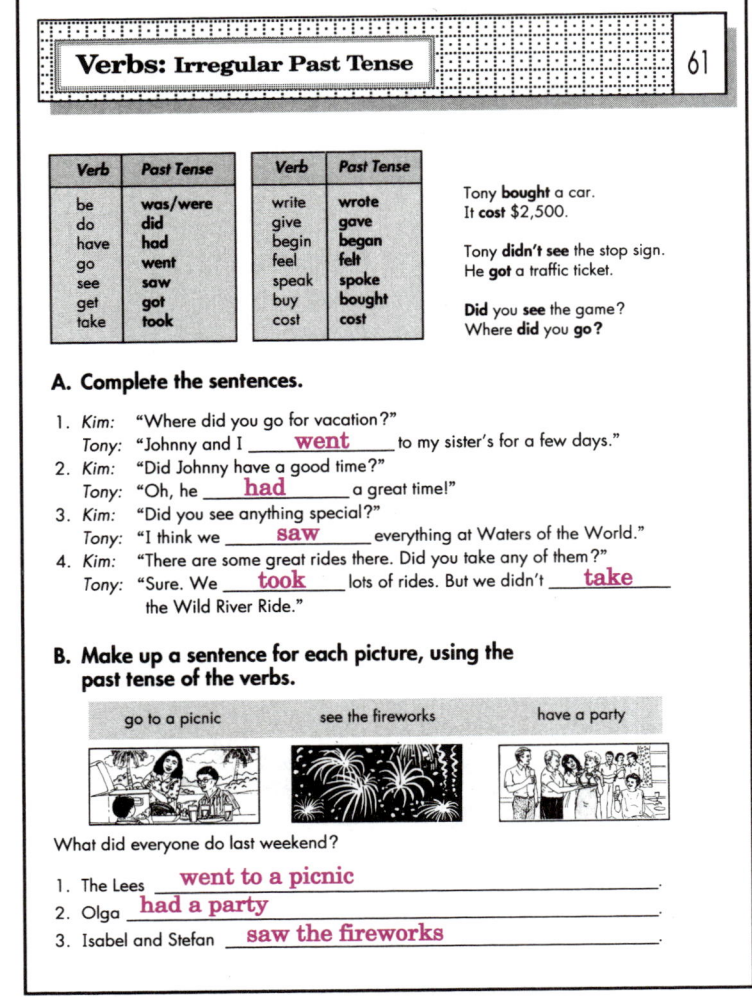

2. Read the sample sentences under the chart. Point out the use of *did/didn't* with the simple form of the verb.
3. Have learners complete exercise A individually. Then ask a pair of volunteers to read the completed conversation aloud. Ask questions, such as *Where did Tony go on vacation?* (He went to his sister's.) *What did Johnny see while on vacation?*
4. Have learners complete exercise B. Ask volunteers to read their answers aloud. Based on the answers, have learners make up questions, using the past tense. (FOR EXAMPLE: "Did Isabel and Stefan enjoy the fireworks?" "What did the Lees do at the picnic?")

Expansion/Extension

- Distribute copies of a weekly calendar or small notebooks. Tell learners to record their activities for the next week. When they have completed their logs, have learners talk about their activities with one another, using appropriate forms of the past tense.

Verbs: Past Continuous Tense

Purpose: To give practice with the formation and use of the past continuous tense

Teacher Preparation and Materials
Magazines with pictures of actions, such as walking, riding a bike, and smiling; scissors for all *(Expansion/Extension)*

Warm-up
1. Tell the class to watch while you read a book. Then ask *What was I doing while you watched me?* (You were reading a book.) Write the question and answer on the board and read it with the class. Explain that *was doing* and *were reading* are examples of the past continuous tense. They tell about something that was *going on* in the past.
2. Have volunteers act out something while you watch. Ask the rest of the class to describe it, using the past continuous. Write some responses on the board. Have learners look at the two verbs that make up the past continuous in each example. Lead them to conclude that these examples use *was* or *were* plus an *-ing* verb form.

Presentation
1. Have learners turn to page 62. Read the examples of the past continuous tense in the first chart. Use a substitution drill to practice the correct choice of *was* or *were*. Then say a verb (*work, move, paint, study, look, cook*) and have various learners each say a sentence, using one of the pronouns in the chart.
2. Read the examples labeled "Past Continuous Tense" and "Past Tense" on the charts. Compare and contrast the formation and uses of the past continuous and the simple past. If learners need more examples of the past and past continuous, use the verbs from the substitution drill in sentences for further comparison.

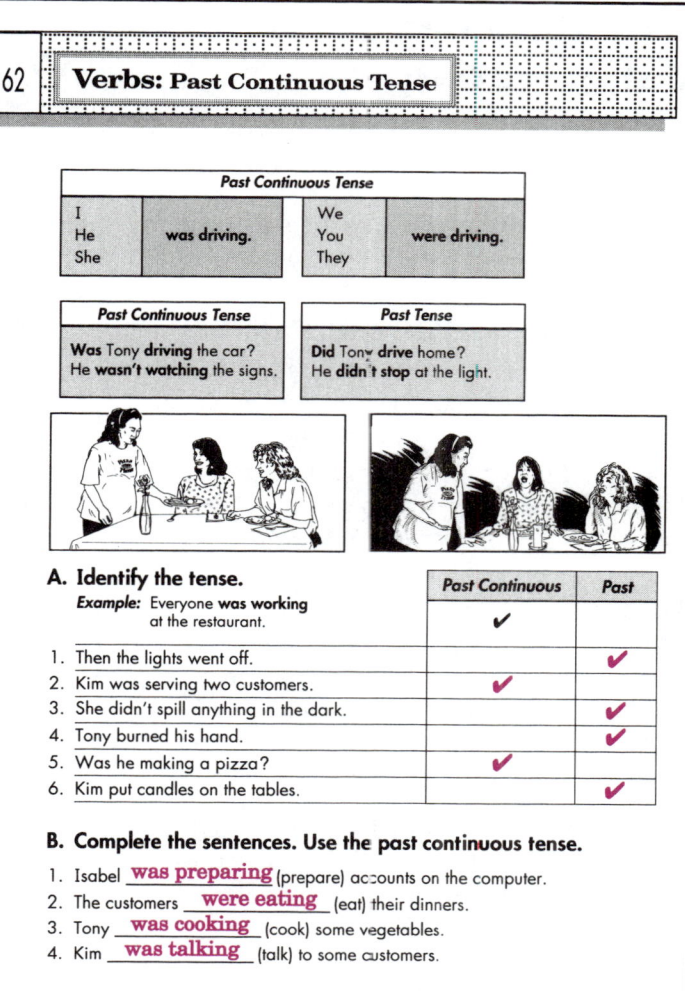

3. Have learners complete exercises A and B individually or in pairs. Ask volunteers to read their answers aloud.
4. Ask questions about the story to elicit either the past or the past continuous tense. Have learners identify the tenses they use in their answers. FOR EXAMPLE: *What happened at the restaurant?* (The lights went off. Past.) *How did Tony burn his hand?* (He was cooking. Past continuous.) *What did Kim do to help everyone see? What was Isabel doing when the lights went out?*

Expansion/Extension
- Put the class in pairs and distribute magazines and scissors. Tell learners to cut out pictures that show actions, such as walking, riding a bike, and smiling. Ask them to show and describe all of the actions in their pictures, using structures such as *When this picture was taken, the girl was walking down the street.* Emphasize the importance of the clause *when this picture was taken.*

UNIT 6 • 101

Adjectives: Comparative

Purpose: To give practice in identifying, forming, and using comparative adjectives

Teacher Preparation and Materials

1. Objects of various contrasting sizes and appearance (FOR EXAMPLE: old, small, cheap books; large, new, expensive books)
2. Copies of pages from store catalogs or fliers showing various styles and prices for similar items *(Expansion/Extension)*

Warm-up

1. Choose several pairs of items in the classroom to compare. FOR EXAMPLE: books, desks, chairs, maps. As you hold up or point out each pair of items, ask *Which one is smaller? bigger? more expensive? less expensive? Which one looks better? worse?* Ask learners to describe the pairs of items in greater detail, using their own words. Have them describe other objects in the room in a similar way.
2. On the board, write the comparative adjectives learners used. You might want to point out that they are called *comparative adjectives.* Have learners use comparative adjectives in other statements, referring to cars, apartments, friends, clothing, and so on.

Presentation

1. Have learners turn to page 63 and look at the chart at the top of the page. Read the examples aloud while learners repeat after you. Explain the spelling changes if learners ask about them. However, do not expect learners to master all spelling changes at this time.
2. Ask learners to find examples in the chart where the comparative adjective is not formed simply by adding *-er*, not counting spelling changes. Explain the use of the irregular forms *good/better* and *bad/worse* and the use of *more* and *less* with longer adjectives, such as *expensive*. Have volunteers read the example sentences aloud.

Adjectives: Comparative — 63

Adjective	Comparative	Adjective	Comparative
small	smaller	pretty	prettier
cheap	cheaper	good	better
large	larger	bad	worse
big	bigger	expensive	more expensive
			less expensive

Examples: This television is too **small.** Do you have anything **larger?**
These shoes are very **expensive.** Do you have anything **less expensive?**
The baseball game was **exciting.** It was **more exciting** than the parade.

A. Underline the comparative adjectives.

1. The sale at Franklin's is bigger than at S-Mart.
2. Franklin's is more expensive.
3. S-Mart is more crowded than Franklin's during sales.
4. Franklin's has a better selection than S-Mart.
5. S-Mart is closer than Franklin's.

B. Write the comparative adjective.

1. *Althea:* "Look at this. The prices are a lot ___cheaper___ (cheap) at S-Mart than at Franklin's."
2. *Olga:* "I like S-Mart's prices, but that store is ___noisier___ (noisy) than Franklin's."
3. *Althea:* "Yes, but S-Mart has ___better___ (good) buys. That's for sure."
4. *Olga:* "Well, the service is ___faster___ (fast) at Franklin's than at S-Mart."
5. *Althea:* "I don't know. I think the salesclerks are ___nicer___ (nice) at S-Mart."
6. *Olga:* "Well, I feel ___more comfortable___ (comfortable) at Franklin's. I'm going shopping there this weekend."

---

3. Have learners describe the picture and then complete exercises A and B individually or in pairs. Ask volunteers to read aloud the adjectives they underlined in exercise A. Then have volunteers read aloud the completed conversation in exercise B.
4. Make two columns on the board with the headings *S-Mart* and *Franklin's.* Elicit adjectives for each store and write responses in the appropriate columns. Then ask learners where they would shop and why.

Expansion/Extension

- Put learners in small groups and distribute copies of pages from store catalogs or fliers to each group. Ask them to find five pairs of items they can compare, using adjectives such as *more/less expensive; better/worse; bigger/smaller; prettier/uglier.* Ask learners to show and describe the pictures to the class.

Modals: *Can, Could, Would, Should*

Purpose: To give practice in understanding and using the modals *can, could, would, should*

Teacher Preparation and Materials
Pictures of people, animals, and objects (Expansion/Extension)

Warm-up
1. Ask learners *Can a duck drive a car?* On the board, write *A duck can't drive a car.* Ask *Who can drive a car?* Write *I can drive a car.* Ask *When I was a baby, could I drive a car?* Write *I couldn't drive a car when I was a baby.*
2. Pretend to drop your book. Ask a learner *Can you pick up my book for me?* Repeat, dropping two other items and asking *Could you pick up my pen? Would you pick up my chalk?* Write all three questions on the board.
3. Ask learners what things they should do if they want to learn English faster. (watch TV, read the newspaper, read books, talk more in English) Write their suggestions on the board under *To learn English faster, we should . . .*

Presentation
1. Have learners turn to page 64 and look at the chart at the top of the page. Read through the chart while learners follow along silently. Have them repeat the modals and example sentences after you. Clarify vocabulary as necessary. Point out the formation of the negative forms of *could* and *should*. Ask learners how to form the negatives of *can* and *would*. (can't, wouldn't) If necessary, explain that *can't* is a short way of saying/writing *cannot*.
2. Ask learners to describe the picture next to exercise A. Then read the directions and have learners underline the correct form of each modal. Have volunteers read the complete sentences aloud, using the correct modals.

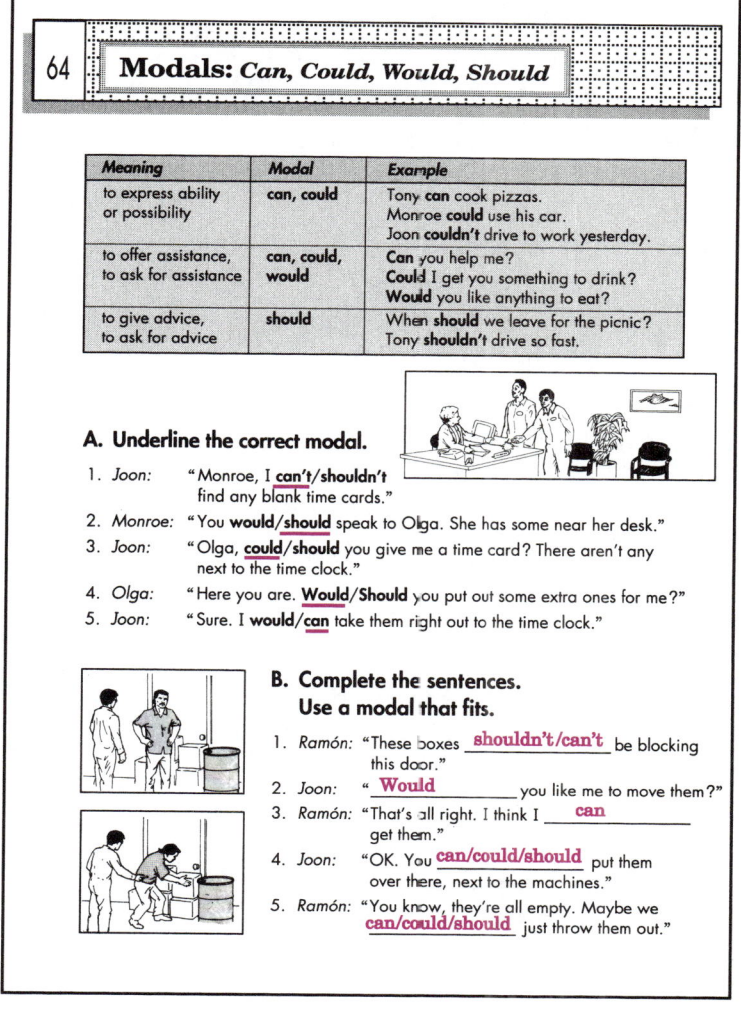

3. Have learners describe the pictures next to exercise B. Ask *What are they doing? Why?* Then ask them to complete the exercise with a partner. Point out that more than one answer can be correct. Have volunteers read the completed conversation aloud. Afterward, ask others to give alternative answers.

Expansion/Extension
- Put the class in pairs and distribute pictures of people, animals, and objects. Ask partners to make up statements about what the people/objects/animals can and can't do. Suggest that they consider both serious and funny statements. (FOR EXAMPLE: *A dog can bark. A dog can't make good pizza.*) Have volunteers show and describe their pictures to the class.
- Put the class in pairs to create short role plays offering or asking for assistance and using *can, could,* or *would*. Give a model if needed. Have volunteers role-play their situations in front of the class.

1 2 3 4 5 6 7 8 9 10 11 12 Summary
Wash and Wear

Objectives

Functions
- Comparing and contrasting
- Asking for information
- Expressing needs
- Expressing preferences
- Following directions

Life Tasks
- Buying clothing
- Caring for clothing
- Examining the cost of clothing

Structures
- Comparative adjectives
- Future tense: *will*
- Imperatives

Culture
- U.S. department stores and discount stores
- Sales and discounts
- U.S. sizes

Vocabulary

Key words:

blend	perfect
buttons	practical
(take) care (of)	price
cotton	rayon
dark	remove
department	sale
department store	shop
dry-clean	shopping
dryer	shirt
durable	shrink
fabric	size
fit	sleeve
formal	stain
important	style
iron	suit
label	tag
look (their) best	try on
mall	washer
outfit	wool

Related words:

ammonia	permanent
bleach	racks
blood	removal
casual	rinse
checked	rub
collar	scrape
delicate	shade
dressing room	snag
dressy	soak
fancy	sponge
frustrated	tweed
gum	washable
hair spray	wash and wear
ink	wedding
irregular	

Does It Fit?

Purpose: To give practice in stating needs and in comparing and contrasting

Teacher Preparation and Materials

1. Samples of clothes that are stained, too small or too big for you, and torn or damaged in some way
2. Catalogs/fashion magazines *(Expansion/Extension)*

Warm-up

1. Show learners an article of clothing that is too big or too small for you. Ask *Why can't I wear this? What should I do?* Repeat with stained or torn clothing. Write *too small, too big, stained,* and *torn* on the board.
2. Ask learners what they might do with clothing that is too small, stained, or torn. (Give it away, donate it to charity, take it to a professional cleaner, repair it, replace it with a similar or same item, etc.)

Presentation

1. Have learners turn to page 65 and describe the different clothes and characters in the picture. Ask *What's going on? What is Monroe doing? What is Althea looking at? Why do you think Jody looks unhappy? What kinds of clothing do you see in the picture?*
2. Ask learners to tell why they think the Bonners are looking over their clothes. Do the clothes look casual or dressy? Do they think Monroe, Jody, and Althea wear these outfits often? Why or why not?
3. Have learners work with partners to discuss possible answers to the questions at the bottom of the page. Suggest that learners consider where the Bonners might be going, what their problems are with their clothes, and what they might do about them. Have partners use their predictions to write a brief description of the situation to share with the class.
4. Ask learners if they have ever planned to wear a particular outfit to a special event and then found a problem with

the clothes. Have them describe the event, the problem, and what they ended up doing about the situation.

Expansion/Extension

- Tell learners to prepare for a class "Funny Fashion Show." They should bring in clothes that are too small or big, mismatched, and so on. Have learners take turns modeling their clothes while the rest of the class identifies the problems. Help with vocabulary as necessary. You may wish to have the class vote on the funniest outfit.
- Name some different problems that people can have with clothes. Say *My shirt is wrinkled. My skirt is too long. The zipper on my jacket is broken. The soles of my shoes are worn*, and so on. Have learners suggest solutions for these problems. Have different volunteers take notes on individual problems and suggested solutions. Keep the notes as the beginning of an ongoing class Clothing Care Guide.

More *Expansion/Extension* on page 116

Looking Their Best

Purpose: To give practice in comparing and contrasting, and in stating needs

Teacher Preparation and Materials

1. Torn apron, sweater, or coat
2. Catalogs/fashion magazines; posterboard, tape, and scissors for all (*Expansion/Extension*)

Warm-up

1. Describe a situation in which you wanted to look your best. FOR EXAMPLE: *I once went to a party at a very fancy restaurant. I was going to see many people I hadn't seen in a long time. I wanted to look my best.* Continue by describing the outfit you wore. Ask learners to name situations in which they wanted to look their best. (special party, important job interview, meeting someone important, etc.)
2. Ask the class what they would wear if they were going to a wedding. (best suit, dress, blouse, new outfit, etc.) Have learners provide details such as color, style, and accessories they would wear with their outfits.
3. Tell learners to imagine the following situation: *You have a wedding to go to next week. You had planned to wear your best outfit. When you take it out of the closet, you notice a large stain or tear. What would you do?* (buy a new outfit, wash it or try to have it fixed, borrow an outfit from a friend, wear something else, and so on)

Presentation

1. Have learners turn to page 66. You may want to review what happened on page 65. Ask questions to elicit known vocabulary about the picture. For example: *What is Monroe's problem? How does Althea look? Do they look their best? Why or why not?*
2. Have learners read the paragraphs silently. Check comprehension by asking different volunteers to read a sentence that describes each person's problem/solution.

3. Put learners in small groups to read, discuss, and write some possible answers to the questions at the bottom of the page. Ask the groups to share their answers with the class. Elicit several suggestions for questions 2 and 3, and write the responses on the board. Ask learners to identify the suggestions they think are the most/least expensive, most/least time-consuming, easiest, and so on. You may wish to vote on the most popular suggestion for Althea.

Expansion/Extension

- Put learners in groups of three to create and then to role-play possible dialogues between Monroe, Althea, and Jody. ◼ In a one-to-one situation, discuss possible conversations between the characters.

More *Expansion/Extension* on page 116

What Store Should We Go To?

Purpose: To give practice in comparing and contrasting, in asking for information, and in expressing preferences

Teacher Preparation and Materials
1. Audiotape for Level 2
2. Copies of clothing ads (Expansion/Extension)
3. Copies of TRF Handout 7.1, *People and Places at the Mall (Expansion/Extension)*
4. Copies of TRF Handout 7.2, *Shopping at the Mall (Expansion/Extension)*

Warm-up
1. Ask learners to name different kinds of stores that sell clothing. (department store, boutique or specialty shop, discount store, children's clothing store) If they mention specific store names, help learners identify the category each store fits in. Discuss the stores' features, asking *What kinds of stores sell inexpensive clothing? What stores sell one-of-a-kind outfits / children's clothing?*
2. Tell learners *I want to buy a new outfit. I would like to get something that is on sale. Where can I find ads for clothes? What stores should I go to in this area?* Write learners' comments on the board, including the names of local stores and/or malls. For those who are unfamiliar with the area, identify newspapers that carry ads for local retail stores. Mention the yellow pages of the phone directory as another source.

Presentation
1. Have learners turn to page 67. Ask questions about the picture. For example: *What is Monroe looking at? Why do you think he's looking at ads? What is Althea doing? What do you think they are talking about?*
2. Tell learners to find the four store names. Then ask them to listen carefully to the conversation on the audiotape to find out where Monroe, Althea, and Jody will go to buy their clothes. Play the audiotape

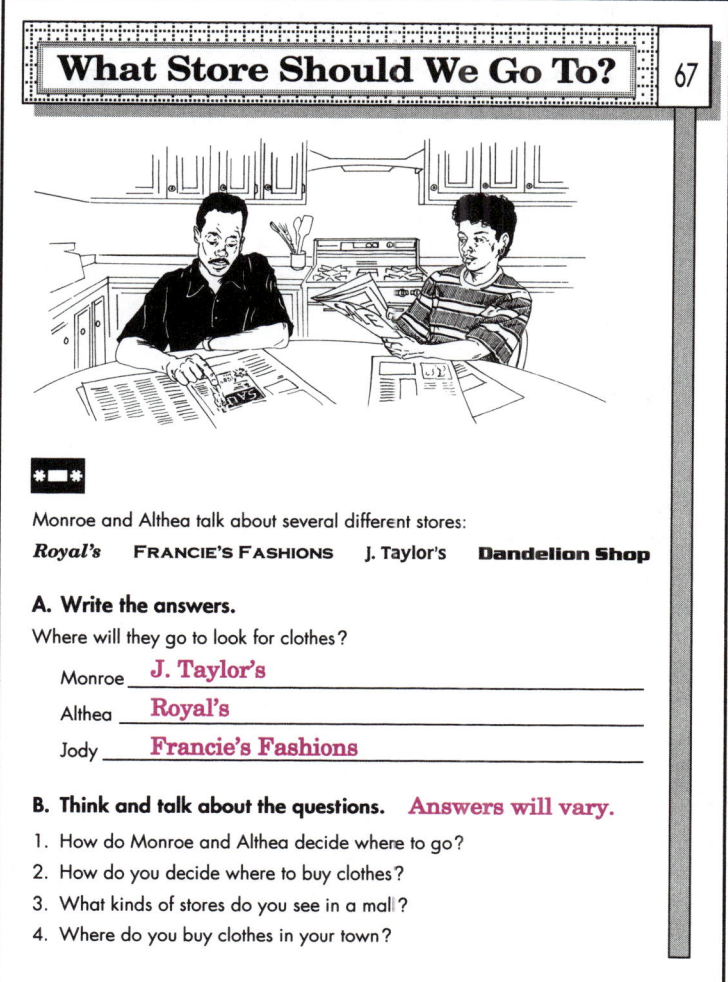

and have them complete the chart in exercise A. Replay the audiotape so learners can check their work and fill in missing information.
3. Put learners in groups to check their answers for exercise A and then to discuss the answers to exercise B. Ask groups to share their ideas with the class, giving advice to one another for making clothing purchases. List their suggestions on the board, followed by brief descriptions, such as *discount store* and *department store*. Include comments about each of the stores. (good quality clothing for cheap prices, largest selection around for children's clothing, etc.)

Expansion/Extension
See **TRF HANDOUT 7.1,** *People and Places at the Mall*
TRF HANDOUT 7.2, *Shopping at the Mall*

- Discuss and decide with learners how to organize the information from the board into a class shopping guide. (by store type, by prices, in alphabetical order, etc.)

More *Expansion/Extension* on page 116

Looking through the Racks

Purpose: To give practice in comparing and contrasting, in stating needs, and in expressing preferences; to give practice with *prefer*

Teacher Preparation and Materials

1. Samples of clothes made of different fabrics and with different patterns
2. Pages from clothing catalogs *(Expansion/Extension)*
3. Arrange a visit to a local department store. *(Expansion/Extension)*
4. Copies of TRF Handout 7.5, *Best Clothes for Me (Expansion/Extension)*
5. Copies of TRF Handout 7.7, *Let's Go Shopping! (Expansion/Extension)*

Warm-up

1. Ask learners how a store organizes the clothing it sells. Introduce the phrase *looking through the racks* by asking *Do most stores display clothes on hangers? Where do they hang them?* If necessary, mime the action.
2. On the board, write the headings *Colors, Fabrics,* and *Patterns.* Name examples from each category and ask learners where each belongs. (brown, blue; blends, wool, polyester, cotton; tweed, checks, stripes, plaids, and so on) As you write words under the categories, show learners samples of the appropriate colors, fabrics, and patterns. Ask learners to add words they know already. Have volunteers describe their own clothing, using color, fabric, and pattern names.
3. Ask learners if they have ever bought suits for men. Elicit descriptions of different styles. (business, dressy, casual) Ask *Did you find fitted jackets/loose-fitting jackets, long/short jackets, pants with cuffs/no cuffs, baggy/tight pants?* Have them describe the styles, fabrics, colors, and patterns they looked for, what they ended up buying, and why.

Presentation

1. Have learners turn to page 68. Ask questions to elicit known vocabulary about the picture. FOR EXAMPLE: *What is Althea doing? What sizes are these suits? What fabrics/patterns do you see?*
2. Read the paragraphs aloud with learners, one at a time. Ask literal and inferential questions after each one. After the first paragraph, ask *Which suit does Jody prefer? Which suit do you think is most suitable for a wedding? Which one do you think Monroe should buy? Do you think Monroe will get the suit Althea prefers? Why or why not?* Continue with the other paragraphs.
3. Have learners answer the questions in exercise A and share their answers in small groups. Have them continue in groups to discuss the questions in exercise B. Ask volunteers to state individual preferences, along with reasons. Suggest that they consider such factors as purpose for buying clothes (work, special events), climate/season, and so on.

Expansion/Extension **on page 116**

In the Men's Department

Purpose: To give practice in comparing and contrasting, in expressing needs and preferences, and in asking for information; to give practice with *will*

Teacher Preparation and Materials

1. Clothing tags that give fabric and care information
2. Audiotape for Level 2
3. Copies of TRF Handout 7.4, *Where's the Housewares Department? (Expansion/Extension)*

Warm-up

1. Ask learners to name some departments found in various clothing stores and items that could be found in each.
2. If possible, pass around clothing tags or labels. Discuss some of the fabric and care information, using examples from learners' (and your) clothing. Ask which fabrics usually last a long time (cotton, polyester) and point out that these fabrics are "durable." Ask which fabrics need careful treatment (rayon, silk) and point out that these are "delicate."
3. Discuss with learners how men's clothing is sized, pointing out which are smaller and which are larger sizes. Have them compare these sizes with those in their native countries. You may wish to make a chart on the board.

Presentation

1. Have learners turn to page 69. Ask questions to elicit known vocabulary about the picture. FOR EXAMPLE: *What is Monroe looking at? Who's he talking to? What does the tag say?*
2. Ask learners to read through the statements in exercise A. Clarify vocabulary as necessary. Tell learners to listen carefully to the conversation on the audiotape to find the word or words that complete each statement in exercise A. Play the audiotape and have them

write the correct answers. Replay the audiotape so learners can check their work and fill in missing information. Ask volunteers to read each completed statement. Continue with a discussion about the conversation on the audiotape. Ask *What did Monroe like about the suit? Did he like the fabric? Do you think he'll buy the suit? Why or why not?*

3. Have a volunteer explain how to figure the sale price of $135, using the regular price ($150) and the percentage discount (10%). If there is a clothing tax in your area, calculate the final cost, including tax.

Expansion/Extension

See **TRF HANDOUT 7.4,** *Where's the Housewares Department?*

More *Expansion/Extension* on page 116

UNIT 7 • 109

Choosing a Shirt

Purpose: To give practice in comparing and contrasting, in stating needs and preferences; to give practice with *Yes/No* questions

Teacher Preparation and Materials

1. Samples or pictures of four shirts of varied colors and styles
2. Audiotape for Level 2
3. Copies of ads for shirts *(Expansion/Extension)*
4. Copies of size charts for men's clothing *(Expansion/Extension)*

Warm-up

1. Tell learners that you want to buy a shirt. Discuss the features of the shirt samples/pictures. (long or short sleeves, light or dark shade, formal or casual, cotton or rayon, etc.) Ask which shirt learners would recommend and why.
2. Ask learners what features they look for in the clothes they buy. (easy-care, wash-and-wear fabrics; dry-clean-only fabrics; no-iron fabrics, etc.) Ask if they are concerned about shrinkage. Explain the word *shrink* if necessary. Have learners give reasons for their preferences. List some of the pluses and minuses for the various care features mentioned.
3. Elicit/explain the meaning of an "irregular" label on an article of clothing. Brainstorm with learners some advantages and disadvantages of buying irregulars. Discuss what things to look for and how to get a good deal on irregulars.

Presentation

1. Have learners turn to page 70. Ask literal and inferential questions about the picture. FOR EXAMPLE: *What are Althea and Monroe doing? Why do you think they are looking at shirts? What do you think Althea and Monroe might be talking about? Which shirts do you think Althea will like? Which do you think Monroe will prefer?*
2. Ask different learners to read aloud the six statements under the picture. Tell

them to listen carefully to the conversation on the audiotape to determine which statements are true and which are false. Explain that they may have to interpret the information given to arrive at the correct answer. Play the audiotape and then have learners work in pairs to complete the chart. Replay the audiotape so learners can check their work and fill in missing information. Have volunteers read the answers aloud. Continue with a discussion, asking if learners would have chosen the same shirt as Monroe or if they would have bought something different. Ask them to give reasons for their answers.

Expansion/Extension

- Distribute ads for different kinds of shirts and blouses. Put learners in small groups to discuss their preferences with respect to fabric, style, pattern, and color. Whenever possible, they should explain or give reasons for their preferences.

More *Expansion/Extension* on page 117

Jody's New Dress

Purpose: To give practice with vocabulary used in buying clothing, in caring for clothing, and in following directions

Teacher Preparation and Materials

1. Samples or pictures of various children's outfits
2. Copies of size charts for children's clothing *(Expansion/Extension)*
3. Copies of ads for children's clothing *(Expansion/Extension)*
4. Copies of TRF Handout 7.6, *At the Laundromat (Expansion/Extension)*

Warm-up

1. Show samples or pictures of various children's outfits. Lead a discussion on the sizes, colors, patterns, fabrics, and care required. Review the concept of *shrinkage*. Ask *Which clothes are easiest to clean? Which are most difficult? Which are best for children? Why? Why is it important to pay attention to shrinkage?*
2. Talk about sizes of children's clothing, including infants (0–24 months), toddlers (2T–4T), girls (4–14), and boys (4–18). Talk about the sizes or ranges of sizes that usually fit children of different ages and the importance of knowing size ranges when buying clothes for children.

Presentation

1. Have learners turn to page 71. Ask questions to elicit known vocabulary about the pictures. FOR EXAMPLE: *What is Jody looking at? What does the tag say? What kind of information on the label does Althea seem most interested in? What do you think each character likes best about the dress?*
2. Have learners read the information on the tag. Then ask volunteers to read aloud details that you ask for. FOR EXAMPLE: *What was the original price of the dress? What is the percentage discount?* Repeat with information from the care label. FOR EXAMPLE: *What fabric is the dress made of? How should you care for the dress?*

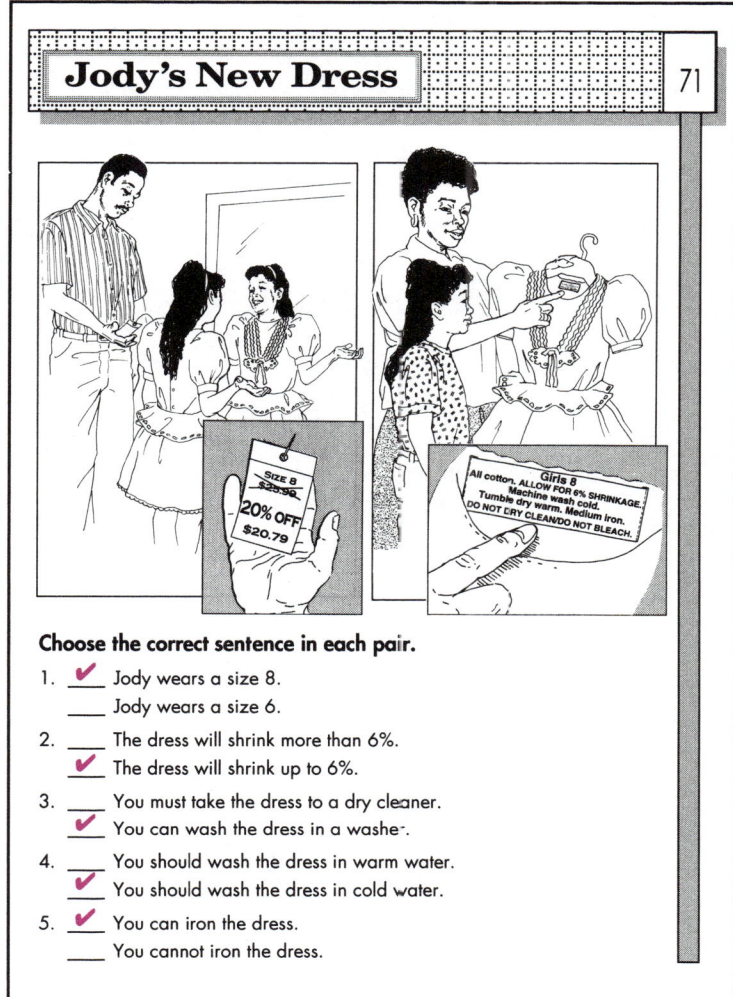

3. Pair learners to complete the exercise. After volunteers read the correct answers aloud, ask why each feature might be good/bad for a girl's dress, considering price, style, and care features. Have learners tell whether or not they think the dress is an overall good choice for Jody and why.

Expansion/Extension

See **TRF HANDOUT 7.6**, *At the Laundromat*

- In small groups, have learners discuss and list where to get clothes for children. Suggest that they consider price and selection. Group recorders should write their lists on the board. Ask volunteers to name stores where they usually shop and give reasons why.
- Distribute size charts for children's clothing from a catalog. Have learners work in small groups, choosing the right sizes for their sons, daughters, nieces, nephews, and so on. If necessary, have learners take measurements at home and bring them to the next class to determine the right size.

More *Expansion/Extension* on page 117

What's Important to You?

Purpose: To give practice in comparing and contrasting, and in expressing preferences about buying clothing

Teacher Preparation and Materials

1. Chart of important features of clothing (copied from page 72 onto the board)
2. Copies of the chart of important features of clothing *(Expansion/Extension)*

Warm-up

1. Tell learners to think about the last time they shopped for clothes. Ask *What did you look for? What was most important to you? Was it price, style, fabric, easy care? What else was important?* Write learners' comments on the board.
2. Talk about situations where each of the features could be most important. (easy care for clothes that are worn and washed often, nice style when you want to look good, durable fabric if you want something to last for a long time, etc.)

Presentation

1. Have learners turn to page 72. Ask if they think Monroe, Althea, and Jody have different or similar ideas about the important features of clothes. Have them guess which features are most important to each character.
2. Have learners read the first paragraph silently. Then ask volunteers to read key words or phrases that describe what is important to Monroe. ("sales," "hates to pay full price," "good material," "not wear out," etc.) Suggest that learners underline these words and phrases. Continue in this manner with the two remaining paragraphs and then have learners complete the chart.
3. Read aloud the question *What's most important to you?* On the board copy the chart, as described above. Interview one or two learners and then have learners interview each other in the same way. Suggest that they add more features to the chart if they wish. ◼ In a one-to-one situation, interview the learner, have the learner interview you and three of his or her friends or family members, and discuss the results.
4. Tell learners to tally the number of people who voted on each feature as important. Explain that more than one item can be important. As a class, discuss the results and possible reasons for them. Talk about what those interviewed do for work or in their free time and how this affects their choices. Ask volunteers to share any interesting comments from their interviews.

Expansion/Extension

- Distribute copies of the chart. Have learners use the chart to interview their family members and/or friends. They can report on the results in small groups, tallying and comparing the results with the interviews conducted in class to determine if the most important features are the same or different.

More *Expansion/Extension* on page 117

---

72 What's Important to You?

Monroe always looks for sales when he goes shopping. He hates to pay full price for anything. When he buys clothes, he wants good material that will not wear out quickly. He also wants to look good, so he looks for nice styles.

When Althea goes shopping, she looks for the same things that Monroe looks for. But she also wants materials that are easy to take care of. She doesn't like to iron, so she doesn't like to buy materials that wrinkle easily, like cotton.

The only thing that is important to Jody is style. She wants to look good all the time. She doesn't care about the price or if the material is durable and strong or if it's easy or difficult to care for. She just wants to look good!

Interview. **Answers will vary.**
What's important to you?

		Easy Care	Good Price	Nice Style	Durable Fabric
1.	Monroe		✓	✓	✓
2.	Althea	✓	✓	✓	✓
3.	Jody			✓	
4.	_____				
5.	_____				
6.	_____				
7.	_____				
8.	_____				
	Totals				

Looking for Another Blouse

Purpose: To give practice in comparing and contrasting, in asking for information, in stating needs and preferences, and in talking with a salesclerk

Teacher Preparation and Materials

1. Samples or pictures of three or four blouses in various styles
2. Audiotape for Level 2
3. Copies of size charts for women's clothing *(Expansion/Extension)*

Warm-up

1. Display the samples or pictures of blouses in the front of the room. Tell the class that you are a salesclerk. Ask a volunteer to pretend to be a customer looking for a blouse. Point out the different features of the blouses. Ask the customer what she is looking for, make suggestions, and then try to close the sale. Have other volunteers be customers and clerks.
2. Ask learners *Have you ever looked in several stores for a very specific piece of clothing and not found what you were looking for? How did you feel?* Introduce the word *frustrated* and have volunteers describe their own frustrating shopping experiences. Discuss the option of calling various stores in advance to see if they have the item you are looking for.

Presentation

1. Have learners turn to page 73. Ask questions to elicit known vocabulary about the picture. FOR EXAMPLE: *What is Althea doing? Who is she talking to? What do you think they are saying? What do you think Althea wants?*
2. Have different learners read aloud the statements in exercise A. Tell them to listen carefully to the conversation on the audiotape to find the missing words from each sentence. Play the audiotape and then ask learners to work with partners to complete the statements.

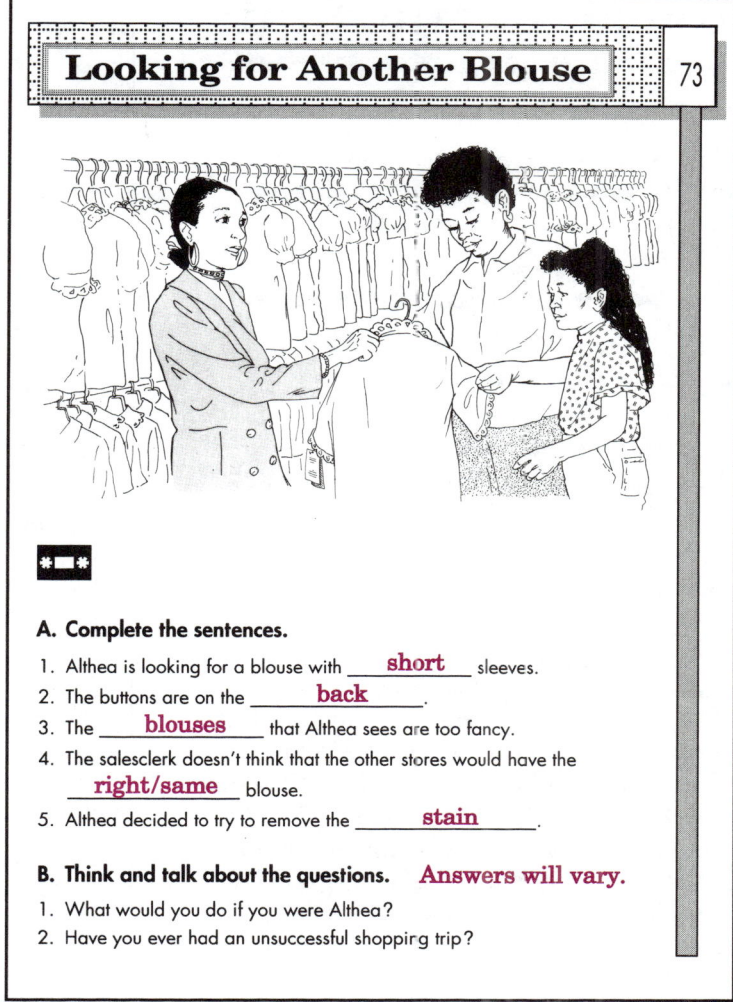

Replay the audiotape so learners can check their work and fill in missing information.

3. After volunteers read their completed statements, have learners think of Althea's different options. (buy a different blouse, continue to look in other stores, try to remove the stain, etc.) Ask if they think Althea made a good choice and why.
4. Put learners in groups to discuss the questions in exercise B. Ask the groups to share their most interesting Unsuccessful Shopping Trip stories with the class.

Expansion/Extension

- Have learners work in pairs, pretending to be a salesclerk and a customer. They should prepare a conversation between these two characters. The customer provides details about what he or she is looking for, and the salesclerk describes the items that are available. Ask volunteers to role-play their conversations in front of the class.

More *Expansion/Extension* on page 117

Removing the Stain

Purpose: To give practice in following directions and in caring for clothing; to give practice with imperatives

Teacher Preparation and Materials
1. Samples of fabrics; ink; hair spray
2. Articles of clothing (optional)
3. Copies of stain removal guides *(Expansion/Extension)*
4. Copies of TRF Handout 7.3, *Where Can You Find It? (Expansion/Extension)*

Warm-up
1. Mark a piece of fabric with some ink from a pen, reviewing the word *stain*. Ask learners *Can I get out/remove the ink? How?* Elicit different answers. Tell them that one way to remove ink is to spray it with hair spray and then sponge it off. Demonstrate, if possible.
2. Ask learners what other kinds of stains they and family members have had on their clothes. Have them describe methods they have used for removing different kinds of stains. If you have any interesting stain removal methods, share them with the class.
3. Ask learners what they would do with a stain on a dry-clean-only fabric. Would they try any of the methods described in the discussion? Why or why not?

Presentation
1. Have learners turn to page 74. Ask questions to elicit known vocabulary about the pictures and text. FOR EXAMPLE: *What is the first stain shown? What are the other stains shown on the page?*
2. Name one of the stains and have learners read aloud the removal directions. Elicit/explain the asterisks and statements at the bottom of the page. Ask literal and inferential questions. FOR EXAMPLE: *What is the first step for removing gum? What are all the things you need to remove fruit stains? What is one thing that should not be used on fruit stains? Why not? Which stain seems to be the easiest/most difficult to remove?*

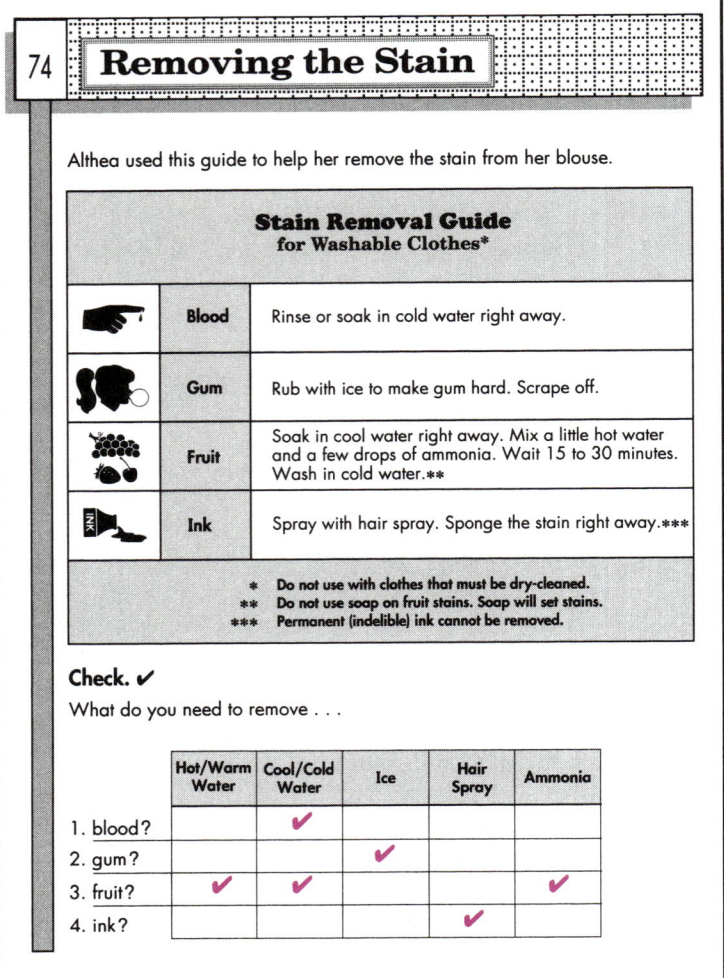

3. Put learners in pairs to complete the chart at the bottom of the page. Group the pairs together and have them check their answers.
4. Learners can work in pairs and take turns giving each other directions for removing the different stains. One learner gives directions, and the other learner pantomimes the directions given. If possible, provide each pair with an article of clothing to use in the pantomime.

Expansion/Extension
See **TRF HANDOUT 7.3**, *Where Can You Find It?*

- Distribute stain removal guides or ask learners to bring some in. Put learners in small groups to discuss the guides. Ask *Do you agree with the removal techniques? Why? Why not? Do you have better techniques?*

More *Expansion/Extension* on page 117

Making the Connection

Purpose: To give practice in comparing and contrasting, and in caring for clothing; to give practice with skills, functions, and vocabulary from Unit 7

Teacher Preparation and Materials
Pictures or samples of laundry-related items, such as bleach, detergent, washer, dryer

Warm-up
1. Tell learners a brief story about the last time you had problems doing the laundry. Describe what you did and what happened. Write your story on the board.
2. Use pictures or samples to review important vocabulary.
3. Ask one or two volunteers to tell about a laundry experience they have had or have heard about. Ask *What went wrong? What happened to the clothes? Were they ruined? Could the problem be fixed?* Assist with vocabulary. On the board, write words or phrases that learners may need in their written stories.

Presentation
1. Have learners turn to page 75. Ask questions to elicit known vocabulary about the pictures. FOR EXAMPLE: *What happened to Monroe's sweater? What is wrong with the blouse Althea is holding? What might have happened to the clothes Jody is holding?*
2. Have volunteers read the sentences aloud. Check comprehension by reading one of the results and asking a learner to read the sentence that describes the cause.
3. Tell learners to write their own stories about shrinking, fading, or ruining clothing in the laundry. Have them share their stories in small groups.
4. Discuss the importance of following the care instructions on clothing labels. Ask learners if any of the problems they wrote about were the result of not following proper laundering instructions.

Expansion/Extension
- Have learners draw washer and dryer dials on the board. Discuss the settings used for different kinds of clothes. Ask *What kinds of fabrics can be washed in hot water? With what kinds of fabrics do you usually use cold water? Why? What is the delicate cycle used for? What kinds of settings are available on most dryers?*
- Create a chain story. Divide the class into two teams: Team A and Team B. Appoint a scorekeeper and a timekeeper. Start a story by saying *One day I did the laundry and . . .* Have learners continue the story, alternating teams. Each team member must provide an appropriate sentence within 15 seconds. Score one point for each acceptable addition to the story. When the story is complete, you may wish to start with a different line. (FOR EXAMPLE: *When I looked in the dryer, . . . When I did the laundry last week, I heard the washer making strange noises.*)

UNIT 7: Wash and Wear
Expansion/Extension

Does It Fit?
More *Expansion/Extension* for SB page 65

- Discuss with learners when is it OK to wear stained clothes and when is it not OK. (You might wear old or stained clothes when doing yard work, cleaning, or any other activity in which the clothes might get dirty or damaged. You would not want to wear stained clothes to a special event, social gathering, or job interview.)

Looking Their Best
More *Expansion/Extension* for SB page 66

- Pair learners and distribute catalogs or fashion magazines. Have them look for pictures of clothing that would be appropriate to wear to a wedding. Encourage creativity and imagination. Suggest that learners look for outfits to wear to different kinds of weddings. (very formal weddings; informal gatherings; weddings that take place at strange places, such as at the beach or on a ski slope; outdoor weddings vs. indoor weddings; weddings that take place during different seasons) Ask partners to show and describe their pictures to the class.

- On the board, write the categories *Business, Special Events, Physical Work, Sports, At Home*. Ask learners to describe appropriate clothing for each. Then divide the class into five groups. Assign each group one category and have members make a poster with pictures of appropriate clothing. Have them show and describe their posters to the class.

What Store Should We Go To?
More *Expansion/Extension* for SB page 67

- Put learners in groups and assign each group the task of recording information for one of the stores in the class shopping guide. They may make additional comments about the individual stores already listed. Allow learners to add to the guide as they learn about different stores.

- Have each learner choose one article of clothing to use for comparison shopping. Ask them to visit different stores and check on the prices for that item. Have them note details that may affect the price, such as quality/workmanship, fabric, and style. Have volunteers report their findings, stating what they think is the best value and why.

Looking through the Racks
Expansion/Extension for SB page 68

See **TRF HANDOUT 7.5,** *Best Clothes for Me*
TRF HANDOUT 7.7, *Let's Go Shopping!*

- Distribute pages from clothing catalogs. Have learners work in pairs to identify and list the different styles and fabrics.

- Have learners select favorite styles and fabrics from the pages, and then compare prices. They should decide which prices are reasonable and which are unreasonable, and why.

- Visit a department store with learners. As you walk around, talk about the different kinds of clothing, fabrics, sizes, and prices. Ask learners to rate the store as inexpensive, moderate, or expensive.

In the Men's Department
More *Expansion/Extension* for SB page 69

- Have learners work in small groups to name places that sell clothing at discounted prices. (second-hand or thrift shops, garage sales, factory outlets, etc.) Ask them to list reasons why these items are sold at discounted prices. (FOR EXAMPLE: The styles are being discontinued. The clothing is from past seasons. The clothing is irregular or slightly damaged. The clothing may be slightly damaged or not damaged at all after fires or other disasters. The items have been used.)

- Ask learners to give pros and cons for shopping at places with discounted/used clothing. (pros: savings, support causes, interesting/different clothing; cons: lesser quality, may be damaged, not as many sizes/styles to choose from)

- Play a percentages game. Divide the class into two teams. Have a member of Team A name a price and a percent off that price; FOR EXAMPLE: 10% off a price of $25. The first member of Team B must give the discount price. Ask learners to stick with even dollar amounts and percentages that are multiples of five (5%, 10%, 15%, 20%, etc.). Continue with the game, alternating teams. Score one point for each correct answer. When the game is over, review how to figure percentages that are not multiples of five. Make up a few examples for learners or find some in store fliers.

Choosing a Shirt
More *Expansion/Extension* for SB page 70

- On the board, make a chart with the names of different fabrics as the headings. Ask learners to discuss the advantages and disadvantages of each fabric. Tell them to consider care, different weather conditions, lifestyles, and so on. Fill in the chart with their comments. Ask learners to name appropriate and inappropriate situations for wearing these various fabrics. (FOR EXAMPLE: Wool clothing is more suitable for cooler weather. Don't wear suede on a rainy day. Cotton is not a good fabric for people who don't like ironing. Wear a fabric that is easy to wash if you are going to do something that might get you dirty.)
- Distribute size charts for men's clothing from a catalog. Have learners work in small groups, choosing the right sizes for their fathers, husbands, brothers, or sons. If necessary, show them how to take measurements. Have learners take measurements at home and bring them to the next class to determine the right size.

Jody's New Dress
More *Expansion/Extension* for SB page 71

- Distribute ads for children's clothing. Have learners work in small groups to talk about the features and styles. Tell them to imagine that they want to buy clothes for their own child, to select some favorite outfits from the ads, and to give reasons for their choices.

What's Important to You?
More *Expansion/Extension* for SB page 72

- Have learners work in small groups to compare and contrast buying clothes in the United States and in their native countries. Ask learners to discuss any reasons for differences in buying habits.

Looking for Another Blouse
More *Expansion/Extension* for SB page 73

- Distribute size charts for women's clothing from a catalog. Have learners work in small groups, choosing the right sizes for their sisters, wives, daughters, or friends. If needed, have them take measurements at home and bring them to the next class to determine the right size.

Removing the Stain
More *Expansion/Extension* for SB page 74

- Have learners create stain removal guides to add to the class Clothing Care Guide. They can compile ideas generated during the Warm-up, Presentation, and Expansion/Extension activities. Assign small groups the task of writing directions for removing a set of stains. Compile the directions from the various groups and make copies for class members.
- Put learners in small groups. Ask that learners, in turn, describe one problem they have had in cleaning clothes. The rest of the group should give each learner advice.

1 2 3 4 5 6 7 **8** 9 10 11 12 Summary
What the Doctor Said

Objectives

Functions
- Reporting
- Following directions
- Clarifying
- Interrupting
- Sequencing
- Identifying causes
- Describing symptoms

Life Tasks
- Talking to a doctor
- Following medical directions
- Completing a medical history

Structures
- *Wh-* questions
- Past tense
- Adverbs of frequency
- Imperatives
- Sequence words

Culture
- Medications
- Prenatal care
- Health care
- Preventive medicine
- Diet and nutrition
- Causes of and treatments for stress

Vocabulary

Key words:

alcohol	hospital
allergy	medical
anemia	medicine
aspirin	(family) member
blood	operation
blood pressure	patient
care	pill
cause	pounds
checkup	pregnant
deal (with)	prenatal
diet	reduce
disease	relax
event	serving
exam	smoke
examine	snack
exercise	stomachache
habit	stress
headache	stressful
health	trouble
healthy	weigh
history	weight (gain/lose)

Related words:

break a habit	marriage
caffeine	medication
cavity	meditate
dairy	overweight
death	penicillin
dentist	poor
diabetes	preventive
divorce	protein
drugs	quite
excellent	sore
eye drops	starch
fair	stethoscope
fats	support group
hired	tuberculosis
in-laws	upset
iron	worry

Checkups

Purpose: To give practice with *Wh-* questions; to introduce a discussion of preventive medicine in the United States

Teacher Preparation and Materials

1. Pictures of a doctor, nurse, stethoscope, blood pressure cuff, needles, scale, and so on
2. Copies of local medical directories or copies of the yellow pages for your area *(Expansion/Extension)*

Warm-up

1. Display the pictures of health-care workers and instruments (or use the picture on page 76). Introduce key vocabulary. Be sure to include *stethoscope, blood pressure,* and *prenatal care.*
2. Ask learners where they go when they are sick and whom they see. (doctor's office, clinic, hospital; doctor, nurse) Introduce the word *checkup* by asking why someone who is not sick might visit the doctor and what the doctor would look for. Talk about the reasons people go for checkups. (to stay healthy, job requirement, insurance requirement)

Presentation

1. Have learners turn to page 76. Ask questions to elicit known vocabulary about the picture. FOR EXAMPLE: *What's going on? Where is this? Why is Kim at the doctor's? Do you think Kim is happy? Why or why not? What do you think the doctor will say to Olga?*
2. Put learners in small groups to discuss the questions at the bottom of the page. Ask volunteers to share their responses. Follow up with a discussion of the importance of regular checkups and preventive medicine. Ask learners what they can do on a daily basis to stay healthy. (eat a well-balanced diet with plenty of fruits and vegetables, exercise, etc.)
3. Talk about the necessity of prenatal care for both the mother and the baby. Ask learners why they think it is especially important for pregnant women to see a doctor regularly and to take other preventive health measures.

Expansion/Extension

- Put learners in small groups. Ask them to think of all the reasons why they might go to see a doctor. Have the recorder in each group write down the reasons. Afterward, have the reporter in each group share the group's list with the class. Ask learners to classify the responses as *preventive* or *treatment.*
- Distribute copies of medical directories or local yellow pages for your area. Review the format and content with learners. Have them work in small groups to decide what kinds of doctors they would go to for particular problems.

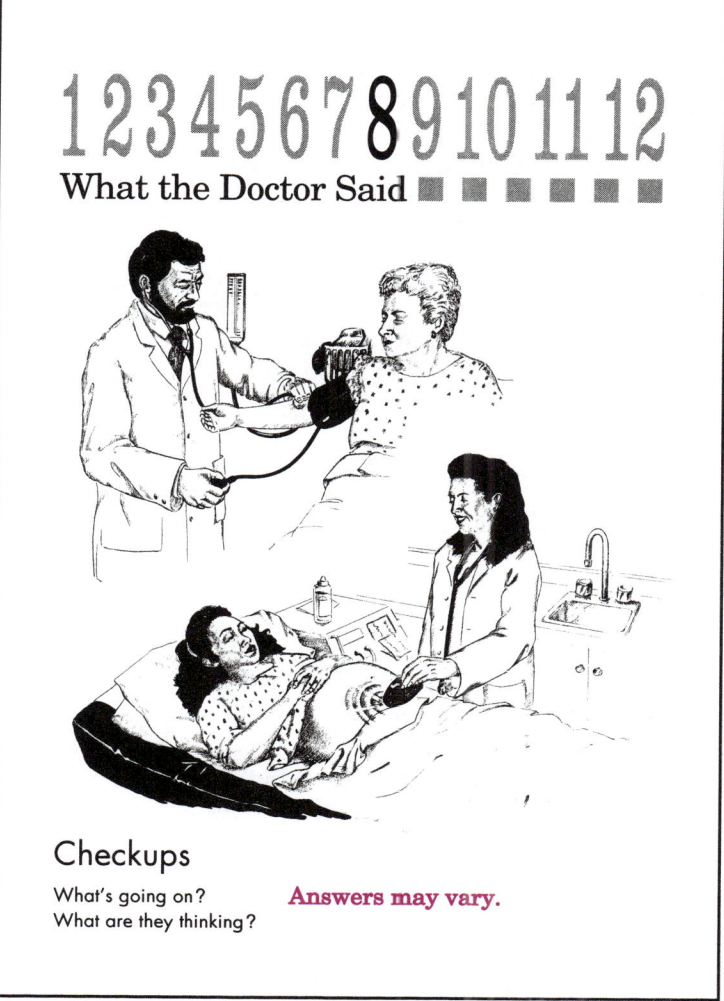

Checkups
What's going on?
What are they thinking?

Answers may vary.

Prenatal Care

Purpose: To give practice in sequencing and in discussing preventive medicine; to give practice with the past tense

Teacher Preparation and Materials

1. Arrange for a health-care worker to visit the class. *(Expansion/Extension)*
2. Blood pressure cuff, scale, blood sample kit brought by the health-care worker *(Expansion/Extension)*

Warm-up

1. Refer learners back to the picture of Kim on page 76. Review the concept of *prenatal care.* Elicit other words with the prefix *pre-* if helpful.
2. Depending on the age and interests of your learners, lead a discussion about how to stay healthy through regular checkups, in general or during pregnancy. Ask a volunteer to describe health care during a pregnancy in the United States. If not mentioned, point out that for most of a pregnancy, women should go for checkups once a month. During the last several weeks before the baby is due, women should usually see their doctor every other week or every week. Ask learners to suggest reasons for the frequency of these checkups.
3. Ask learners *What does a doctor usually check during a prenatal or other visit?* Elicit words such as *blood pressure, weight,* and *blood/urine samples.* Use the pictures on page 77 to clarify meaning. Ask more experienced learners to describe the kinds of tests and procedures used in prenatal visits.

Presentation

1. Have learners turn to page 77. Ask questions to elicit known vocabulary about the picture. FOR EXAMPLE: *Where is Kim? What is the nurse doing? Who is the doctor talking to?*
2. Read the first paragraph aloud while learners follow along silently. Ask questions, such as *What do Kim and Joon want?*

Kim and Joon wanted to have a baby. They wanted to have a brother or sister for their son, Han. They are very happy because Kim is pregnant. Naturally they want to have a healthy baby, so Kim sees the doctor often for checkups. These checkups are an important part of prenatal care.

 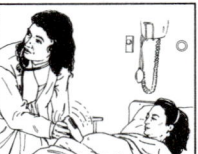 

First, a nurse weighs Kim. Then she takes her blood pressure. She takes a blood sample too. The doctor listens to the baby's heart, and then she lets Kim listen too. After the checkup, the doctor talks to both Kim and Joon. She asks them if they have any questions.

Think and talk about the questions.   **Answers will vary.**

1. Why is Kim having prenatal care?
2. Do you think it's a good idea?
3. Do you think it's important for men to learn about prenatal care?
4. Is there prenatal care in your native country?

How do they feel? Why does Kim see the doctor often? Have learners read the second paragraph silently. Then point to the various pictures on the page and ask learners to read the sentence that describes each one.

3. Put learners in small groups to discuss the questions at the bottom of the page. Have them consider the possible consequences of not seeing a doctor regularly during a pregnancy.
4. Ask learners to work in their groups to create and then present possible conversations for each picture.

Expansion/Extension

- Invite a health-care worker to talk to the class about prenatal and preventive care. If possible, have the worker bring a blood pressure cuff, blood sample kit, and scale to demonstrate to the class. Have the health-care worker take volunteers' blood pressure readings. Ask the guest to describe for learners how to find good, reasonably priced health care.

More *Expansion/Extension* on page 130

A Medical History

Purpose: To give practice in following directions, in reporting, in clarifying, and in filling out medical history forms; to give practice with adverbs of frequency

Teacher Preparation and Materials

1. Samples or pictures of aspirin/pain killers, eye drops, antacids, penicillin
2. Audiotape for Level 2
3. Copies of medical history forms *(Expansion/Extension)*

Warm-up

1. On the board, write the word *Diseases*. Ask volunteers to help you create a semantic web with different names of diseases, briefly describing the diseases for others. Repeat this procedure with *Medications*. Be sure to include words such as *anemia, tuberculosis, heart problems, high blood pressure, penicillin, aspirin/pain killers, antacid, eye drops*. If possible, clarify meanings with pictures and/or real medications.
2. Tell learners that information about the items on the board is commonly included in people's medical histories. Elicit/explain other categories or questions that might be asked on a medical history form. Be sure to include *operations, allergies, height, weight, general health, smoking/drinking habits,* and *family health information*. Ask learners why they think it is important for a doctor to have a patient's medical history and why it is helpful for a doctor to know about health problems in their families.

Presentation

1. Have learners turn to page 78. Ask questions to elicit known vocabulary on the form. FOR EXAMPLE: *Who is the form for? What is Kim's last name? What is today's date? Why do you think the doctor needs all this information about Kim?*
2. Read all the categories and information aloud while learners follow along silently. Clarify vocabulary as necessary. Tell learners they are going to hear a conversation between Kim and the nurse who is helping her fill out the form. Have learners use the incompleted portions of the form to predict the questions the nurse might ask.
3. Play the audiotape, having learners listen for and fill in the information needed to complete the form. Replay the audiotape so learners can check their work and fill in missing information. Review answers by naming categories and asking volunteers for the appropriate information.
4. Have learners write their own brief medical history in exercise B. Assist with vocabulary as necessary. Follow up with a discussion of health problems, including causes and treatments, that learners have experienced. Ask if any other family members have had the same problems. Talk about these and other health problems that tend to run in families.

---

78 **A Medical History**

A. Finish Kim's form.

Patient's name:				
Lee	Kim		Kang	8/23/94
Last	First	Middle	Maiden	Today's date

General Health: ☑ Excellent ☐ Good ☐ Fair ☐ Poor
Height: 5'3" Weight: 132
Do you smoke? ☐ Yes ☑ No If yes, how many packs a week? ____
Do you drink alcohol? ☐ Yes ☑ No If yes, how many glasses a week? ____

Check all that apply.	You	List family member(s)
High blood pressure	☐	grandfather, an aunt
Heart problems	☐	father, uncle
Diabetes	☐	
Tuberculosis	☐	
Anemia	☐	
Operations	☐	father, uncle (open-heart surgery)

Do you take any medication? (Include aspirin, eye drops, and over-the-counter drugs.)

Drug name	Dose	Reason
aspirin	2	headaches
antacid		stomachaches

Are you allergic to any medication? If yes, list:
penicillin

B. What's your medical history? Answers will vary.
1. Diseases _____
2. Medications _____
3. Operations _____
4. Allergies _____

***Expansion/Extension** on page 130*

Taking Medication

Purpose: To give practice in clarifying information, in following directions, and in interrupting for more information

Teacher Preparation and Materials

1. Samples (or pictures) of different over-the-counter and prescription medications, including iron/vitamin pills
2. Audiotape for Level 2
3. Pictures of patients and doctors (*Expansion/Extension*)
4. Arrange a class trip to a drugstore. (*Expansion/Extension*)
5. Copies of TRF Handout 8.2, *How Often Do I Take This?* (*Expansion/Extension*)
6. Copies of TRF Handout 8.6, *Home Remedies* (*Expansion/Extension*)

Warm-up

1. Show learners examples (or pictures) of different kinds of medications. Tell them that these are drugs that can be good for you if a doctor has told you to take them. Ask volunteers to name the medications you hold up and then talk about what the medications are used for. Introduce and explain the words *prescription, medicine,* and *over-the-counter medicine* and point out examples of each.
2. Tell learners that some drugs are neither prescribed nor recommended by doctors: caffeine, alcohol, and nicotine. Ask them to identify the substances that contain these drugs. Lead a discussion about attitudes toward alcohol, cigarettes, and coffee in the United States vs. learners' native countries.

Presentation

1. Have learners turn to page 79. Ask questions to elicit known vocabulary about the picture. FOR EXAMPLE: *Who is Kim talking to? Where are they? What do you think they are talking about?*
2. Put learners in pairs to read through the sentences at the bottom of the page. Have them discuss possible answers. You may suggest that they write their answers in

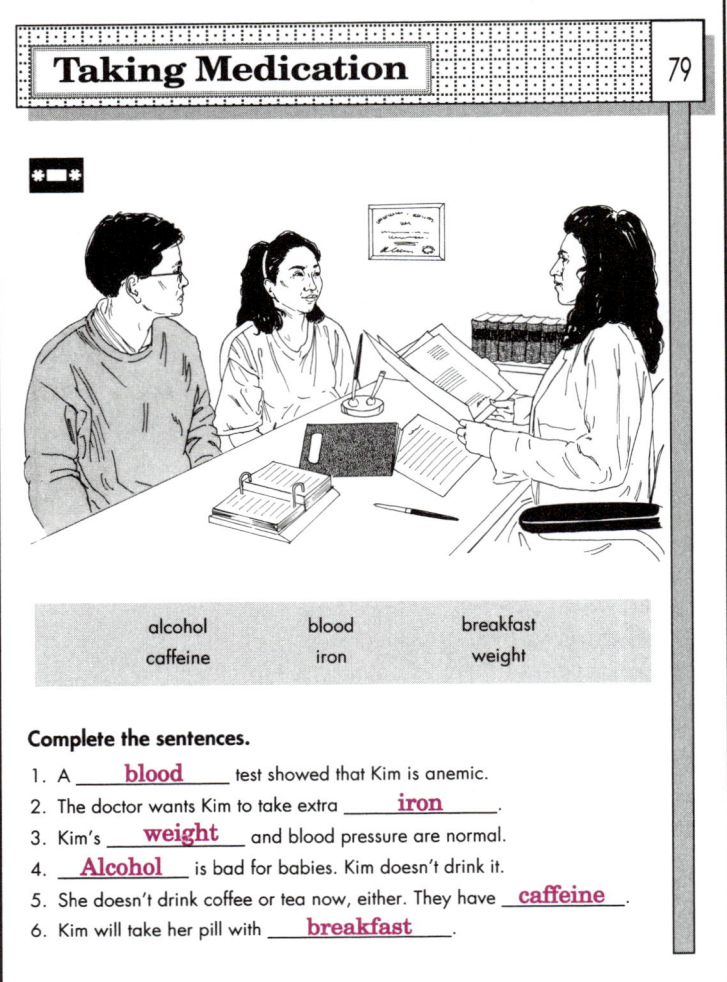

pencil. Then have learners listen to the conversation on the audiotape to check the answers they wrote and fill in missing words. Replay the audiotape if necessary.

3. Continue the topic of conversation on the audiotape by discussing the doctor's suggestions and other things that are good/bad for pregnant women. Ask *Why do you think alcohol and caffeine are not good for babies? Why do babies need iron? What kinds of foods/drinks should pregnant women eat/drink? Should pregnant women exercise? What kinds of exercise do you think would be good?*

Expansion/Extension

See TRF HANDOUT 8.2, *How Often Do I Take This?*
TRF HANDOUT 8.6, *Home Remedies*

- If suitable for your group, discuss the important *do's* and *don'ts* for pregnant women. Have learners compile this information into a Prenatal Care Guide, which they can share with friends and family members.

More *Expansion/Extension* on page 130

Olga's Exam

Purpose: To give practice in following directions, in interrupting for clarification, and in discussing health issues and healthy habits

Teacher Preparation and Materials
1. 🔲 Audiotape for Level 2
2. Toy or real telephones *(Expansion/Extension)*
3. Copies of TRF Handout 8.4, *You Are What You Eat (Expansion/Extension)*

Warm-up
1. Tell the class about a recent experience you had when a doctor, nurse, or dentist gave you advice. Then ask learners to summarize your experience by asking *What was the problem? What did the doctor/nurse/dentist say? What did I do?* Ask volunteers to share similar experiences.
2. If it has not been mentioned, talk about high blood pressure. Ask if learners know anyone who has high blood pressure, what caused it, and what the person is supposed to do about it. Be sure to talk about the effects of eating too much salt, being overweight, having too much stress, and not getting enough exercise.

Presentation
1. Have learners turn to page 80. Ask questions to elicit known vocabulary about the picture. FOR EXAMPLE: *Where is Olga? Who is she talking to? Do they look happy or unhappy? Why do you think they look this way?*
2. Read the paragraph aloud while learners follow along silently. After they have identified Olga's problem, ask volunteers to predict the doctor's suggestions from the list at the bottom of the page. Discuss the reasons for their predictions.
3. Tell learners to listen to the conversation between Olga and her doctor. 🔲 Play the audiotape and have learners underline the suggestions Olga's doctor makes. 🔲 Replay the audiotape so learners can check their work. Review the correct

answers, discussing why they make sense, not only for people with high blood pressure but for general well-being.
4. Have learners describe Olga's attitude during her conversation with the doctor. Ask *Did Olga interrupt the doctor, or did she listen quietly? Why do you think she interrupted him? How did she sound? Did the doctor get mad? What did the doctor say?*

Expansion/Extension
See **TRF HANDOUT 8.4,** *You Are What You Eat*

- Use a pair of telephones and ask a volunteer to pretend to be a patient with a problem. Take the role of the doctor and give advice over the phone. Ask pairs of other volunteers to do the same.
- Tell learners to review the choices at the bottom of page 80. Ask *For what health problems would a doctor give each piece of advice?* (FOR EXAMPLE: A doctor may suggest exercise if a patient has to lose weight. Eating fish may be a suggestion for reducing fat in your diet.)

More *Expansion/Extension* on page 130

Olga's Healthy Diet

Purpose: To give practice in following medical directions and in discussing preventive medicine; to give practice with adverbs of frequency

Teacher Preparation and Materials

1. An apple and a candy bar
2. Cereal box, yogurt container, or other containers that include serving-size information
3. Arrange for a health-care worker to visit the class. *(Expansion/Extension)*
4. Pictures of different kinds of food *(Expansion/Extension)*
5. Copies of recipes from learners *(Expansion/Extension)*
6. Copies of TRF Handout 8.5, *The Best Diet for You (Expansion/Extension)*

Warm-up

1. Pick up an apple and show it to the class. Ask what kind of food it is and if it is good for you. Then pick up a candy bar and tell the class *I like to eat a lot of candy. Is that good for me?* Have learners suggest why eating too much candy is bad for you.
2. On the board, make a chart with the heading *Healthy Foods*. Ask volunteers to name food categories and write them along the vertical axis of the chart. Include *Protein* (meat, fish, eggs), *Fruit, Vegetables, Starch* (bread, rice, cereal), *Fat* (oil, nuts, olives), and *Dairy* (milk, cheese). Elicit/provide examples of healthy food for each category. Continue with a chart labeled *Unhealthy Foods*. (candy, chocolate, sweets, too much oil/fat, too much salt, and so on)
3. Introduce the word *moderation*, contrasting it with *too much*. Elicit ideas about healthy eating based on the concept of moderation. (FOR EXAMPLE: *A little salt/sugar/oil in your diet is OK. Too much of anything can be bad.*)
4. Explain that many foods are measured in *serving sizes,* and these measurements vary for different foods. Show some examples of different food containers

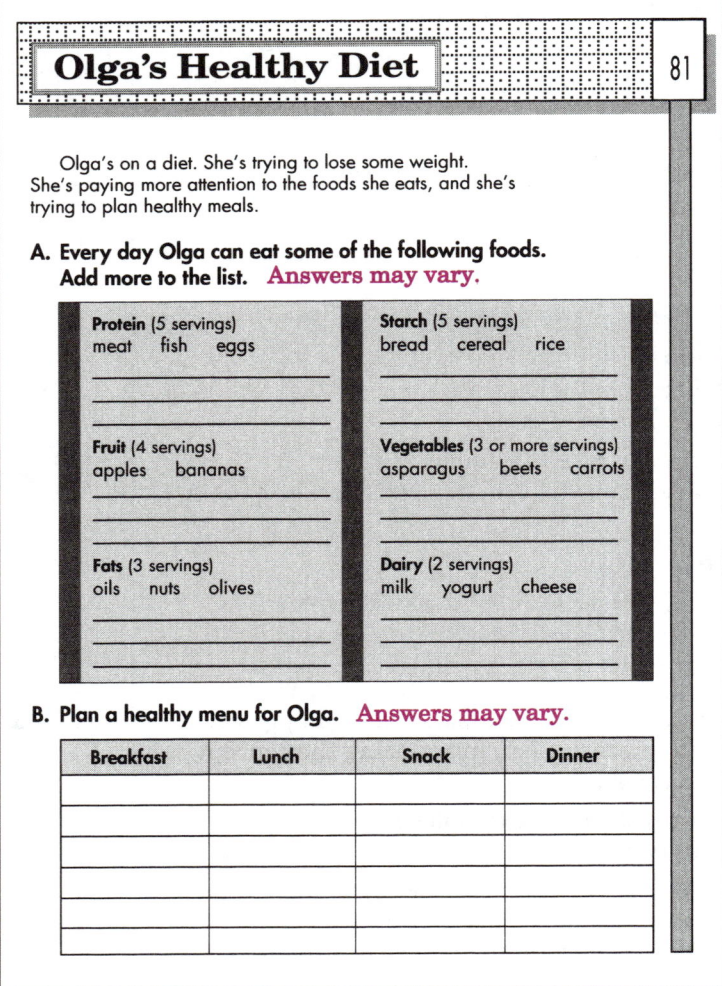

and read through the information provided about serving sizes.

Presentation

1. Have learners turn to page 81. Ask questions to elicit known vocabulary about the diet. FOR EXAMPLE: *How much protein can Olga have every day? Do you think this sounds like a healthy diet? Why or why not?*
2. Have volunteers read the categories and examples aloud. Then have learners work in pairs to add examples to the categories. Refer learners to the food examples on the board for ideas. Have them continue on a separate sheet of paper if they want to add lines to the categories on the page. Ask volunteers to read their examples aloud as you add new items to the chart on the board.
3. Have learners continue in pairs to create a healthy menu for Olga. Tell them to mix and match food groups to create more exciting meals. Combine pairs into small groups to compare their meals.

***Expansion/Extension* on page 130**

124 • UNIT 8

What Causes Stress?

Purpose: To give practice in reporting; to give practice with the past tense

Teacher Preparation and Materials
Copies of monthly calendar (Expansion/Extension)

Warm-up
1. Tell learners to imagine themselves in the following situation: *You just got a promotion at work. It means you have to work longer hours; you also have more responsibilities and more problems. Meanwhile, your son is having trouble in school. He needs more of your time. You have also been trying to take care of all the minor repair work that your house needs.* Ask learners how they might feel in this situation, introducing the concept of *stress*.
2. Provide a few examples of positive events (buying a house, getting married, etc.) and negative events (job loss, a death, etc.) that can lead to stress. Explain that any big change in life, whether it is good or bad, can cause stress. Have learners suggest reasons why change can cause stress. (disrupts your normal routine, requires you to make new plans or to change your daily life, etc.)
3. Ask volunteers to describe changes in their lives that created stress for them, mentioning moving to the United States as a starter. Include new vocabulary from the checklist on page 82, such as *spouse getting hired or fired, in-laws, divorce, special recognition or award.*

Presentation
1. Have learners turn to page 82. Ask *What causes stress for you?* Refer to the discussion from Warm-up #3. Write key ideas on the board.
2. Have volunteers read aloud the items in exercise B. Clarify vocabulary as necessary. Tell learners to check off any items that apply to them, adding their own ideas for numbers 11 and 12. Ask

---

82 What Causes Stress?

Olga's doctor wants her to reduce stress.
Stress can make you sick.

A. What causes stress for you? Answers will vary.

B. Read this list. Check anything that happened to you in the last 12 months. Answers will vary.
   ☐ 1. death in the family
   ☐ 2. marriage or divorce
   ☐ 3. pregnancy
   ☐ 4. a new family member
   ☐ 5. getting hired or fired from a job
   ☐ 6. spouse getting hired or fired from a job
   ☐ 7. moving
   ☐ 8. son or daughter leaving home
   ☐ 9. trouble in the family or with in-laws
   ☐ 10. winning special recognition or an award
   ☐ 11. _____
   ☐ 12. _____

C. Think and talk about the questions. Answers will vary.
   1. Did you check many events?
   2. Do you think your life is stressful?
   3. What do you think you can do to reduce stress?

---

learners to share their experiences, discussing general and specific reasons why these particular events caused stress.
3. Put learners in small groups to discuss the answers to exercise C. Ask them to give suggestions for reducing stress, based on personal experiences. Have each learner suggest a tip for reducing stress.

Expansion/Extension
- Have learners compile their tips for stress reduction in an ongoing Guide to Stress Management. Learners can add ideas as they experience different situations.
- Ask learners if they experienced a lot of stress in their native countries. Ask *Was life more or less stressful in your native country than in the United States? What were the causes of stress? How were they similar or different?* Lead a discussion. (**Note:** This could be a sensitive topic for some learners.)

More *Expansion/Extension* on page 131

UNIT 8 • 125

Dealing with Stress

Purpose: To give practice with adverbs of frequency; to give practice in reporting

Teacher Preparation and Materials
None

Warm-up
1. Tell learners *When I'm feeling under stress, I'm worried and nervous. Sometimes I get headaches and an upset stomach.* Ask volunteers to describe their own reactions to stress.
2. Ask learners what they do to control stress in their lives, introducing the phrase *dealing with stress*. Be sure to include the methods on page 83. Have them suggest why it is important to develop methods for dealing with stress. (FOR EXAMPLE: to stay healthy; to be able to have friendly relationships with family/friends/co-workers)

Presentation
1. Have learners turn to page 83. Read the paragraph aloud while learners follow along silently. Clarify vocabulary as necessary. Ask literal and inferential questions. FOR EXAMPLE: *Why isn't Olga sleeping well? What is she always thinking about? Who does she worry about? Why does she worry about them? What other problems does she have? Do you think she worries too much? Why?*
2. Start a class discussion by posing the questions *What seems to be Olga's biggest cause of stress? How could she possibly help all of the people she is worried about? What would you suggest she do?* Remind learners that there is no single way to reduce stress. List their ideas on the board and suggest that learners add to the checklist on the page.
3. Tell learners to complete the checklist independently. Then take a class survey. On the board, write the suggestions for dealing with stress from page 83. Include suggestions added by learners. Then have learners raise their hands for each method they use. Tally the numbers on

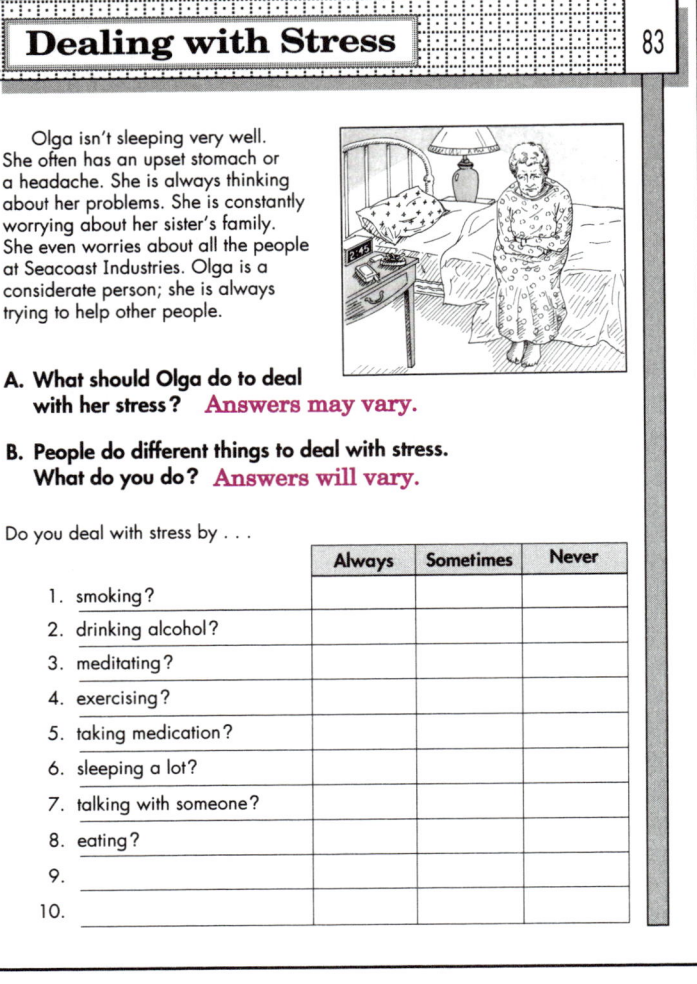

the board next to each method to determine which methods are most popular.

4. As a class, evaluate the different methods used for dealing with stress. Have learners discuss the following: *What are the short- and long-term effects of using each method? Could these effects change if the method is used only sometimes instead of always? Which effects are good and bad? Does the method really help to deal with stress, or is it just an escape?*

Expansion/Extension
- As a result of the discussions, allow learners to add tips to the Guide to Stress Management.
- Ask learners to discuss in small groups how they dealt with stress in their native countries. Ask *How is that different from what you do in the United States? Which way was better for you?*

More *Expansion/Extension* on page 131

Breaking Bad Habits

Purpose: To give practice in sequencing and in discussing preventive medicine

Teacher Preparation and Materials
1. Copies of ads for programs or products specializing in breaking bad habits, such as weight-loss programs or products to help a person stop smoking *(Expansion/Extension)*
2. Copies of TRF Handout 8.7, *Be a Healthy Winner (Expansion/Extension)*
3. Copies of TRF Handout 8.1, *Take Care of Yourself (Expansion/Extension)*

Warm-up
1. Tell learners that smoking is considered a bad habit. Have them explain what makes it a bad habit. (FOR EXAMPLE: It's bad for your health. It can annoy other people and be bad for their health too.)
2. Ask volunteers to describe a bad habit they had and then stopped. Introduce the phrase *breaking bad habits*. Ask *Was it hard to break the habit? Did you try different ways before you finally broke it? What worked for you? Why?*

Presentation
1. Have learners turn to page 84. Ask questions to elicit known vocabulary about the picture. FOR EXAMPLE: *What is Olga doing in the first picture? Do you think she looks happy? Why or why not? Why do you think she is doing all these different things?*
2. Ask volunteers to take turns reading the sentences aloud. Then mention each of the strategies Olga tried and ask learners what the effect was. Help learners conclude that sometimes when we try to break one bad habit, we can have other kinds of problems. Ask literal and inferential questions. FOR EXAMPLE: *What finally helped Olga? Why do you think this worked? Do you think the same method would work for you? Why or why not?*
3. Put learners in small groups to answer the questions at the bottom of the page. Tell them to consider why people have these habits. (FOR EXAMPLE: Some people bite their nails because they are nervous.

People may smoke more in some situations.) These reasons may help learners think of ways to break a habit. Have the reporter in each group share the group's ideas with the class.

Expansion/Extension
See **TRF HANDOUT 8.7,** *Be a Healthy Winner*
TRF HANDOUT 8.1, *Take Care of Yourself*

- Put the class in small groups to conduct a chain drill. Model the following: Turn to the person next to you, state a bad habit, and ask *What can I do to break my bad habit?* The person gives you advice, then turns to the following person and states a bad habit, asking for advice. Have learners continue the chain drill in their small groups.
- Take a class survey of bad habits learners have. Write some of the most common ones on the board. (smoking, biting fingernails, eating too much, etc.) Then have learners suggest ways to break these habits and discuss which methods are likely to be successful/unsuccessful.

More *Expansion/Extension* on page 131

It's a Girl!

Purpose: To give practice in reporting and sequencing

Teacher Preparation and Materials
1. Audiotape for Level 2
2. Arrange for a trip to a local hospital. *(Expansion/Extension)*
3. Paper for sentence strips; scissors for all *(Expansion/Extension)*
4. Copies of TRF Handout 8.3, *What Happened First? (Expansion/Extension)*

Warm-up
1. Tell learners *Something exciting happened the other day. I won a prize!* Give details of your exciting experience. Then ask *Has something exciting happened to you? Tell us about it.* While different volunteers are telling their stories, interject exclamations such as *Oh, how wonderful! I'm so happy for you!*
2. Ask if any learners and/or their family members have had a baby in the United States. Have learners describe their experiences.
3. Have learners describe people's attitudes in their native countries about having boy babies or having girl babies. Ask if there seems to be a preference for one sex or the other and why.

Presentation
1. Have learners turn to page 85. Explain that the pictures on the page are not in order. Ask questions to elicit known vocabulary about the pictures. FOR EXAMPLE: *Where is Joon in the first picture? What is he doing? What do you think is going on in these pictures?*
2. Ask learners to predict the correct order of the pictures and to write the numbers in pencil if they wish. Tell them to listen carefully to the phone conversation on the audiotape to see if they were right. Play the audiotape and have learners fill in the correct order. Replay the audiotape so that learners can check their work and fill in missing information.
3. Put learners in pairs. First have them retell the story to one another. Then tell them to write their own sentences about the pictures, adding descriptive details, such as the characters' emotions. Have volunteers read their stories to the class.
4. Put learners in groups to discuss the questions in exercise C. Remind them that although this is a very happy occasion, a new baby is a very big change in the Lees' lives. It is likely to cause a variety of emotions. Then have groups use the outcome of the discussion to write a conversation to go with the pictures. Ask learners to role-play their conversations for the class.

Expansion/Extension
See **TRF HANDOUT 8.3**, *What Happened First?*

- Visit a hospital together. Tour the different areas with a guide. Have learners ask questions about admitting procedures.

More *Expansion/Extension* on page 131

It's a Girl!

A. Put these pictures in order. Write the numbers.

(Pictures numbered: 3, 5, 1, 4, 2, 6)

B. Write sentences about the pictures.   *Answers may vary.*

1. _____
2. _____
3. _____
4. _____
5. _____
6. _____

C. Think and talk about the questions.   *Answers may vary.*
1. How do you think Kim and Joon feel?
2. How do you think Han feels?

Making the Connection

Purpose: To give practice with the past tense and adverbs of frequency; to give practice with skills, functions, and vocabulary from Unit 8

Teacher Preparation and Materials
None

Warm-up
1. Remind learners of Olga's visit to the doctor. Ask *What were her problems? What did the doctor tell her to do? What did Olga do as a result?*
2. Tell learners that it has been six months since Olga's examination. Ask them to imagine what has happened to her in this time.

Presentation
1. Have learners turn to page 86. Tell them to read the story to see whether their predictions about Olga were accurate.
2. Ask literal and inferential questions about the story. FOR EXAMPLE: *How was Olga six months later? What things does Olga do now? How does she feel? Do you think she will continue to do these healthy things? Why or why not? How do you think Olga will be doing in another six months?*
3. Ask volunteers to read aloud the questions below the story. Have learners work in pairs to discuss the questions, taking notes on key ideas.
4. On the board, write a brief story about a personal experience. Tell learners to use this and Olga's story as models for their own stories. Have them read their stories aloud in small groups.

---

86 · Making the Connection

Olga was overweight and had high blood pressure. She was under stress. She went to see her doctor. He told her to lose weight, stop smoking, and exercise. He told her to relax. He gave her some medication too.

Six months later Olga went back to her doctor. She stopped smoking and she still lost 12 pounds. She walks home from work every day. Sometimes she walks to work too. She takes her medication, and her blood pressure is down. She feels healthier.

What about you?
What are some medical problems you've had?
What did you do?
Have you ever been under stress?
What did you do about it?

Write a story about yourself. *Answers will vary.*

I was _____

Then I _____

Now I'm _____

Expansion/Extension

- Have learners interview a family member or friend, using the questions on page 86. Have them report back to the class on what they learned about how to solve medical problems and/or handle stress. They may wish to add this new information to the Guide to Stress Management.

- State a health problem. FOR EXAMPLE: *My brother is overweight. What should he do?* Ask learners to give you advice. Suggest that they ask for additional details about your brother to help them determine appropriate action. Then have volunteers state other problems, while learners follow the same procedure to offer advice.

- Tell learners about a problem you have had finding a doctor, filling out insurance forms, and so on. Ask them to discuss other problems in getting good health care in the United States. Try to find solutions together.

UNIT 8: What the Doctor Said
Expansion/Extension

Prenatal Care
More *Expansion/Extension* for SB page 77

- Have learners write class, group, or individual stories about the health-care worker's visit to share with the class.
- On the board, write *The Best Place in Town for Good, Reasonably Priced Health Care*. Lead a discussion about this topic, including suggestions from the guest speaker. Write learners' (and your own) suggestions and comments on the board.
- Ask learners about care for pregnant women in their native cultures. Ask *Who takes care of women before, during, and after childbirth? What do pregnant women do differently in your native country than in the United States? Are men usually involved in the prenatal care and delivery of babies in your native country? What do you think of prenatal care in the United States?* (**Cultural note:** This may be a sensitive issue in some cultures.)

A Medical History
Expansion/Extension for SB page 78

- Distribute copies of medical history forms. Learners can work in pairs to discuss the meanings of the categories and to fill out the forms.
- Put learners in pairs. Have one partner take the role of a nurse and the other the role of a patient, to create a conversation about the patient's medical history. Ask volunteers to role-play their conversations in front of the class.
- Review family relationship terms. Show learners how to make a family tree by creating one on the board for your family. Then have learners work in pairs to help each other create their own family trees.
- Elicit learners' opinions about their general health. (excellent, good, fair, poor) Ask them to give reasons for their responses.

Taking Medication
More *Expansion/Extension* for SB page 79

- If possible, visit a drugstore as a class. Discuss the choices of drugs for various purposes that are available over the counter. If possible, introduce learners to the pharmacist and explain the procedure for filling a prescription.
- Discuss how learners get medication in their native countries. Ask *Are most drugs prescribed by doctors? Do you buy drugs at drugstores or in other places?* Compare and contrast medication from different countries.

Olga's Exam
More *Expansion/Extension* for SB page 80

- Put learners in pairs. Have them each think of one person whose health they worry about. Ask *Why do you worry about that person's health? What should that person do? What shouldn't he or she do?* Have them discuss these questions with their partners.

Olga's Healthy Diet
Expansion/Extension for SB page 81

See TRF HANDOUT 8.5, *The Best Diet for You*

- Have learners remain in their small groups and use their responses to exercise B to create a five-day menu plan for Olga.
- Invite a health-care worker to speak to your class about diet and nutrition.
- Ask learners to compare eating habits in their native countries with those in the United States. Have learners group the foods in their native country's diet into the food groups on page 81. Lead a discussion about which country's eating habits they feel are healthier and why.
- Provide or have learners bring in pictures of different kinds of food. Put learners in small groups to conduct a chain drill. Show a picture and ask a member of a group *What is this food? Do you think it's healthy? Why or why not? Would you eat it?* Let them continue the chain drill in their groups.
- Use the food pictures for a variety of activities. Learners could make food group charts or collages, plan menus, or sort the pictures into the categories *Healthy* and *Unhealthy*.

- Divide the class into five groups. Assign each group one of the following categories: Protein, Starch, Fruit, Vegetables, and Dairy. Tell them to write a list of as many foods as they can in their category. Set a time limit. When they finish, have each group recorder write the group's list on the board. Read each list aloud and determine who has the longest correct list.
- Have the class plan a healthy full-day menu, using a wide variety of foods from their native countries. Include three meals and a snack.
- Have learners each bring in one healthful dish for the class to sample. They should bring in the recipe in English for you to copy and distribute.

What Causes Stress?
More *Expansion/Extension* for SB page 82

- Discuss with learners how stress can affect health. Ask *What bad effects can it have?*
- Distribute copies of the monthly calendar. Have learners fill in the dates for the present month. Ask that during the next week they keep a record of stressful events. At the end of the week, they can share their calendars with a partner, discuss the effects of stress in their lives, and suggest ways to reduce stress in the coming weeks.

Dealing with Stress
More *Expansion/Extension* for SB page 83

- Divide the class into four groups. Assign each group one method for dealing with stress: meditating, exercising, taking medication, talking with someone. Each group should plan a presentation on why its way is the best way to deal with stress. Have each group make a presentation before the class. ◘ In a one-to-one situation, allow the learner to select one method and present to you as many reasons as possible why this is a good way to deal with stress.

Breaking Bad Habits
More *Expansion/Extension* for SB page 84

- Distribute copies of ads for programs or products specializing in breaking bad habits, such as weight-loss programs or products to help a person stop smoking. Put learners in small groups to discuss the product claims or methods that the programs describe and whether or not they think the products or programs would work.
- Have learners describe an experience in trying to break a bad habit. Ask *What happened first? What happened next? What finally happened? Do you still have the bad habit?* Ask them to write individual stories titled "How I Tried to Break My Bad Habit." If they broke the habit, tell them to explain why their method worked. They can use the story on page 84 as a model. Have volunteers read their stories in class.

It's a Girl!
More *Expansion/Extension* for SB page 85

- Develop a group LEA story about the hospital visit.
- Choose a few of the stories learners wrote about the pictures of Kim's delivery. Rewrite them so they can be cut into sentence strips. Duplicate the stories and cut each story into strips; then distribute one story at a time to learners. Have them reconstruct each story.

1 2 3 4 5 6 7 8 **9** 10 11 12 Summary
Going to School

Objectives

Functions
- Expressing concern
- Expressing agreement and disagreement
- Asking for clarification
- Describing problems
- Reporting successes

Life Tasks
- Understanding the U.S. school system
- Understanding expectations of students
- Understanding parental rights and responsibilities
- Talking to a child's teacher
- Reading a class schedule and course descriptions

Structures
- Modals: *must, may*
- *If/then* statements
- Future tense: *will*

Culture
- Expectations of children in U.S. schools: behavior, attitudes
- Special school programs
- Grade levels of U.S. schools
- Adult education in the United States

Vocabulary

Key words:

adult	grade
agree	grade level
American	high school
basic	history
basics	homework
citizen	kindergarten
classroom	learn
college	meeting
computer	note
conduct	quiet
counselor	registration
course	schedule
culture	schooling
education	sign up
elementary	subject
ESL	understand
exam	yoga

Related words:

art	offered
attention	reason
citizenship	serious
civics	shock
classmate	special
district	education
fail	spelling
guidance	stress
gym	management
holidays	term
joke	transportation
left out	trouble
middle school	worried
music	writing
newspaper	yell

At School

Purpose: To give practice in describing problems and successes

Teacher Preparation and Materials
None

Warm-up

1. Ask learners to describe the educational level of the course they are attending. (community college, adult education, tutoring program, etc.) Ask *What kinds of schools do children of different ages go to?* (elementary, middle school/junior high, high school) Write the words on the board in the form of a flowchart and ask learners about the approximate ages and/or grade levels for each. Write these on the board under the appropriate school category.

2. Ask learners *Have you or any of your children had exciting moments at school?* Have volunteers describe those moments. *How did you feel? Have you or your child had difficult moments? What happened? How did you feel then?*

Presentation

1. Have learners turn to page 87. Ask questions to elicit known vocabulary about the picture. FOR EXAMPLE: *Where is Han? What is he doing? How do you think he feels? Why might he feel this way? Who do you think Johnny is talking to? What are Olga and Isabel looking at?*

2. Remind learners of what happened at the end of the last unit. (The Lees had a new baby.) Ask how this might affect Han. Have learners think about this as they read and discuss in small groups the questions at the bottom of the page.

3. Have different groups describe what they think is going on in each picture. Then ask them to predict what might happen next with each of the characters. Ask questions, such as *What do you think Han's teacher will do? Do you think Kim and Joon know what's going on with Han in school? What do you think Johnny's father will say and do about his paper? Do you think Isabel and Olga will take a class? What kinds of classes might they take?*

Expansion/Extension

- Refer learners back to the flowchart from the *Warm-up*. On the board, have them create similar flowcharts for schools in their native countries. Talk about the similarities and differences among the various flowcharts.

- Put learners in pairs. Ask *Do you think U.S. schools offer a good variety of courses? Are the courses challenging enough? Do you think teachers do their jobs well? Is there anything you would like to see changed in the educational system?* Have learners discuss how they feel about education in the United States, for themselves and their family members.

More *Expansion/Extension* on page 144

Han Lee's Class

Purpose: To introduce information about U.S. elementary schools; to give practice with ordinal numbers

Teacher Preparation and Materials

1. Map of the world
2. Arrange for an elementary ESL teacher to visit your class. *(Expansion/Extension)*
3. Arrange for a tour of a local elementary school. *Expansion/Extension)*

Warm-up

1. Ask learners what countries they are from. Write the country names on the board. Have them describe something about their native countries that make them very different. Ask questions, such as *What is the food like? How do people dress? What kind of social events are popular?* As learners respond, introduce the concept of *culture*.
2. Ask learners what languages are spoken in their native countries. Ask *Do you speak your native language at home? Do you think that's good or bad for your children? Why?*
3. Introduce these country names: *Korea, Philippines, Mexico*. Locate the countries on a map and ask what languages are spoken there.
4. Review the ordinal numbers first through 12th. Line up twelve books and ask volunteers to choose the 10th, the third, and so on. Have learners write ordinal numbers on the board. Show them how to write ordinals in both word (*second*) and abbreviated (*2nd*) forms.
5. On the board, write the titles *Mr., Mrs., Ms.,* and *Miss*. Ask learners to explain what each one stands for. Use people in class to provide examples of the different titles.

Presentation

1. Have learners turn to page 88. Ask questions to elicit known vocabulary about the picture. FOR EXAMPLE: *Where is Han sitting? Who do you think the other children are? Where do you think they are from?*

2. Ask learners to read aloud the paragraphs, one at a time. After each paragraph, have volunteers find and read different sentences. FOR EXAMPLE: *Read a sentence that tells what Ms. Hunter likes. Read a sentence that describes the children in Han's class.*
3. Ask if learners have ever seen or heard about classrooms like this one. Have them describe elementary classrooms they have seen, either in the United States or in their native countries. Ask how those classrooms are similar to or different from the one in the picture.
4. Put learners in small groups to discuss the questions at the bottom of the page. Have each group think of ways that children can learn about other cultures. Have the reporter in each group share some of the group's ideas with the class.

Expansion/Extension

- Have learners write individual or group stories about the visit. Afterward, ask them to read their stories aloud to the class.

More *Expansion/Extension* on page 144

Welcome to District 5 Elementary School

Purpose: To introduce reading a school handbook; to give practice with *will* and *should*

Teacher Preparation and Materials

1. Copies of handbook pages from local elementary schools *(Expansion/Extension)*
2. Arrange for an elementary school counselor to visit your class. *(Expansion/Extension)*
3. Copies of handbook pages from your college or school *(Expansion/Extension)*
4. Copies of TRF Handout 9.1, *A New School Year (Expansion/Extension)*

Warm-up

1. Ask learners with children if they know what school district they are in. Elicit/explain that most towns and cities are divided into school districts, usually identified by number or by name, each with its own special rules.
2. Ask learners to share any rules and other information they know about children's schools in your area. On the board, write the words *staff, calendar, grade levels, conduct, subjects, transportation, safety rules,* and *after-school activities.* Discuss how all these terms relate to elementary schools and elicit/provide ideas about each. Tell learners that many school districts put together a handbook that includes this kind of information.
3. Ask why they think an elementary school handbook is needed. Ask *Who might be interested in the book? Who do you think schools give the books to? Why?*

Presentation

1. Have learners turn to page 89. Identify the page as a sample first page from a school handbook. Ask *What would you want to know about your child's elementary school? Could you find it in this handbook?*
2. Read the page aloud while learners follow along silently. Clarify vocabulary as

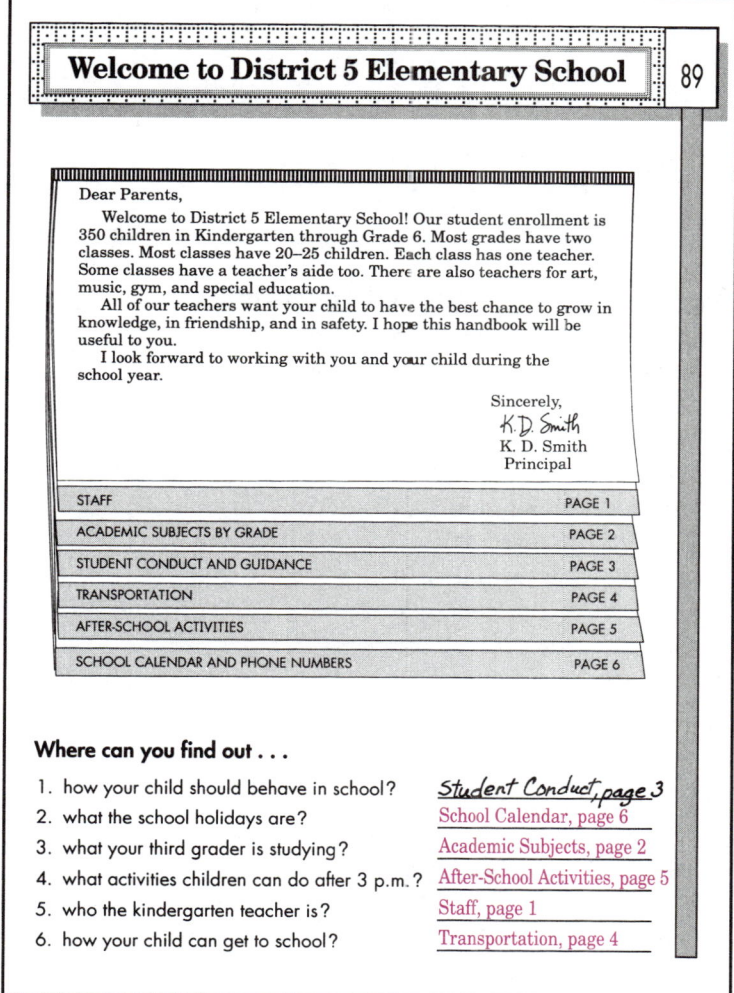

necessary. Ask questions to check comprehension. FOR EXAMPLE: *Who is the principal? How many children attend the school? What might the section called "Staff" cover? What would you expect to read about in the "Transportation" section?*

3. Have learners answer the questions at the bottom of the page. Then put them in small groups to share their answers.

Expansion/Extension

See **TRF HANDOUT 9.1,** *A New School Year*

- Invite a local elementary school counselor to talk with learners about school policies and rules. Have learners ask questions. Afterward, clarify information as necessary.
- Have learners work in small groups. Assign each group one of the sections of the handbook on page 89. Ask the groups to think about what might be in their section and to develop a paragraph or piece of information that they would expect to see in this section.

More *Expansion/Extension* on page 144

A Note from School

Purpose: To introduce expressing concern; to give practice in asking for clarification and in describing problems

Teacher Preparation and Materials

1. Copies of sample letters and forms for parents from elementary schools *(Expansion/Extension)*
2. Copies of sample letters from your institution *(Expansion/Extension)*
3. Toy or real telephones *(Expansion/Extension)*
4. Copies of TRF Handout 9.2, *School Supply List (Expansion/Extension)*

Warm-up

1. Ask learners what a teacher might do if a child was having trouble in school. Ask *How would the teacher let the parent know about the trouble? What would you want a teacher to do if your child was having trouble? Why do teachers send notes home to parents?*
2. Have volunteers describe notes they have received from their children's teachers. Ask them how they felt about the notes and what they did or how they responded.
3. On the board, write *parent-teacher conference*. Ask *Why might teachers meet with parents? What kinds of things would parents and teachers talk about?* As volunteers give their ideas, write them on the board. Include key vocabulary from the note on page 90.

Presentation

1. Have learners turn to page 90. Explain that this is a note from Han's teacher to his parents. Give them time to look at the note and to share comments among themselves.
2. Read the note aloud while learners follow along silently. Clarify vocabulary as necessary. Ask literal and inferential questions. FOR EXAMPLE: *Why does the teacher want to meet with Han's parents? What problems is Han having? Why do you think Han is having problems? When can the teacher meet with Joon and Kim? How do you think Joon and Kim should respond to the note?*
3. Tell learners to read the paragraph below the note. Clarify vocabulary as necessary. Ask *What problems do the Lees have? Why can't they go to the meeting?*
4. Put learners in pairs to discuss the question at the bottom of the page. Tell them to brainstorm several possible solutions. As a class, discuss all of the different options, identifying the pros and cons. Then have learners vote on the best solution.

Expansion/Extension

See **TRF HANDOUT 9.2**, *School Supply List*

- Put learners in pairs and have them pretend to be Joon and Kim. Tell them to write a note back to the teacher asking for a different meeting time. You may wish to write a model note on the board. Ask volunteers to read their notes aloud to the class.

More *Expansion/Extension* on page 144

Meeting Ms. Hunter

Purpose: To introduce expressing agreement and disagreement; to give practice in expressing concern, in describing problems, and in asking for clarification

Teacher Preparation and Materials
1. ▄▄ Audiotape for Level 2
2. Copies of TRF Handout 9.7, *Be a Winner in School!* (Expansion/Extension)

Warm-up
1. Ask learners to imagine what could happen in a child's life that might affect his or her schoolwork in a negative way. (new friends, parents' divorce, sickness, etc.) Be sure to include having a new baby in the family as a possible factor. Then ask learners to suggest possible results of these changes relating to a student's schoolwork. (failing tests, not paying attention, acting up in class, not doing homework, not participating, etc.)
2. Have volunteers describe situations they have experienced regarding a child's change in behavior or performance. Ask *What was the cause? What happened as a result? Was the problem resolved? How?*

Presentation
1. Have learners turn to page 91. Ask questions to elicit known vocabulary about the picture. FOR EXAMPLE: *Where is Joon? Who is he talking to? What do you think they will talk about?* Review with learners what Ms. Hunter said in her note about Han's behavior. Ask *Why do you think Han is having problems in school?*
2. Tell learners to listen carefully to the conversation on the audiotape to find out what the teacher and Joon talk about. ▄▄ Play the audiotape, suggesting that learners make notes of key points. Ask questions, such as *Is Han giving the teacher any trouble? Does Joon agree with the teacher about Han? What big change has there been at home? What does the teacher think about this change? What should Joon and Kim do?*

3. Read the first question aloud. ▄▄ Tell learners to listen for several answers to this question while you play the audiotape again. Have them write the answers.
4. In pairs, have learners think of and list several possible answers to the second question. Tell them to imagine the conversation that might occur between Joon and Kim when Joon tells her about the meeting with the teacher. Ask learners to create and then to role-play conversations that include Joon's summary of the meeting and then Kim and Joon's discussion of what to do about the problem. Suggest that they include their ideas about possible solutions as a part of the Lees' discussion. They should try to end the conversation with some kind of conclusion.

Expansion/Extension
See TRF HANDOUT 9.7, *Be a Winner in School!*

More *Expansion/Extension* on page 144

High School Years

Purpose: To give practice in describing problems and successes, and in understanding the U.S. school system

Teacher Preparation and Materials

1. Copies of important pages from a local high school handbook, including a high school schedule *(Expansion/Extension)*
2. Arrange for a high school ESL teacher to address your class. *(Expansion/Extension)*
3. Arrange for a tour of a local high school. *(Expansion/Extension)*
4. Copies of TRF Handout 9.4, *She's Going to Take Music (Expansion/Extension)*

Warm-up

1. Have learners describe what they know about high school. Ask *What are the grade levels? What are some of the courses offered? What are students' schedules like? What special activities and sports are offered? How is high school different from elementary or middle school?*
2. If learners have (or have had) any children in high school, ask them to give their impressions.

Presentation

1. Have learners turn to page 92. Ask questions to elicit known vocabulary about the picture. FOR EXAMPLE: *Where is Johnny? Who is he talking to? What do you think they're going to do?*
2. Tell learners to read the first paragraph silently and then have volunteers summarize it in their own words. Repeat with the second paragraph. Ask learners to identify the differences between elementary school, middle school, and high school. Then ask questions about high school. FOR EXAMPLE: *What do you think this sentence means: "There is more to high school than just taking classes"? What else does Johnny do in high school? What other activities are available in high school? Do you think these other activities are good for high school students? Why or why not?*

3. Put learners in small groups to discuss the questions at the bottom of the page and to list their ideas. As a class, compare and contrast high schools from around the world. As learners offer suggestions, categorize them on the board. (courses, rules, requirements, grade levels, public vs. private, etc.) Elicit learner opinions about the pros and cons of these different characteristics.

Expansion/Extension

See **TRF HANDOUT 9.4**, *She's Going to Take Music*

- Distribute copies of important pages from a local high school handbook. Read through the pages with the class. Put learners in small groups to review the policies and procedures. Clarify vocabulary as necessary. Tell groups to discuss the reasons for certain policies and to compare the policies with those in high schools in their native countries.
- Review the high school schedule with learners. Ask *How does this compare with high school classes in your native countries?* Lead a discussion.

More *Expansion/Extension* on page 145

Johnny Wins a Contest

Purpose: To give practice in describing problems and successes

Teacher Preparation and Materials
Arrange for a counselor from a local high school to visit your class. *(Expansion/Extension)*

Warm-up
1. Ask learners to think about the teacher they admire most. Ask *What was special about that teacher? Why did you admire him or her? How did that teacher help you?* Have one or two volunteers tell the class about their special teachers.
2. Ask the class what characteristics are important in a teacher and how a teacher can help a student. Write the word *Teacher* on the board. Have learners help you develop a semantic web. Elicit words such as *teaching, understanding, helping, caring,* and *listening.* Ask volunteers to describe ways teachers use these qualities with students.

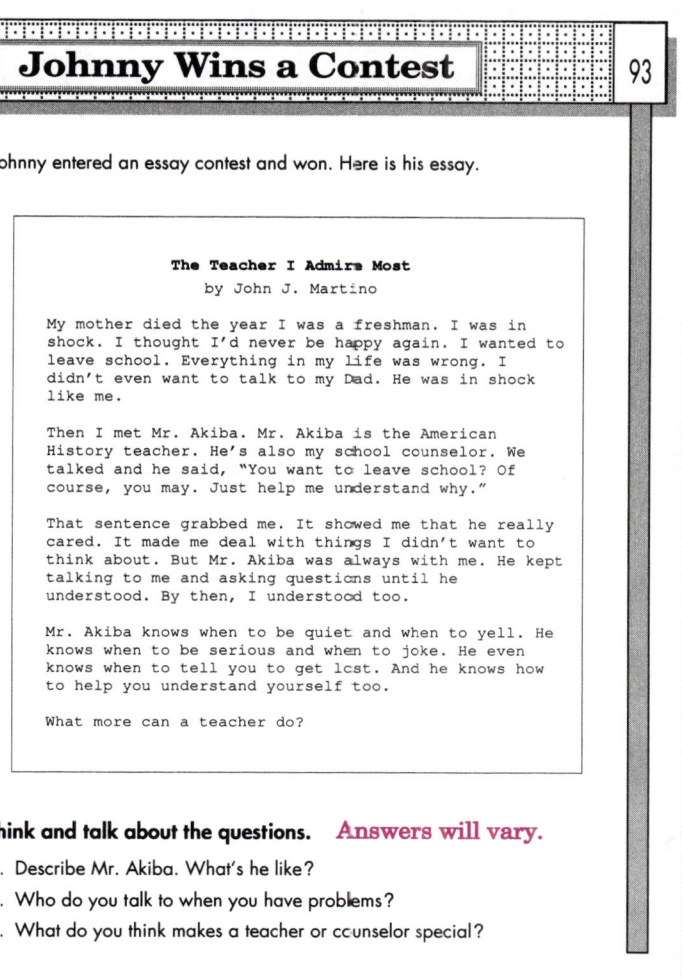

Presentation
1. Have learners turn to page 93. Explain that the story is in the form of an essay that Johnny wrote, which won the prize in a school essay contest.
2. Read the essay aloud while learners follow along silently. Clarify vocabulary as necessary. Have learners guess the meanings of idiomatic phrases in the essay. ("in shock," "grabbed me," "get lost") Provide explanation as necessary.
3. Ask questions to elicit learners' ideas about Johnny's feelings. FOR EXAMPLE: *Why didn't Johnny want to talk about his mother's death? Why couldn't he talk to his father? Why do you think talking helped Johnny?*
4. Discuss the qualities that make Mr. Akiba special. Ask learners how he helped Johnny and how he did more than is usually expected of a teacher.
5. Put learners in pairs and ask them to discuss the questions at the bottom of the page. Ask each learner to write a sentence about a special teacher. Have volunteers read their sentences aloud.

Expansion/Extension
- Ask learners to think about a difficult time in their lives. Ask *What happened? Who helped you during that time?* Have them write individual stories about the special person or persons. Have volunteers share their stories with the class.
- Ask learners what two jobs Mr. Akiba had. Write the titles on the board. If necessary, explain that a counselor helps students with school and personal problems. Ask learners to name other positions at high schools. (FOR EXAMPLE: coach, principal, dean, aide, librarian.) Talk about the job each person has and why learners think so many different positions are needed in a high school.

More *Expansion/Extension* on page 145

Adult Education Courses

Purpose: To introduce course offerings in adult education in the United States

Teacher Preparation and Materials

1. Pictures of a dessert, quilt, guitar, vase, computer, dress, exercise outfit
2. Map of the world
3. Copies of a local community college or adult education program schedule *(Expansion/Extension)*
4. Arrange for a counselor from a local community college to visit your class. *(Expansion/Extension)*
5. Arrange for a tour of a local college. *(Expansion/Extension)*
6. Copies of TRF Handout 9.3, *What Is the Subject?* *(Expansion/Extension)*

Warm-up

1. Ask learners why adults take classes and list the reasons on the board. (to learn a new skill, to study for a degree, to take up a hobby, to learn English, to study for a citizenship exam, etc.)
2. Have learners name some courses adults might like to take. Write their suggestions on the board. Be sure to include course names from page 94. Ask volunteers to describe the courses. If necessary, clarify meaning with pictures such as a dessert, quilt, guitar, vase, computer, dress, and exercise outfit.
3. Write *Adult Education* on the board. Use the categories from the bottom half of page 94 to create a semantic web. Ask learners to add names of courses that would fit in those categories.

Presentation

1. Have learners turn to page 94 and identify where the page came from. (a community college or adult education catalog) Give them time to read through the page. Clarify vocabulary as necessary. You may wish to point out Thailand, Texas, Mexico, and Africa on a world map to show the ethnic backgrounds of some of the courses.
2. Ask literal and inferential questions, such as *Which courses offer musical instrument lessons? Which courses might interest people looking for exercise? Why do you think someone might study quilting or bread baking? Why might someone take a course in civics?*
3. Put learners in small groups and model a chain drill, asking *When can you take (course name)?* Tell learners to continue the drill in their small groups, asking and answering questions about the catalog page.
4. Review with learners the sample answers at the bottom of the page. Explain that a course might fit in more than one category. Then put learners in pairs to complete the exercise and to select one or more courses they would like to take. Follow with a class discussion of which categories the courses fit in, why learners chose particular courses, and why people might take the different classes.

Expansion/Extension on page 145

Adult Education Courses (page 94)

Most school systems have courses for adults. Adults go to school for a lot of different reasons. Here are the adult education courses offered at one school.

	Monday	Tuesday	Wednesday	Thursday
6 p.m.	ESL Spanish Résumé Writing	Piano Perfect Pasta Typing	ESL	ESL Gentle Exercise Yoga
7 p.m.	Auto Repair Dressmaking Tex-Mex Cooking	Thai Cooking Bookkeeping	Printmaking Aerobics Baking Breads	American History Healthy Desserts
8 p.m.	Stress Management Job Interview Workshop Business Writing	H.S. Math H.S. Civics Computers I	Pottery Guitar Computers II	Quilting African Dance

Put the courses into categories.

Languages & Adult Basic Education (ABE)	Arts, Crafts, & Skills	Cooking	Business & Careers	Health, Exercise, & Dance
ESL Spanish H.S. Math H.S. Civics American History	Auto Repair Piano Dressmaking Printmaking Pottery Guitar Quilting	Baking Breads Perfect Pasta Tex-Mex Cooking Thai Cooking Healthy Desserts	Typing Résumé Writing Bookkeeping Job Interview Workshop Business Writing Computers I Computers II	Yoga Gentle Exercise Aerobics African Dance Stress Management

At Registration

Purpose: To give practice in expressing agreement and disagreement, in asking for clarification, and in describing problems and successes

Teacher Preparation and Materials
1. Audiotape for Level 2
2. Copies of registration forms from a local community college *(Expansion/Extension)*
3. Arrange to visit a local college on registration day. *(Expansion/Extension)*
4. Copies of TRF Handout 9.5, *What's for Lunch? (Expansion/Extension)*

Warm-up
1. Remind learners of the courses they selected during the last lesson. Then have a volunteer come to the front of the class and ask what courses he or she is planning to take in the future. Make comments and ask for additional clarification, using phrases such as *What will you learn . . . ? Could you tell me about . . . ? Why don't you . . . ?* Then have the volunteer ask you about courses you would like to take.
2. On the board, write *Registration for Adult Education*. Ask learners what it was like to register for this ESL class. Ask *Where did you go? Did you have to wait in line? Did you have any problems? Did you meet anyone you knew?* Ask them to describe their experiences.

Presentation
1. Have learners turn to page 95. Ask questions to elicit known vocabulary about the picture. FOR EXAMPLE: *Where are Olga and Isabel? What are they doing? What do you think they are talking about? What classes do you think they would each like to take?*
2. Remind learners about Olga's visit to the doctor and have them look back at page 94 to predict what classes she will register for. Then have learners listen to the conversation on the audiotape to see if they were right. Replay the audiotape

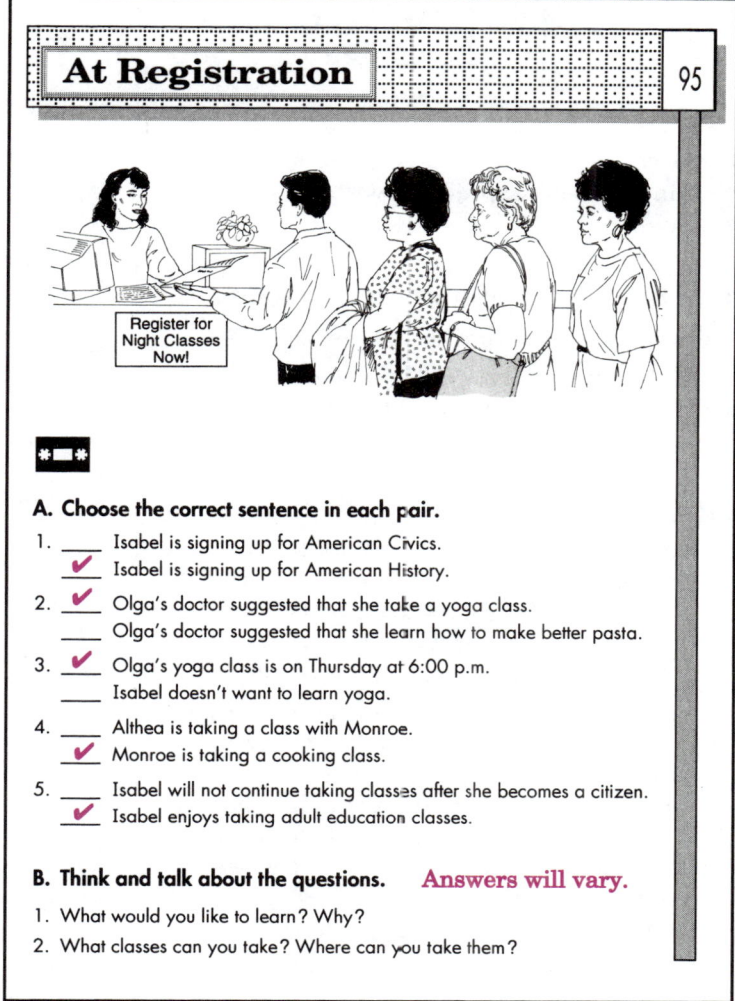

so learners can check their work and fill in any missing information.

3. Continue by discussing the conversation on the audiotape. *What has Isabel been studying? What do you think she wants to learn more about? Why is Olga taking classes? Who else is taking classes? Do you think they are all taking courses for the same reasons? What are some of their reasons?*

4. Put learners in small groups to discuss the questions in exercise B. Refer learners to the courses they selected from page 94. Suggest that they consider those or similar courses and talk about why they would like to take them. Ask volunteers to describe their course selections and make a list of places where learners might find such classes.

Expansion/Extension
See TRF HANDOUT 9.5, *What's for Lunch?*

More *Expansion/Extension* on page 145

UNIT 9 • 141

Adult Education

Purpose: To give practice with *If/then* statements; to give practice with *must* and *will*

Teacher Preparation and Materials

1. Copies of pages from school and college catalogs *(Expansion/Extension)*
2. Copies of TRF Handout 9.6, *Time to Study (Expansion/Extension)*

Warm-up

1. Ask learners *What do we learn in ESL? What materials must we bring to class?* As learners offer their ideas, write them on the board. Repeat with other courses, such as computers, yoga, and cooking.
2. Ask learners *Do you need special knowledge or experience for ESL Level 1?* (No.) *Do you need it for our level of ESL?* (Yes, you should know some English already.) Have them describe any special skills or experience they needed for other classes they have taken.
3. Ask learners how long each ESL class session is and write the answer on the board.

Presentation

1. Have learners turn to page 96 and identify the top half of the page. (descriptions from a course catalog) Point out that these are descriptions of a few of the courses on page 94.
2. Explain that learners do not need to understand every word in the catalog, just the basic meaning. Read the first description aloud, asking learners to underline the following words: *learn, basics, no experience necessary, knowledge of keyboard or typing recommended*. Say that these words tell what you will learn in the class and what skills or experience are needed. Have learners read the other course descriptions, underlining key words. Clarify vocabulary as necessary.
3. Read the direction for the exercise. Do the first example as a class. Then put learners in pairs to complete the exercise.

---

96 Adult Education

BUSINESS
Computers I — Tuesday 8:00–9:00
Learn all the basics of how computers work. No previous computer experience is necessary, but knowledge of the keyboard or typing is recommended. You will interact one-on-one with a computer!

COOKING
Baking Breads — Wednesday 7:00–8:00
Learn the art and techniques of baking all kinds of breads: white, rye, wheat, and fruit breads. The instructor will demonstrate and provide hands-on practice making, kneading, and rolling yeast dough. All supplies included. Bring an apron, though!

LANGUAGES
ESL (English as a Second Language) — Monday 6:00–7:00
This course is for people whose native language is not English and who have very little knowledge of English. The instructor will teach grammar and pronunciation basics and provide many opportunities for conversation. Buy your ESL textbook at the school bookstore before the first class.

HEALTH, EXERCISE, & DANCE
Yoga — Thursday 6:00–7:00
This is a six-session course consisting of practical, gentle exercises for men and women of all ages. Yoga makes you healthier and more physically fit, reduces stress, and raises energy levels. Wear loose-fitting clothing and bring an exercise mat to class.

Complete the sentences.

1. If you take the computer class, then you need to know __about the keyboard or how to type__.
2. If you take the ESL class, then you will learn __grammar, pronunciation basics, conversation__.
3. If you take the yoga class, then you must wear __loose-fitting clothing__ and bring __an exercise mat__.
4. If you take the Baking Breads class, then you will practice __making, kneading, and rolling yeast dough__.
5. If you take the ESL class, then you must buy __a textbook at the school bookstore before the first class__.

As volunteers share their answers with the class, ask further questions about the course descriptions. FOR EXAMPLE: *What can yoga do for you? What should you bring to the Baking Breads class? What kind of person might be interested in the computer course?*

Expansion/Extension

See **TRF HANDOUT 9.6,** *Time to Study*

- Ask learners *Which of the four classes would you take and why? Why would you not take some of the other classes?* Take a class survey. Tally the numbers on the board. Ask *Are the times listed convenient for you? Why or why not?*
- Distribute pages from other school and college catalogs that might be of interest to learners. Have learners discuss the pages in small groups. Ask *Which courses would you like to take?*

More *Expansion/Extension* on page 145

Making the Connection

Purpose: To give practice in asking for clarification; to give practice with skills, functions, and vocabulary from Unit 9

Teacher Preparation and Materials
None

Warm-up
Have a volunteer explain why he or she takes classes or is studying ESL. Write the volunteer's comments on the board in the form of a paragraph. Ask the rest of the learners to brainstorm other reasons and write them on the board under the heading *Reasons for Taking Classes*. Have them consider people of different ages, with different educational backgrounds, and so on.

Presentation
1. Have learners turn to page 97. Read aloud the title and first paragraph. Clarify vocabulary as necessary. Then ask learners to write individual paragraphs. Suggest that they follow the model from the *Warm-up*.
2. When learners have finished, tell them to read their paragraphs aloud in small groups. Have learners ask each other questions if they do not understand something or if they would like to hear more about a particular idea.

Expansion/Extension
- Ask learners to name the most important results of taking classes. (learning English, getting a better job, learning new skills, making friends, etc.) Explain that the results may not be the same as the reasons they first had for taking classes. Have learners describe any changes they found between original reasons for taking classes and the final results.

Making the Connection 97

People go to school for different reasons. Some people need to take classes to help them at work. Some people take classes to learn new things. And some people take classes to relax, have fun, and meet other people.

Write about why *you* take classes. Answers will vary.

- Put learners in pairs. Have them interview each other, asking *What are the most important results of your adult education classes?* Ask volunteers to report on the results of their interviews.
- Play a game with *If/then*. Divide the class into two teams. Appoint a scorekeeper. Start the game by calling on the first member of Team A. Say *If I take a computer class, then I'll . . .* The first member of Team A must finish the sentence appropriately within 10 seconds. Then he or she calls on a member from Team B, saying *If I take ESL, then I'll . . .* , and so on. Continue with the game, alternating team members. Score one point for each correct answer given within 10 seconds.
- Play charades, having each learner act out a different kind of class while the rest guess what it is.

UNIT 9 • 143

UNIT 9: Going to School
Expansion/Extension

At School
More *Expansion/Extension* for SB page 87

- Ask learners to write individual stories titled How I Feel about Education in the United States. You may wish to compose a sample LEA story on the board, interviewing a volunteer and writing the answers in story form. After learners have finished, divide the class into small groups to read their stories aloud.

- Make a semantic web on the board with *U.S. Education* at the center. Ask volunteers to help you fill it out with their ideas and suggestions. Prompt them with categories such as School Levels, Course Titles, and School Jobs.

Han Lee's Class
More *Expansion/Extension* for SB page 88

- Take a class survey. Ask *How many learners think it's an advantage for children to learn their parents' native language or languages? How many think it's a disadvantage?* Tally the responses. Lead a discussion, helping learners see the advantages of knowing two or more languages in a multilingual society.

- Invite an elementary ESL teacher to speak to your class about how to help children do well in school. Have learners prepare questions before the visit and practice asking them.

- If possible, arrange to tour an elementary school together with your class. Visit the office, the gym, the special activity rooms, the playground, and the nurse's office. Discuss how each is run. Have learners prepare questions ahead of time.

Welcome to District 5 Elementary School
More *Expansion/Extension* for SB page 89

- Distribute key handbook pages from your local elementary schools' handbooks. Put learners in small groups to read through the pages and categorize the rules and other information. Tell them to discuss and evaluate the information. Suggest that they consider the reasons for particular rules, why the classes are a particular size, and so on. Afterward, have them share important information.

- Distribute copies of the handbook for the learners' own college, program, or school. Have learners read and discuss the handbook. Clarify information as necessary. Afterward, ask each group to share with the class any important information they discovered.

A Note from School
More *Expansion/Extension* for SB page 90

- Have learners work in small groups to develop a telephone conversation between Joon or Kim and first the secretary at Han's school, then Ms. Hunter, to set up a different meeting time. Ask volunteers to role-play their conversations in front of the class.

- Ask learners to bring in notes they have received from their children's schools, or ask local elementary teachers to give you copies of standard notes they send home. Duplicate and distribute them. Put learners in small groups to identify and discuss what, if any, action the parents must take for each kind of note.

- Pretend to be an elementary teacher and ask a volunteer to pretend to be a parent. Using real or toy telephones, tell the parent that you want to talk about his or her child. Ask *When can we meet?* Help learners with appropriate answers.

- Afterward, pair the learners and have them write similar conversations between a teacher and a parent. Encourage them to ask and talk about why the teacher wants to talk to the parent. Ask volunteers to role-play their conversations in front of the class.

Meeting Ms. Hunter
More *Expansion/Extension* for SB page 91

- Ask learners *Have you or any of your children ever had problems in school? What did the teacher say? What did you do? Did things get better?* Have volunteers describe their experiences.

- Have learners write individual stories titled "Problems in School." You may wish to compose a model on the board, interviewing a volunteer and writing the answers in story form. Ask volunteers to read their stories aloud.

- Tell learners you are going to pretend to be an elementary school teacher. Ask a volunteer to be a parent. Role-play a parent-teacher conference in front of the class. Brainstorm a list of questions to ask during a parent-teacher conference and a list of some things a teacher might tell parents. Then put learners in pairs and have them prepare the same kind of conversations to role-play in front of the class.
- Ask learners *Have you ever had problems with a new baby in the house? How was each member of the family affected? Did they have problems? Could they solve them? How?* Have volunteers share their experiences.

High School Years
More *Expansion/Extension* for SB page 92

- On the board, write the high school grade levels. (freshman, sophomore, junior, senior) Ask volunteers to write "first," "second," "third," or "fourth year" and the grade number (9th, 10th, 11th, 12th) next to each. Ask *What are some courses usually taken at each level?* Write learners' suggestions on the board.
- Invite a high school ESL teacher to talk to your class about various aspects of high school in the United States and in your community in particular. Have learners prepare questions beforehand.
- Visit a local high school with your class. Take learners on a tour of the offices, classrooms, and various departments. If possible, sit in on an ESL class.
- Have learners write individual stories about the visit. Have volunteers read their stories aloud to the class.

Johnny Wins a Contest
More *Expansion/Extension* for SB page 93

- Ask learners to compare teachers in the United States with those in their native countries. Ask *How are they the same? How are they different?* Have them carry on discussions in small groups.
- Invite a counselor from a local high school to visit your class and explain how the counseling department works.

Adult Education Courses
***Expansion/Extension* for SB page 94**

See **TRF HANDOUT 9.3,** *What Is the Subject?*

- Distribute copies of your local community college or adult education program schedule. Continue the discussion about course categories and individual interests.
- Have each learner interview at least one or two others, asking *What classes would you like to take? Why?* When they have finished, ask volunteers to report their findings to the class.
- Invite a counselor from your local community college to visit the class and to describe courses learners might be interested in. Have learners prepare questions beforehand.

At Registration
More *Expansion/Extension* for SB page 95

- Have learners discuss in small groups the similarities and differences between adult education in the United States and in their native countries.
- Have each learner work with a partner, pretending they have met in line on registration night. Ask them to create a conversation like the one on the audiotape, using the course selections on page 94 as a reference. Have volunteers role-play their conversations in front of the class.
- Distribute copies of registration forms from your local community college. Go over the forms orally, clarifying vocabulary as necessary. Then have learners work in pairs to fill out the forms.

Adult Education
More *Expansion/Extension* for SB page 96

- Have a volunteer come to the front of the class. On the board, write two column headings: *Need To* and *Want To (But Don't Need To)*. Ask the volunteer to describe which courses he or she needs to take (for a job, for survival) and which courses he or she wants to take. (for fun, for interest) Write the volunteer's answers under the heading he or she indicates. Explain that some courses can fit in both categories. Repeat this procedure with another volunteer. Then pair the learners and have them help each other fill out similar charts.

1 2 3 4 5 6 7 8 9 10 11 12 Summary
Becoming a Citizen

Objectives

Functions
- Reporting
- Persuading
- Expressing agreement and disagreement
- Clarifying

Life Tasks
- Learning about U.S. history and government
- Understanding civic duties
- Becoming familiar with immigration categories and citizenship requirements

Structures
- Past tense vs. past continuous tense
- Reported speech with *that*
- *Wh-* questions
- Modals: *can, should, must*
- Tag questions

Culture
- U.S. history and government
- Civic duties

Vocabulary

Key words:

branch	Independence Day
citizen	INS
citizenship	interview
colonies	judge
Congress	law
court	miss
Declaration of Independence	obey
duties	permanent
election	resident
famous	place of birth
flag	president
government	ready
history	representatives
Immigration and Naturalization Service	revolution
	Senate
	taxes
	vote

Related words:

Alien Registration Card	judicial
armed forces	legislative
discharge	maiden name
executive	naturalization
fingerprint	petition
House of Representatives	"The Star-Spangled Banner"

Citizenship

Purpose: To give practice with *Wh-* questions; to introduce the INS and preparing for citizenship

Teacher Preparation and Materials

1. Copies of descriptions of citizenship courses offered locally *(Expansion/Extension)*
2. Copies of TRF Handout 10.1, *The Best Classes for You (Expansion/Extension)*

Warm-up

1. Write on the board the abbreviation *INS,* explaining that it stands for the Immigration and Naturalization Service. Ask volunteers to share whatever they know about this organization. Ask questions, such as *What does* immigration *mean? What does* naturalization *mean? Where is the closest INS office? What does INS do? What happens when you apply for citizenship?*
2. Ask *Have any of you become U.S. citizens or are you preparing for citizenship?* Have them share their experiences.
3. Refer learners back to the course names and descriptions on pages 94 and 96. Talk about the differences between general adult education courses and citizenship classes.

Presentation

1. Have learners turn to page 98. Ask questions about the pictures to elicit known vocabulary. FOR EXAMPLE: *What's going on in these pictures? Where is Isabel? Who is she in class with? What are they studying? What is happening in the ceremony?*
2. Put learners in small groups to discuss the questions at the bottom of the page. Have them make lists of the things they think Isabel and the other students in her class will need to learn to become citizens. As groups share their lists, discuss why it is important to know these things and why those students might want to become U.S. citizens.

Expansion/Extension

See **TRF HANDOUT 10.1,** *The Best Classes for You*

- Ask *How do you become a citizen in your native country? Can foreigners become citizens in your native country? What do they have to do to become citizens?* Lead a discussion, comparing and contrasting laws in learners' native countries with those in the United States.
- If any of the learners have become citizens of the United States, have them describe the process, while you write the steps on the board.
- Ask learners to name other agencies or organizations (besides INS) in the United States and in the world that use abbreviations for their names. (UN, UNESCO, etc.) Write a few examples on the board. Then put learners in small groups to think of as many other similar abbreviations as they can. Have them discuss what the letters stand for and what these organizations do.
- Distribute copies of local course offerings that prepare learners for citizenship tests. Discuss when and how learners could take these classes.

UNIT 10 • 147

Members of the Class

Purpose: To give practice in reporting personal information; to give practice with *Wh-* questions and with the past tense

Teacher Preparation and Materials

1. Map of the world; pushpins *(Expansion/Extension)*
2. Copies of TRF Handout 10.4, *Becoming U.S. Citizens (Expansion/Extension)*
3. Copies of TRF Handout 10.5, *What Do You Want to Do in the United States? (Expansion/Extension)*

Warm-up

1. Ask one or two volunteers *When you came to the United States, how did you feel at first? Do you feel any differently now?* On the board, write their key comments. Ask the volunteers *Are you U.S. citizens or do you plan on becoming U.S. citizens? Why do/don't you want to be U.S. citizens?*
2. Ask learners what a *permanent resident* is and what the differences are between a permanent resident and a citizen. (FOR EXAMPLE: A citizen can vote, but a permanent resident cannot.) Explain that in this unit, they will learn more about the duties and rights of citizens.
3. Tell learners they are going to read about Isabel, who is from El Salvador, and Stefan, who is from Poland. Ask learners to locate these countries on a world map.

Presentation

1. Have learners turn to page 99. Ask questions about the pictures to elicit known vocabulary. FOR EXAMPLE: *What do you know about Isabel? What do you know about Stefan?*
2. Ask learners to read aloud the paragraph about Isabel. Clarify any unfamiliar vocabulary. Then have learners find and read sentences that give different details. FOR EXAMPLE: Say *Read the sentence that tells why Isabel came to the United States. Read the sentences that tell what Isabel did when she got to the United States.* Repeat this procedure with the paragraph about Stefan.

Members of the Class — 99

Isabel Santos came to the United States 10 years ago. She came because she couldn't find work in her country. Isabel got a job here. She also went to school to become a U.S. citizen. At first Isabel wasn't sure she wanted to be a U.S. citizen. She thought things might change in El Salvador. But then Isabel began to love the United States. She was proud to live here and wanted to become a citizen.

Stefan Zolonski came to the United States six years ago. He wasn't happy in Poland. He thought life in the United States was better for him. Some of his Polish friends remained permanent residents of the United States. They wanted to return to Poland. But Stefan wanted to stay in this country. He wanted to become a citizen.

Think and talk about the questions.   Answers will vary.

1. When did you come to the United States?
2. Why did you come here?
3. How are things different here from your native country?

3. Ask learners *How are Isabel and Stefan similar? How are they different?* Then have volunteers describe how their own situations are similar to or different from Stefan's and Isabel's. Discuss the fact that there are many different reasons why people immigrate to this country.
4. Put the class in small groups. Ask them to talk about the questions at the bottom of the page. Have volunteers share their answers with the class.

Expansion/Extension

See **TRF HANDOUT 10.4,** *Becoming U.S. Citizens*
TRF HANDOUT 10.5, *What Do You Want to Do in the United States?*

- Using a world map, locate the native countries of all learners. Mark them with pushpins. Ask *Can you go back to visit your native country? How often? How do you feel when you go back? Would you like to go back to live?*

More *Expansion/Extension* on page 158

What You Need to Become a Citizen

Purpose: To give practice with *must*; to introduce requirements for becoming a U.S. citizen

Teacher Preparation and Materials

1. Samples of recent photographs, fingerprint forms, money orders, Petition for Naturalization forms, Alien Registration Cards
2. A list of true/false statements (based on information on page 100) *(Expansion/Extension)*
3. Arrange a trip to a photo studio (to have photos taken) and to the police station (to register fingerprints). *(Expansion/Extension)*
4. Arrange for an INS representative to visit the class. *(Expansion/Extension)*

Warm-up

Ask learners what materials are needed to apply for citizenship. Elicit as much information as you can from them, writing their comments on the board. If possible, show recent photographs, actual forms, cards, and so on. Include key materials that they do not mention, such as photographs, fingerprint form, Petition for Naturalization form, and Alien Registration Card.

Presentation

1. Have learners turn to page 100. Read the title aloud and give them a few moments to look over the page.
2. Ask learners *Besides actual photographs, cards, and forms, what else does the INS require?* Then ask questions and have volunteers read the corresponding requirement. FOR EXAMPLE: *What must you send to the INS? What should you not send? What must you be able to do to become a U.S. citizen? What must you know? How old must you be?*
3. Read aloud the direction line and choices at the bottom of the page. Have learners complete the exercise in pairs. Then have

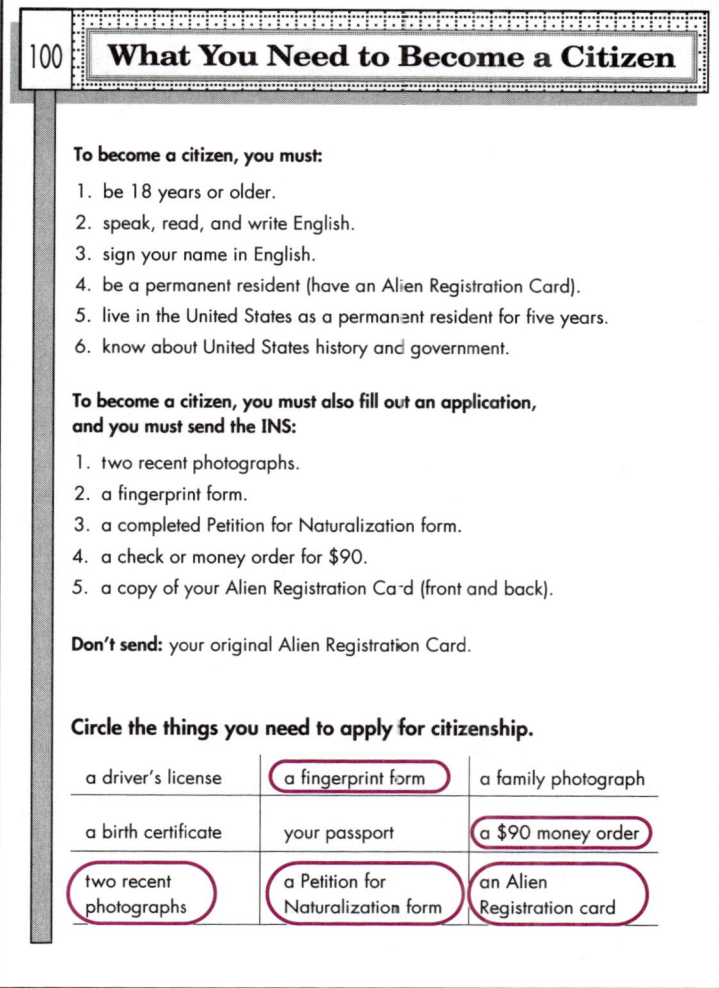

them take turns role-playing an INS worker and a phone caller asking for information. The caller asks questions, such as "What do I need . . . ? Do I need . . . ?" The INS worker answers the questions, trying not to look at the page. The caller can check off things the worker mentions. Then have them switch roles and repeat the activity.

4. With the class, discuss the possible reasons for rules and requirements for citizenship. Ask *Why do you think two photographs are needed? Why should you not send your original Alien Registration Card? Why do you think you have to live in the United States for five years before becoming a citizen?*

Expansion/Extension

- Invite a representative from the INS to address your class about the process of becoming a U.S. citizen. Have learners prepare questions ahead of time.

More *Expansion/Extension* on page 158

Who's Ready?

Purpose: To give practice with *Why* questions; to give practice in reporting and in understanding requirements for becoming a U.S. citizen

Teacher Preparation and Materials
None

Warm-up

1. Ask learners *Who's ready to become a U.S. citizen? Why do you think you're ready?* Write their comments and ideas on the board. Then interview those volunteers, asking about the items on the checklist on page 101.

2. Ask *Have any of you decided to remain a permanent resident? Why?* (Perhaps they hope to return to their native countries to live; perhaps they do not want to serve in the U.S. Armed Forces in time of war; perhaps they do not care about voting.) Point out that there are many things to think about before making the decision to become a citizen and that everyone must do what seems best for himself or herself.

Presentation

1. Have learners turn to page 101 and give them time to look over the checklist.

2. Read the categories aloud or have a volunteer do so. Refer learners back to the stories on page 99. Ask *How do you know Isabel/Stefan is ready to become a citizen?* Have learners look at the chart. Ask *What must Joon do to get ready?*

3. Tell learners they are going to interview five other people, asking them questions about the different categories on the checklist. Demonstrate with a volunteer at the front of the class. Then have learners prepare the questions they will need to ask and proceed with the interviews. You may suggest that they ask an additional question about whether people prefer to become citizens or to be permanent residents and why. (This information can help with the questions

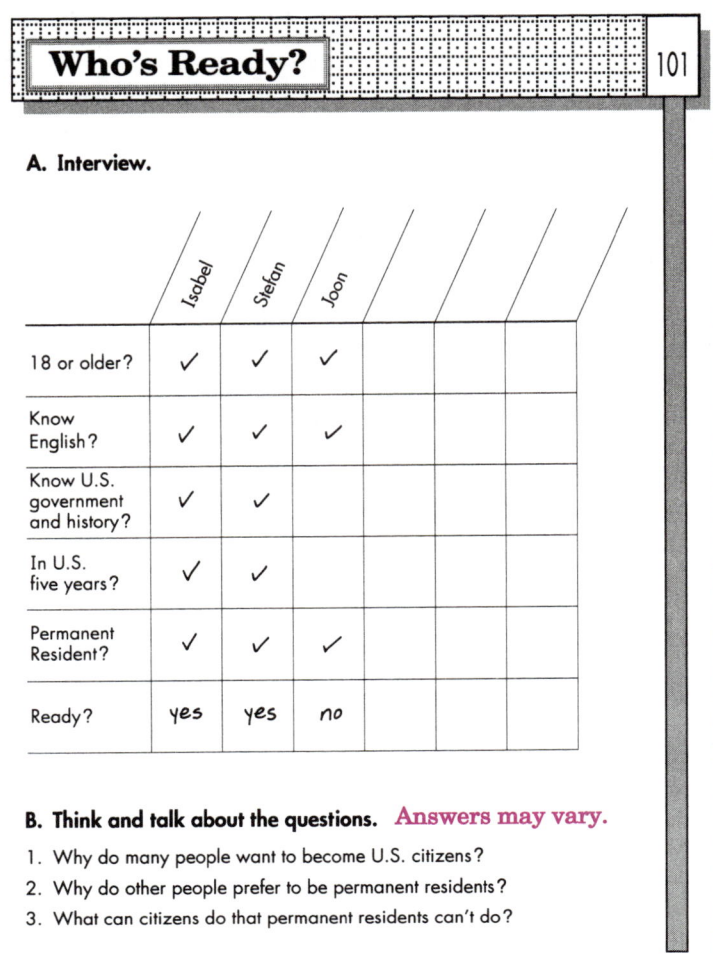

in exercise B.) Afterward, ask volunteers to report the information they discovered during one of their interviews. ◼ In a one-to-one situation, interview the learner. Have the learner interview you and four friends or family members and discuss the results.

4. Put the class in small groups to discuss the questions in exercise B. Afterward, discuss the reasons why people choose to either be citizens or permanent residents. Use this information to re-emphasize the point that this is an individual decision.

Expansion/Extension

- Have learners use the checklist on page 101 to interview some friends and family members, and to ask their preference for citizenship or permanent residency and why. Ask volunteers to share any new reasons they discovered for these preferences.

Petition for Naturalization

Purpose: To give practice in reading and filling out a form, and in understanding requirements for becoming a U.S. citizen

Teacher Preparation and Materials
Copies of a complete Petition for Naturalization form *(Expansion/Extension)*

Warm-up
1. Review the requirements for applying for U.S. citizenship. Then write on the board *Name, Alien Registration card number, Other names you have used,* and *Place of birth,* leaving space to fill in the information. Ask for a volunteer who has an Alien Registration card to come to the board and to fill in the information. To provide additional examples, ask learners what other names they have used and where they were born.

2. Point out that this is some of the information included on a Petition for Naturalization form, explaining that a *petition* is a formal request, often used in legal matters. Ask *Have any of you ever filled out a petition? Do you have any questions about it?*

3. Note that many learners may not have Alien Registration cards. They may be in the United States on a student's or worker's visa, or as refugees. Explain that in these cases, they should leave the second line on this form blank, but they would have to supply copies of any visas or other documents to the INS. They may wish to call the INS for further information. Provide the telephone number.

Presentation
1. Have learners turn to page 102. Identify the form as a shortened version of the Petition for Naturalization. Give learners time to look over the page.

2. Review the information on the petition by asking learners to locate different items. FOR EXAMPLE: *Read the questions that ask about the requirements for citizenship. Read the line that tells you not to write anything in that space. Read a line that might not apply to many applicants.* Point out that applicants should leave the line blank if the question does not apply to them. (FOR EXAMPLE: numbers 12 through 13)

3. Have learners complete the petition with their personal information. Assist as necessary.

4. Lead a discussion on why some immigrants might change their names. (FOR EXAMPLE: Some names are long or difficult for English-speakers to pronounce. Some people might want a more American-sounding name.) Elicit/provide examples of names that people may have shortened or changed. (Martínez/Martin) Point out that this was common years ago, but it is not done very often today.

---

102 Petition for Naturalization

Answers will vary.   This block for government use only.

1. Your name (exactly as it appears on your Alien Registration Card)
2. Your Alien Registration Number
3. Your Social Security Number
4. Your name (full, true, and correct name, if different from above)
5. Any other names you have used (including maiden name)
6. Your place of birth (city/town) (county/province/state) (country)
7. Can you read and write English? ☐ Yes ☐ No
8. Can you speak English? ☐ Yes ☐ No
9. Can you sign your name in English? ☐ Yes ☐ No
10. How long have you continuously lived in the state where you now live?
11. Have you served in the United States Armed Forces? ☐ Yes ☐ No
12. Branch of service
13. Type of discharge (honorable, dishonorable, etc.)

You may change your name when you become a U.S. citizen. If you wish to do so, please sign and print or type that name below.

Your signature _____
New name _____

***Expansion/Extension* on page 158**

Learning American History

Purpose: To give practice with the past tense and with *Wh-* questions; to give practice in listening for key points

Teacher Preparation and Materials

1. Pictures or films about the American Revolution *(Warm-up, Expansion/Extension)*
2. 📼 Audiotape for Level 2
3. Arrange a visit to a public or school library. *(Expansion/Extension)*
4. Copies of TRF Handout 10.7, *All Around the United States (Expansion/Extension)*

Warm-up

1. Ask learners what they know about the beginning of the United States. Write key comments and vocabulary on the board. Elicit/present information about the 13 original colonies, George Washington, the Revolutionary War, England, the Declaration of Independence, and Thomas Jefferson.
2. If possible, show a film or pictures about the American Revolution to the class. Help learners identify important figures and events. If you show a film, shut off the sound and narrate it yourself, adjusting your narration to learners' needs and levels of ability.

Presentation

1. Have learners turn to page 103. Ask questions about the picture to elicit known vocabulary. FOR EXAMPLE: *Where are Isabel and Stefan? What is the teacher talking about? What did the teacher write on the board? What class do you think this is?*
2. Have learners read the questions silently. Assist with vocabulary as necessary. Suggest that they write the answers they know in pencil, in case they need to change them later.
3. Tell learners to listen to the lecture about the American Revolution on the audiotape. 📼 Play the audiotape and then have them answer the questions.

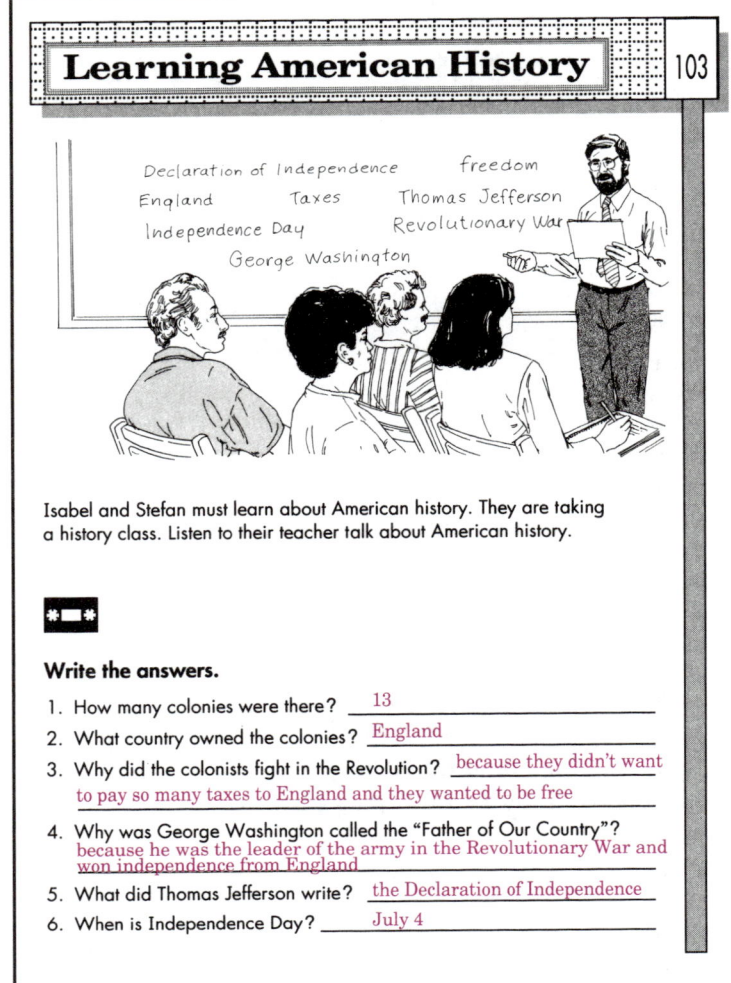

📼 Replay the audiotape so learners can check their work and fill in missing information. Ask volunteers to share the correct answers with the class.

4. Elicit/provide further details about the facts presented on the audiotape. Ask questions, such as *Why did the colonists come to this country in the first place? What do you think the English made them pay taxes for? Who won the Revolutionary War? After the Declaration of Independence was written, the leaders began working on a document that formed the basis of the new country. What was this document called? Why do you think this was an important document?*

Expansion/Extension

See TRF HANDOUT 10.7, *All Around the United States*

- Show a different film about the Revolutionary War. After the film is over, discuss the main events with learners.

More *Expansion/Extension* on page 158

The United States Government

Purpose: To introduce the branches of the U.S. government and information to prepare learners for a citizenship interview

Teacher Preparation and Materials

1. Pictures or a filmstrip about the branches of the U.S. government (FOR EXAMPLE: The judicial branch can be represented by a picture of the scales of justice or a picture of the Supreme Court.)
2. Arrange for a local representative from the state legislature to visit the class. *(Expansion/Extension)*
3. If possible, arrange a trip to your state capital *(Expansion/Extension)*
4. Arrange a trip to your local town or city hall. *(Expansion/Extension)*
5. Copies of TRF Handout 10.3, *100 Questions Game (Expansion/Extension)*

Warm-up

1. Ask learners what responsibilities they think a government should have for its people. Discuss the importance of law and order. Ask *What should the government do to keep law and order in the country?* As you listen to learners' comments, write on the board these responsibilities: *make laws, enforce and carry out laws,* and *decide if laws are fair and legal.*
2. Ask learners what they know about these three responsibilities and how the U.S. government handles them. Write their ideas in a semantic web around the three categories. Elicit/provide information that the U.S. government is made up of three branches, each with its specific responsibilities.
3. If possible, show a filmstrip about the branches of the U.S. government. Turn off the sound and narrate the film yourself, using a level of language appropriate for learners.

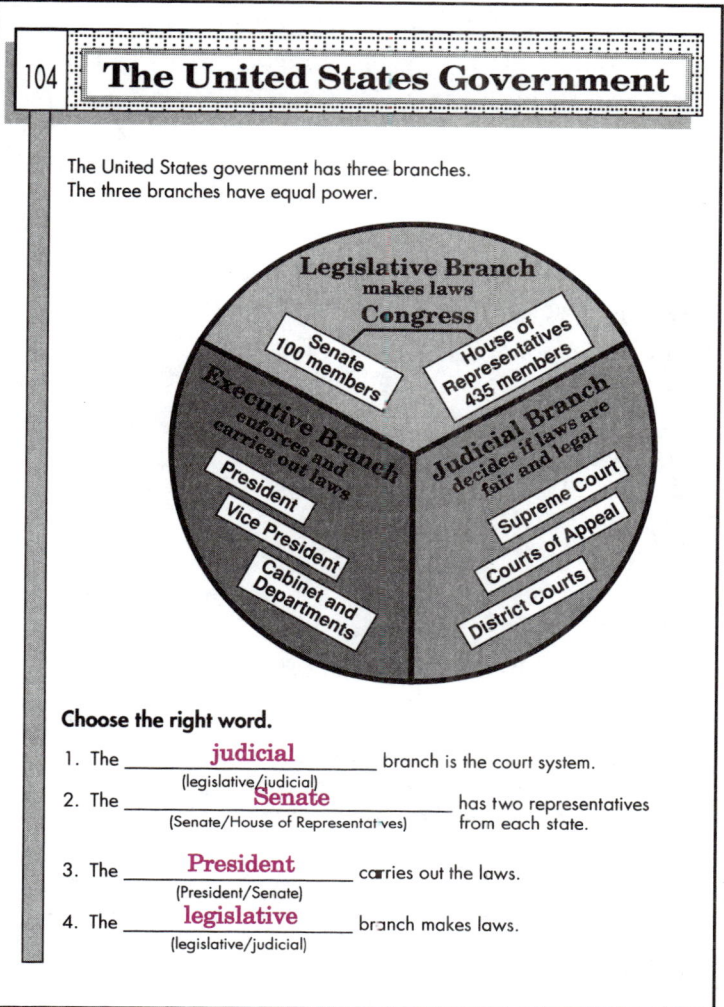

Presentation

1. Have learners turn to page 104 and read the first two sentences. Point out that the pie chart demonstrates that the government is divided into three equal parts. Ask volunteers to come to the board and label the semantic web with the appropriate branch names.
2. Ask volunteers to read the names of the people or groups that belong to each branch. Explain that one major idea for the organization of this government is that the groups will "check up on each other" to be sure that decisions they make are constitutional. Ask *How do you think the Senate and the House of Representatives work together to make a law? Why do you think there are courts at different levels? Does the President make decisions on his own? How do the other groups help him in making decisions?*
3. Put learners in pairs to complete the exercise at the bottom of the page and ask volunteers to share their answers with the class.

Expansion/Extension on page 159

UNIT 10 • 153

Duties of U.S. Citizens

Purpose: To give practice with *can* and *must,* and with *Wh-* questions; to introduce civic duties

Teacher Preparation and Materials

1. The address of the representative for your area, or a local phone book.
2. Arrange for a member of the League of Women Voters (or a similar organization) to visit your class. *(Expansion/Extension)*
3. Copies of TRF Handout 10.2, *Some Important Rights (Expansion/Extension)*

Warm-up

1. Write on the board the words *can* and *must*. Have learners consider an occupation, such as waiter/waitress. Ask them to name different things that a waiter/waitress *must* do as part of the job. (take customers' orders, answer questions, serve food, etc.) Now ask them to name different things that a waiter/waitress *can* do as part of the job. (carry on brief conversations/be friendly with customers, offer advice, make suggestions to restaurant managers, etc.)
2. Tell learners that citizens of the United States also have things that they can do and must do. Introduce the terms *rights* and *duties,* and then brainstorm with the class some important rights and duties of U.S. citizens. Ask *What are the duties of citizens regarding laws? What rights do citizens have about choosing government leaders? What about paying taxes? Is this a right or a duty for citizens?* Write learners' responses on the board and then lead a discussion about why citizens have these duties and rights.

Presentation

1. Have learners turn to page 105. Read the three duties aloud. Then ask learners to read the reasons silently. Clarify vocabulary as necessary.

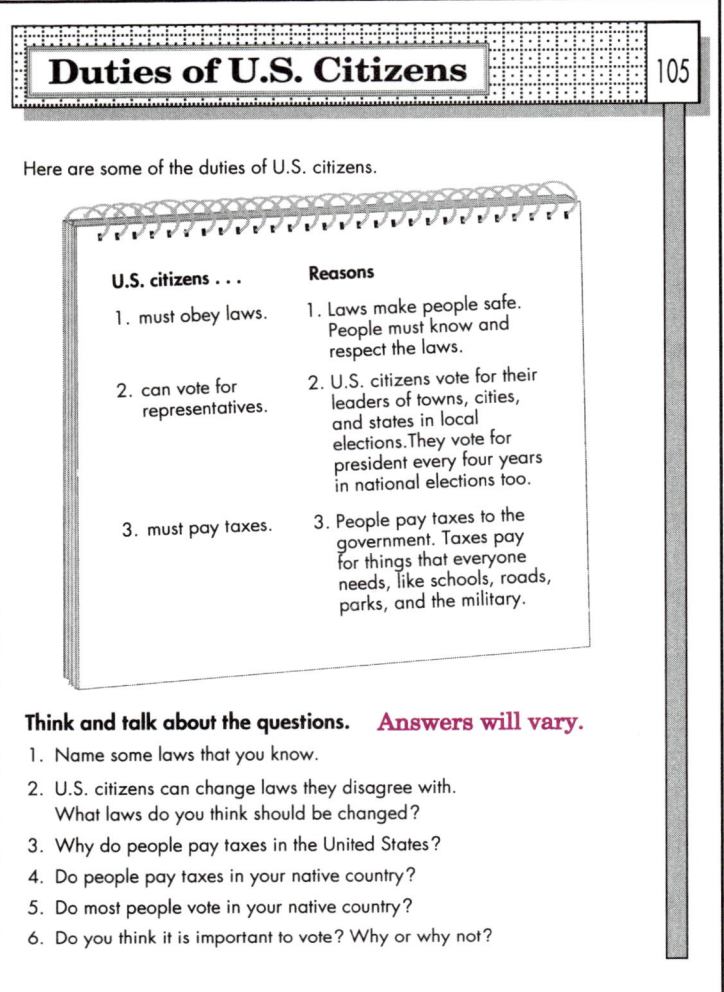

2. Refer learners to the ideas on the board. Suggest that they add to the reasons on the page any additional information they discovered during the *Warm-up* discussion. Expand the discussion by asking questions, such as *What are some important laws? What can happen if you break a law? Who do citizens vote for? What are some things taxes pay for?*
3. Put the class in small groups to discuss the questions at the bottom of the page. Ask volunteers to tell the class which laws they do not agree with and to say why. Elicit different opinions about these laws and select a law that several learners feel should be changed. Tell them that a good way to make their opinion known is to write a letter to their representative. Help learners draft a suitable letter on the board. If it is an issue they feel strongly about, a volunteer may want to copy the letter and send it to the local representative. Provide the address if necessary, or show learners where to find the address in the local phone book.

***Expansion/Extension** on page 159*

Before the Interview

Purpose: To give practice with tag questions and with the past tense; to give practice in listening for key points, in persuading, and in clarifying/asking for clarification

Teacher Preparation and Materials
1. Audiotape for Level 2
2. Arrange for a speaker who has gone through the citizenship process to visit the class. *(Expansion/Extension)*
3. Real or toy telephones *(Expansion/Extension)*
4. Copies of TRF Handout 10.6, *The U.S. Flag (Expansion/Extension)*

Warm-up
1. Ask volunteers to describe how they felt just before an interview for an important job, a citizenship interview, a major test, or similar situation. Ask *Did you feel nervous? Why did you feel that way? What helped you deal with your nervousness? Did you talk to a friend? study more? try to think about something else?*
2. Discuss the effects these situations had on learners. Ask if their nervousness caused them to make mistakes, forget things, get into arguments with family members or friends, and the like. Have volunteers describe their experiences.

Presentation
1. Have learners open their books to page 106. Ask questions about the picture to elicit known vocabulary. FOR EXAMPLE: *Who is talking to Isabel? Where are they? What is the customer doing? How do you think Tony feels? Why?*
2. Tell learners that Isabel will be taking her citizenship test next week. Have them predict what has happened in the picture, why the customer looks angry, and why both Isabel and Tony look upset. Elicit several possible scenarios.
3. Tell learners to listen to the conversation on the audiotape to determine if their predictions about Tony and Isabel were accurate. Play the audiotape. Read

through the statements in exercise A with learners. Allow them to work in pairs to answer true or false for each one. Replay the audiotape so learners can check their work and fill in missing information. Call on volunteers to give the correct answers.

4. Have learners discuss the questions at the bottom of the page. Remind them that Tony was both nervous and sad about becoming a citizen. Ask learners if they miss their native countries, if they think they will ever go back, or if they think they will stay here. Talk about the reasons for their feelings.

Expansion/Extension
See **TRF HANDOUT 10.6,** *The U.S. Flag*

- If no one in your class has gone through the citizenship process, invite a speaker who has done so, preferably a speaker from a background similar to the learners'. After the speaker has talked about his or her experience, encourage learners to ask questions and to discuss their fears and doubts.

More *Expansion/Extension* on page 159

Famous Americans

Purpose: To give practice with the past tense and with *must;* to give practice in clarifying/asking for clarification

Teacher Preparation and Materials
1. ▭ Audiotape for Level 2
2. Copies of the words and music to "The Star-Spangled Banner" or other patriotic songs *(Expansion/Extension)*
3. A film about a famous American, such as George Washington *(Expansion/Extension)*

Warm-up
1. Ask learners to name some famous Americans from the past and to explain why they were famous. Write the names and reasons on the board.
2. Tell learners to pretend that you are an examiner for the INS. Ask a volunteer to come to the front of the room for a citizenship interview. Ask various questions related to the material already introduced in this unit. Repeat with other volunteers. Suggest that they rephrase questions or ask for clarification if necessary. At the end, congratulate each volunteer for doing a good job.

Presentation
1. Have learners turn to page 107. Ask questions about the picture to elicit known vocabulary. FOR EXAMPLE: *Where is Isabel? What do you think she is doing? How do you think she feels? Who do you think she is talking to?*
2. Have learners read through exercise A and match items that they know. Then tell learners to listen to Isabel's interview on the audiotape to determine the correct answers. ▭ Play the audiotape and then have learners match the people with appropriate items. ▭ Replay the audiotape so learners can check their work and fill in missing information.
3. Have learners imagine that they are the examiners in a citizenship interview. Have them write other questions they

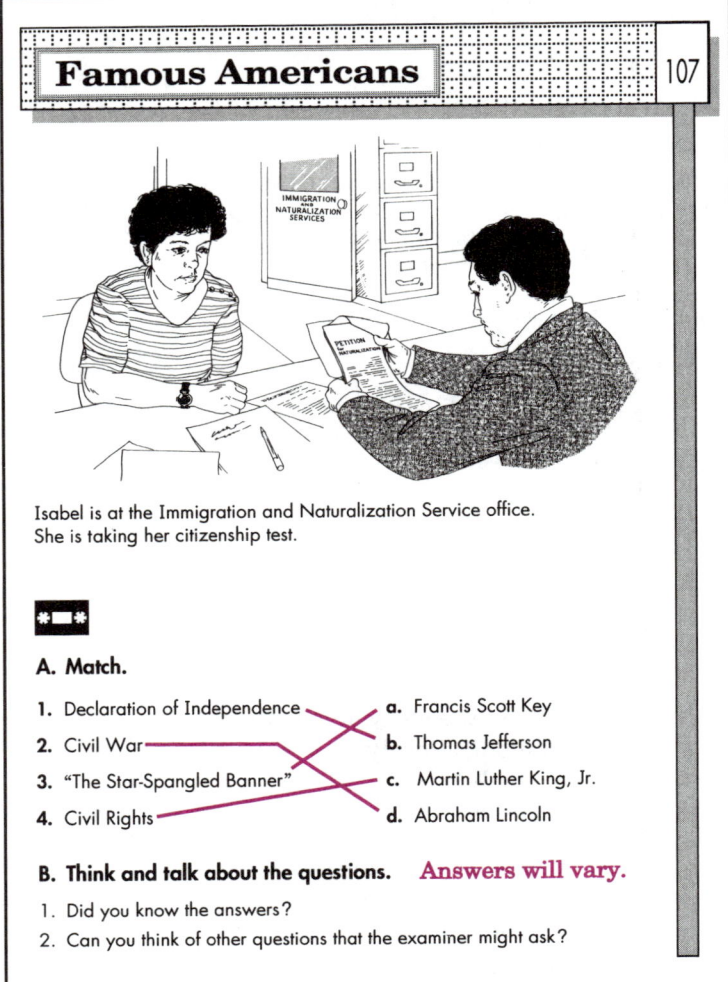

could ask about the information on the page. (FOR EXAMPLE: What famous American was a civil-rights leader? What is our national anthem? Who wrote "The Star-Spangled Banner"?) Put learners in groups to take turns asking and answering questions. Suggest that they answer the questions without looking at their books.
4. Put learners in small groups to complete exercise B. Have them brainstorm some possible questions for number 2. Ask volunteers to read their questions for the class to answer. You may want to have learners write the questions on separate pieces of paper along with the correct answers, for use in an *Expansion/Extension* activity.

Expansion/Extension
- Show a movie about a famous American, such as George Washington. Afterward, lead a discussion about this person's role in American history.

More *Expansion/Extension* on page 159

Making the Connection

Purpose: To give practice with the past tense; to give practice in understanding citizenship concepts; to give practice with skills, functions, and vocabulary from Unit 10

Teacher Preparation and Materials

1. Sheets of construction paper; stapler *(Expansion/Extension)*
2. Arrange a trip to a local library *(Expansion/Extension)*

Warm-up

Ask for a volunteer to be interviewed about coming to the United States. Use the questions on page 108. Write the answers on the board in story form. Read the story aloud while learners follow along silently.

Presentation

1. Have learners turn to page 108. Ask questions about the picture to elicit known vocabulary. FOR EXAMPLE: *Where are Isabel and Stefan? What are they doing? How do you think they feel?*
2. Read Isabel's story while learners follow along silently or ask a volunteer to read it aloud. Ask literal and inferential questions. FOR EXAMPLE: *Where was Isabel born? Who did she come to the United States with? Where are her mother and father? Do you think Isabel would like her parents to come to the United States? Is Isabel a U.S. citizen? What can she do now? How does she feel? How do you think being a citizen will change Isabel's life?*
3. Read the directions beneath the story. Have learners work in pairs to discuss the questions. They may want to ask each other the questions in an interview format. Have learners write their stories individually, using Isabel's story and the one on the board as models. Ask volunteers to read their stories aloud to the class.

---

108 · Making the Connection

Isabel Santos was born in El Salvador. She came to the United States with her sister and brother. Her mother and father still live there and she writes to them often. Isabel is a U.S. citizen now. She can vote, and she knows and respects the law. It took Isabel many years to become a citizen. She's happy and proud.

Write your story.
Here are some questions to help you.   **Answers will vary.**

- What country did you come from?
- Who did you come with?
- Do you still have family or friends in your country?
- Do you want to go back?
- Do you want to become a U.S. citizen?
- How long do you think it will take you to become a citizen?

---

4. Discuss how long it will take learners to become citizens. Try to determine if the time and some of the requirements vary, depending on the native country.

Expansion/Extension

- Ask learners to bring in pictures to illustrate their stories. Have them show and describe their pictures to the class, to a small group, or to a partner.
- Have learners think of special or famous immigrants to the United States who came from their native countries. Ask them to tell the class about these people and what they did that made them stand out. If learners would like more information about immigrants from their native countries, arrange a trip to a local library (or suggest that learners visit the library on their own). The librarian can also suggest related topics to look up in the card catalog.

UNIT 10: Becoming a Citizen
Expansion/Extension

Members of the Class
More *Expansion/Extension* for SB page 99

- Put learners in pairs. Have them interview each other, asking the questions at the bottom of the page and taking notes on the replies. Ask learners to write paragraphs about their partners, using the stories on page 99 as a model. Partners should read each other's work and make any necessary corrections. You may wish to compile learners' work into a book titled Members of the Class.

What You Need to Become a Citizen
More *Expansion/Extension* for SB page 100

- Before class, make up true and false statements from the information on page 100. For example: *1. You must send money to become a U.S. citizen. True or false?* Tell learners to close their books and take out a sheet of paper. Have them listen to each statement, write the item number, and write "true" or "false." Afterward, read aloud each sentence again and have learners say whether it was true or false.

- Ask learners where in the area they can obtain photos for a reasonable price. Have them do some research to find the best place for photos and to report back to the class. Ask *Where can you get fingerprinted?* (at the local police station) If there is interest, visit these places with learners and go through the process of obtaining photos and fingerprints.

- Ask where in your area immigrants go to apply for citizenship. Help learners determine this information and write it on the board.

Petition for Naturalization
Expansion/Extension for SB page 102

- Have learners sign their names, using the alphabets of their native languages. They may enjoy making a class poster with all the signatures. Learners whose alphabets do not use Roman letters may enjoy showing others how their names look.

- Continue the discussion about changing names. Ask *What do you think about the option of changing your name? What are the advantages and disadvantages? Do you think that people in the United States today are used to many different names and cultures?* Lead a discussion, listing *Advantages* and *Disadvantages*. Have learners use the lists to describe situations in which they think people are likely/not likely to change their names.

- Ask *How do you feel about serving in the U.S. Armed Forces?* Discuss the current draft or enlistment policies. Lead a discussion about how this compares with serving in the armed forces in learners' native countries.

- Distribute copies of a complete Petition for Naturalization form. Review the form with learners and have them work in pairs to fill it out.

Learning American History
More *Expansion/Extension* for SB page 103

- Ask *What do you think of the American Revolution? Was it good or bad? Why? What do you think of revolutions in general?* Have learners give reasons for their answers.

- Ask learners to compare U.S. history with the histories of their native countries. Ask *How are they the same? How are they different? Were there any major revolutions? What were they about?* Write key ideas on the board.

- If possible, visit a public or school library with learners. Help them find books about U.S. history that would be of interest to them.

The United States Government

Expansion/Extension for SB page 104

See TRF HANDOUT 10.3, *100 Questions Game*

- Ask *Do you know how many U.S. representatives there are from your state?* Explain that while each state has two senators, the number of representatives depends on the population of the state. Have volunteers find out the number of representatives in your state.
- Ask *Do you know of any U.S. government leaders with your ethnic background? Who are they?* Help learners find out about these leaders. Discuss the importance of having different ethnic and cultural groups represented in the government.
- Have learners compare and contrast the structure of the U.S. government with that of governments in their native countries. Discuss the advantages and disadvantages of the different structures, and the reasons why the governments are set up the way they are. As a result of this discussion, learners may wish to suggest ways that some of these structures might be improved.
- If you are within driving distance of your state capital, plan a class field trip. Contact your state representative ahead of time so that you might visit his or her office, as well as the legislature while it is in session.
- Invite your state representative to address the class about the rights and duties of U.S. citizens and government leaders.
- If possible, organize a visit to your local town hall. Plan to attend a town meeting or city council session with learners. Have them ask questions afterward.

Duties of U.S. Citizens

Expansion/Extension for SB page 105

See TRF HANDOUT 10.2, *Some Important Rights*

- Put learners in small groups. Have them think of additional duties and rights of citizens in the United States. Each group should make a list and later share it with the rest of the class.
- Put learners in small groups to talk about taxes. Ask them if they think taxes are necessary, if they feel Americans are taxed too much/too little, if tax dollars are being spent on the right things, and so on. After the group discussions, ask each learner to write a statement or suggestion about taxes in the United States (or in their city/state). Have volunteers present their statements to the class.
- Ask learners how citizens' rights and duties in the United States compare with those in their native countries. Lead a discussion.
- Ask learners if they have ever voted in a U.S. election. Ask *What was it like? Where did you vote?* Lead a discussion about the importance of voting.
- Invite a member of the League of Women Voters (or a similar organization) to discuss with learners how to register to vote, how to find out where to vote, and how to get more information about candidates, political parties, and so on. Suggest that learners prepare questions before the speaker's visit.

Before the Interview

More Expansion/Extension for SB page 106

- Use a set of real or toy telephones. Pretend to call a volunteer and tell him or her how nervous you are about something. The volunteer should try to calm you down. Have other pairs of volunteers role-play similar situations.

Famous Americans

More Expansion/Extension for SB page 107

- Form two teams to play a question/answer game. Alternate between teams, asking the questions generated in *Presentation #4*. If a team cannot answer a question, they score no points and that question is offered to the other team along with a new question. Each correct answer scores one point. ■ In a one-to-one situation, take turns with the learner asking and answering questions about American history and government.
- Distribute copies of "The Star-Spangled Banner" or other popular patriotic songs. Explain that "The Star-Spangled Banner" was written during a battle of the Revolutionary War. Ask learners to consider the song's origin and to guess what some of the lyrics mean.

1 2 3 4 5 6 7 8 9 10 **11** 12 Summary
Getting Used to a New Land

Objectives

Functions
- Reporting past events
- Expressing surprise
- Comparing and contrasting
- Expressing emotions
- Expressing embarrassment

Life Tasks
- Expressing feelings about being a newcomer to the United States
- Understanding and describing multiculturalism in the United States
- Dealing with embarrassing moments

Structures
- Adverbs of time
- Adverbs of frequency
- Descriptive adjectives
- Prepositions of place
- *When* clauses

Culture
- Customs in the United States and in other countries
- Stereotypes
- American immigrant groups
- Male and female roles in different countries

Vocabulary

Key words:

arriving	immigrants
at home	land
comfortable	lost
confusing	missed
customs	mistakes
directions	newcomers
Ellis Island	opportunities
embarrassing	situation
expected	Statue of Liberty
experience	stereotypes
familiar	strangers
foolish	stupid
freedom	surprised
get used to	treated
grow up	ways

Related words:

care about	inspectors
competitive	island
energetic	lonely
examined	lose
friendly	loud
gateway	love
harbor	rude
hardworking	selfish
hate	smart
helpful	unfriendly
honest	win
independent	worth the wait

Arriving in a New Land

Purpose: To give practice in discussing personal histories and in expressing feelings about arriving in a new land

Teacher Preparation and Materials

1. Copies of learners' stories, cut into sentence strips *(Expansion/Extension)*
2. Photos or magazines with pictures suitable for portraying learners' arrival in the United States; posterboard, glue, markers, and scissors for all *(Expansion/Extension)*
3. Copies of TRF Handout 11.1, *Life in the United States (Expansion/Extension)*

Warm-up

1. Review with learners some key feelings, such as happy, excited, angry, worried, upset, nervous, embarrassed. Have them describe situations in which they have experienced these feelings, giving reasons for their emotions.
2. Use the feelings and situations described to discuss why people can have different feelings about similar situations. Also talk about how a person can have mixed feelings about a situation or event. (feeling both excited and nervous about a new job or about getting married, etc.)

Presentation

1. Have learners turn to page 109. Ask questions about the picture to elicit known vocabulary. FOR EXAMPLE: *What's going on? Where is Isabel? Who is she talking with? What do you think they are talking about? Who do you think the people in the bubbles are? What is happening in the pictures in the bubbles? Why do you think that?*
2. Put learners in small groups to discuss the questions at the bottom of the page. Suggest that they talk about the reasons for the feelings.
3. As a class, discuss some feelings related to first coming to the United States and

feelings about living here now. Write learners' comments under the headings *Then* and *Now*. Discuss the reasons for their feelings, including mixed feelings they have had. Ask *Have your feelings changed after living here for a while? Why? Do you think your feelings will change again in the future?*

Expansion/Extension

See **TRF HANDOUT 11.1**, *Life in the United States*

- Ask learners to bring in any pictures they have of their trip to the United States and their arrival here. Have them describe the pictures in pairs or small groups and discuss the feelings they experienced.
- Put learners in small groups. Have them make collages to represent their arrival in the United States. They can use photos, cut out pictures from magazines, and/or draw pictures. Ask each group to show and describe its collage to the class.

More *Expansion/Extension* on page 172

Ellis Island

Purpose: To introduce information about Ellis Island; to give practice in comparing and contrasting the experiences of immigrants

Teacher Preparation and Materials

1. Map of the United States (or map on Student Book pages 126–127); map of the world
2. Books, pictures, or films about the Statue of Liberty and Ellis Island
3. Colored pins or other individual markers for each learner *(Expansion/Extension)*

Warm-up

1. On a map of the United States, have volunteers locate where they entered the country for the first time. Then on a map of the world, ask volunteers to point to their native countries. On the same map, point to Hungary and explain that this is Olga's native country.
2. Ask learners to share what they know about Ellis Island and the Statue of Liberty. Locate these places on a map of the United States. Use the map to explain the meaning of *harbor* and *island,* if necessary. If possible, show books, pictures, or films about these places.
3. If you know the history of your immigrant ancestors, or if you are an immigrant yourself, tell learners the story of your family's immigration.

Presentation

1. Have learners turn to page 110. Ask questions about the pictures to elicit known vocabulary. FOR EXAMPLE: *Where are these places? Who do you see in the pictures? Where do you think the people are coming from? What are they doing on Ellis Island? Why do you think they came here? Who is examining them?*
2. Ask different volunteers to read each paragraph aloud. Use the pictures to clarify vocabulary as necessary. Ask literal and inferential questions, such as *Why do you think this place was used*

as a first stop for immigrants? How many immigrants arrived there? What happened to the immigrants on Ellis Island? Why do you think the immigrants were examined and questioned? What was Ellis Island called? Why? Today what is Ellis Island part of?

3. Put learners in small groups to read and discuss the questions at the bottom of the page. Have learners tell how they came to the United States. Have the recorder in each group make a list of the places where learners entered the United States. Ask *Why are there many more places to enter the United States today than there were years ago?*

Expansion/Extension

- Use questions 2–4 at the bottom of page 110 as the basis for writing stories. First, do a sample LEA story on the board by interviewing a volunteer and writing his or her answers on the board in story form. Then ask learners to write individual stories and have volunteers read their stories aloud to the class.

More *Expansion/Extension* on page 172

What's the United States Like?

Purpose: To introduce expressing feelings about being a newcomer; to give practice in comparing and contrasting expectations vs. reality and the past vs. the present

Teacher Preparation and Materials
▭ Audiotape for Level 2

Warm-up
1. Ask a volunteer *What did you hear about the United States before you came here? Where did you hear these things?* Write key comments and ideas on the board.
2. Ask *What did you find when you arrived in the United States? Were things exactly the way you expected them to be? How were they different? How did you feel?*
3. On the board write *Ideas about the U.S. before Arrival.* Have learners create a semantic web with their ideas. (good jobs, live well, free speech, travel, etc.) Then make a second web for *First Months in the U.S.* Ask learners to add to the web from their own experiences. Talk about which things in the United States lived up to learners' expectations and which did not.

Presentation
1. Have learners turn to page 111. Remind them of the scene on page 109. Then ask questions about the picture to elicit known vocabulary. FOR EXAMPLE: *Who is in the picture? What are Olga and Isabel doing? What do you think they're talking about?*
2. Have learners read the four questions in exercise A and predict what the answers might be. Tell them to consider how long ago Olga and Isabel came to this country and where they came from. Have them listen to the conversation on the audiotape to find the answers. ▭ Play the audiotape and have learners work in pairs to write the answers. ▭ Replay the audiotape so learners can check their work and fill in missing information.

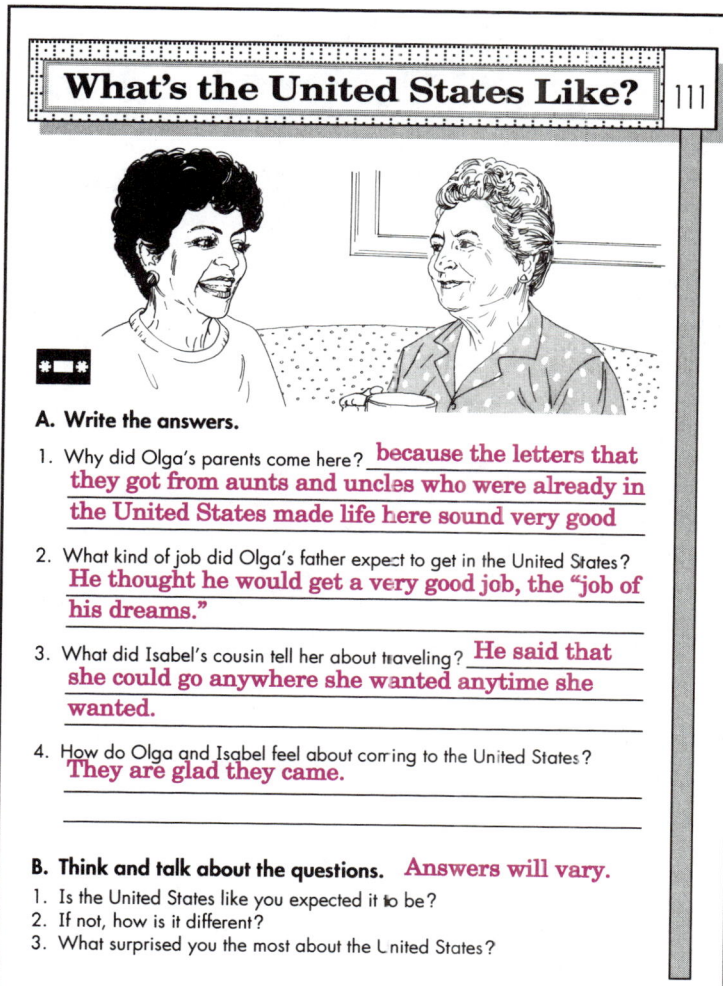

3. Put learners in small groups to discuss the answers. Remind them that there may be more than one way to word an answer.
4. Have learners discuss the questions in exercise B. Refer back to the semantic webs on the board for a more detailed discussion.
5. Ask learners questions to elicit further details about Olga, Isabel, and themselves. FOR EXAMPLE: *Who told Olga that she can live well in this country? Did anyone tell you that? Who told Isabel that there were fantastic jobs and that you could travel anywhere? Did anyone tell you the same thing? Who? What would you consider a fantastic job? What job did Olga's father first get? What job were you able to get?* Ask learners to compare their thoughts about this country during the first few months with their thoughts today.

Expansion/Extension on page 172

UNIT 11 • 163

Making Mistakes

Purpose: To introduce problems recent immigrants experience in the United States

Teacher Preparation and Materials
Copies of TRF Handout 11.2, *Holiday Happenings* (Expansion/Extension)

Warm-up
1. Remind learners about the discussion from page 111 about what their first few months in the United States were like. Ask questions to elicit ideas about common problems or confusions. FOR EXAMPLE: *Could you speak any English at all when you first got here? Did you know your way around? Did you know what to do with money? Did you think that people did things in strange ways or acted differently than what you were used to?*

2. Ask learners to describe situations that resulted from these confusions or problems. Write key comments on the board, such as *getting lost, not being able to ask important questions, not knowing how to open a bank account, making mistakes in giving/taking money*.

Presentation
1. Have learners turn to page 112. Explain that this is a story about the difficulties Olga and Isabel experienced when they first arrived in the United States.

2. Have volunteers read the paragraphs, one at a time. After each paragraph, name a problem (or problems) and ask learners to name the situations that resulted from the problem. FOR EXAMPLE: After paragraph 1, say *Many people don't speak English when they first come to the United States. What happens? People don't understand the customs here. What happens?* Encourage learners to talk about more than just the results mentioned in the text. Continue in a similar manner with the remaining paragraphs.

3. After learners are familiar with the story, have them work with a partner to answer true or false for each statement in exercise A.

---

112 — Making Mistakes

When many people come to the United States, they don't know how to speak much English. They don't feel comfortable speaking the language. They don't feel comfortable with the customs either. They make a lot of mistakes.

Isabel moved to the United States when she was a teenager. She got lost all the time. She was afraid to ask for directions. She walked all over town. She hoped that she would see something familiar. Often she would cry because she missed her country. She never had these kinds of problems there.

Olga remembers that her parents didn't know how to open a bank account. They kept their money in the house. They were always afraid that someone would steal it. When Olga grew older and understood more, she took her parents to the bank and helped them open a bank account.

There are a lot of confusing things about the United States. People don't always act the same way as people from other countries. There is a lot to learn and it's not always easy.

A. Check. ✔

	True	False
1. Many people make mistakes when they come to the United States.	✔	
2. Many people speak English when they come to the United States.		✔
3. Isabel didn't need to ask for directions.		✔
4. Olga's parents kept their money at home.	✔	
5. The United States is a confusing place.	✔	

B. Think and talk about the questions.   **Answers will vary.**
1. When you first came to the United States, were you afraid or confused?
2. What are some things that were confusing to you?
3. What are some ways that people can learn about life in the United States?

---

4. Put the class in small groups to discuss the questions in exercise B. Suggest that they make lists for their answers to questions 2 and 3. Make a class list of confusing situations and try to match each situation with suggestions of ways to learn more about the confusing issues or ways to resolve the problems. Learners may want to take notes from the discussion to share with friends and family members who are experiencing some of the same confusions.

Expansion/Extension
See **TRF HANDOUT 11.2, *Holiday Happenings***

- Have learners interview family members and friends about what they find most confusing in the United States. Ask learners to discuss these confusions in small groups and to give advice to each other. Suggest that they add these ideas to their notes for family and friends.

Being Newcomers

Purpose: To give practice in reading information about recent immigrants to the United States; to give practice with adverbs of time

Teacher Preparation and Materials

1. Copies of TRF Handout 11.4, *Never Dreamed of the United States* (Expansion/Extension)
2. Copies of TRF Handout 11.5, *Before and After* (Expansion/Extension)

Warm-up

1. Ask learners how long they have been in the United States. Write the number of years or months next to each learner's name. Ask a volunteer who has been in the United States about two years to describe how it feels to be living here and what plans he or she has made for the future.
2. On the board, write the adverbs *still, already, yet, only,* and *recently.* Explain the use of each word and provide examples. (*I saw that movie recently. I have already seen that movie. I haven't seen that movie yet. I still haven't seen that movie.*)
3. Ask learners questions using the adverbs on the board. FOR EXAMPLE: *Are you a citizen already? Did you get your passport yet? Are you still homesick?* You may want to write some questions and answers on the board for learners to refer to during the lesson.

Presentation

1. Have learners turn to page 113. Ask questions about the picture to elicit known vocabulary. FOR EXAMPLE: *Who is in the picture? What do you know about the Lees? How long have they lived in the United States? How many children do they have?*
2. Ask volunteers to read different parts of the story aloud. Clarify vocabulary as necessary. Ask literal and inferential questions. FOR EXAMPLE: *Why do you think Kim and Joon came to the United States? How many years will it take for them to become citizens? How do they feel about

the United States? Why do you think they want to raise their family in the United States? Do you think it will be easy for them to become citizens? Why?*
3. Tell learners to read the words in the box, choose the word that best completes each sentence, and write it on the line. Remind them of the samples on the board. Have volunteers read the completed sentences aloud.
4. Ask learners to write sentences of their own using the words in the box. Elicit ideas to get them started. Ask *Have you bought something new recently? Is there some place you would like to visit that you haven't been able to get to yet?*

Expansion/Extension

See **TRF HANDOUT 11.4,** *Never Dreamed of the United States*
  TRF HANDOUT 11.5, *Before and After*

More *Expansion/Extension* on page 172

UNIT 11 • 165

Feeling Foolish

Purpose: To give practice in describing embarrassing moments and the feelings such moments cause

Teacher Preparation and Materials
- Audiotape for Level 2

Warm-up
1. Describe a potentially embarrassing situation. FOR EXAMPLE: *I recently met a man named Tom. I saw him at the store the other day and by mistake I called him Tim.* Ask learners how they think you felt when this happened, eliciting words like *embarrassed, foolish, silly, dumb, stupid,* and so on.
2. Elicit from learners embarrassing moments they have had, asking them to describe how they felt. Point out that embarrassing things can happen to anyone, whether new to the United States or born here. Share with learners embarrassing moments you have had, especially if they occurred in a foreign country or in an unfamiliar place.

Presentation
1. Have learners open their books to page 114. Ask questions about the picture to elicit known vocabulary. FOR EXAMPLE: *Who is Joon talking to? Where are they? What do you think Joon is talking about? What was the cost of the groceries? How much money did Joon have? How do you think he felt? What do you think he did in that situation?*
2. Read the sentences below the picture aloud. Tell learners to listen to the conversation on the audiotape to see how Joon reacted in this embarrassing situation. Play the audiotape and then have learners read the questions at the bottom of the page. Tell them to think about the questions while you replay the audiotape. Suggest that they take notes if they wish.
3. Start a discussion by asking volunteers to give their answers to the questions. Help them understand that this situation could

happen to anyone, no matter how long the person has been in the United States. Ask questions, such as *Why do you think this situation happened? How do you think the clerk felt? Do you think this kind of thing happens often? Why? What could you do to prevent a situation like this?*

4. Put learners in pairs and ask the class what they think about Monroe's suggestion of explaining what happened to the clerk and then putting some things back. Have learners decide what Joon did and create a conversation between Joon and the clerk. Ask volunteers to role-play their conversations for the class.

Expansion/Extension
- Put the class in small groups to conduct a chain drill. Model the drill by having a volunteer ask you "When do you feel foolish?" Provide a sample response, such as *I feel foolish when I forget to do things I promised to do.* Let them continue the chain drill in their small groups.

More *Expansion/Extension* on page 172

A Parking Space

Purpose: To give practice in sequencing events and in discussing feelings about embarrassing moments

Teacher Preparation and Materials
1. ▭ Audiotape for Level 2
2. Copies of learners' stories, cut into sentence strips *(Expansion/Extension)*

Warm-up
1. Discuss the topic of driving and parking. Ask learners to describe different ways that people behave when they are driving, either on the road or in parking lots. Mention that people frequently make mistakes while driving. Discuss why people seem to get angry or upset about mistakes that drivers make.
2. Remind learners of Joon's experience in the grocery store and his feelings of embarrassment. Then ask learners to think of situations involving driving or parking that could be embarrassing. (FOR EXAMPLE: putting on your left-turn signal, realizing that you want to turn right, and changing lanes at the last minute; making several attempts to parallel park on a busy street)

Presentation
1. Have learners turn to page 115 and look at the picture at the top of the page. Read the line next to the picture and ask learners what they think Monroe's embarrassing mistake was.
2. Have learners study the pictures in exercise A. Ask questions to see that learners have a sense of what is going on. FOR EXAMPLE: *Where is Monroe in these pictures? What is he doing? What is the other man doing? How do you think the other man feels? How do you think Monroe feels?*
3. Tell learners to listen to the conversation between Monroe and Joon on the audiotape to determine what is happening in the pictures. ▭ Play the audiotape and have learners check if their guesses were correct.
4. Ask volunteers to retell the story. Check to see that they understand the story and mention any words or parts they have omitted. On the board, write key words they will need for exercise A.
5. Put learners in pairs to write the sentences for exercise A. ▭ You may want to play the audiotape again while they check their work. Ask volunteers to read their sentences aloud.
6. With the class, discuss the questions in exercise B. Continue the discussion by asking *What do you think about the other man? Do you think he had a reason to be upset? Do you think Monroe did the right thing? What would you have done?*

Expansion/Extension on page 173

UNIT 11 • 167

Stereotypes

Purpose: To introduce reasons for cultural stereotypes; to give practice in expressing opinions about others, and in comparing and contrasting the past with the present

Teacher Preparation and Materials

Copies of TRF Handout 11.3, *Questionnaire: Life in the United States* (Expansion/Extension)

Warm-up

1. Ask learners *What did you think of Americans when you first arrived in the United States?* If possible, elicit words from the list on page 116, such as *independent, selfish, hardworking,* and *honest*. Then ask *What do you think of Americans now?* List their comments under the headings *Then* and *Now,* and compare and contrast the lists. Ask learners to explain their opinions.

2. Explain that opinions about groups of people, like the ones discussed, are called *stereotypes*. Ask learners to mention other stereotypes they know of and to tell where they heard this information. Lead learners to realize that these opinions are based on things they heard from others or on experiences with only one or two people. Point out that no two Americans are exactly alike, just as no two people from any country are exactly alike, and that stereotypes can hurt our understanding of each other.

Presentation

1. Have learners open their books to page 116. Read the paragraph aloud while learners follow along silently. Clarify vocabulary as necessary. Ask literal and inferential questions. FOR EXAMPLE: *What did Joon think about Americans when he first came to the United States? Why do you think he thought that? Why do you think he changed his mind about some Americans? What does he still think about some Americans?*

2. Have volunteers read the words in the list. Ask questions to check

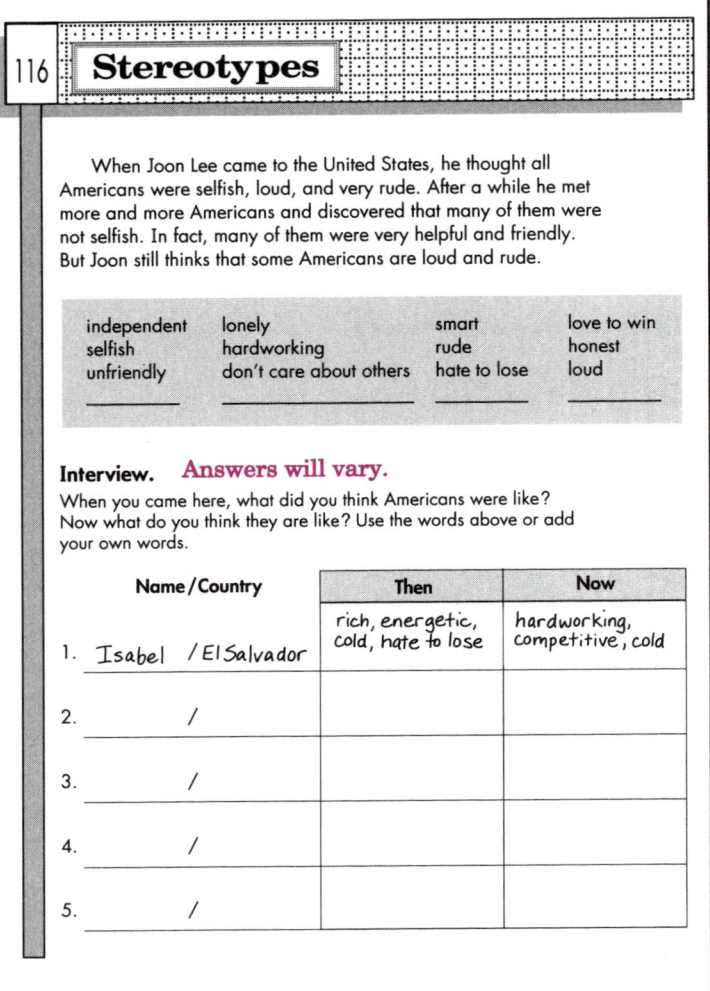

understanding. FOR EXAMPLE: *How would you describe a person who slams a door in your face? people who like to do things by themselves and refuse help?* Have learners add their own words on the blanks.

3. Read through the directions and Isabel's example in the exercise. Ask learners to look back at Joon's opinions and write his ideas in the appropriate columns. Then have learners use the questions to interview three others. ◼ In a one-to-one situation, interview the learner and then have the learner interview friends or family members and report back to you.

4. Put the class in small groups to discuss the results of learners' interviews. Lead a class discussion about how stereotypes develop. Ask *What might happen if people don't understand customs from different cultures?*

Expansion/Extension

See **TRF HANDOUT 11.3**, *Questionnaire: Life in the United States*

More *Expansion/Extension* on page 173

168 • UNIT 11

Old Ways and New Ways

Purpose: To introduce the variation of customs and male/female roles in different countries

Teacher Preparation and Materials
1. ▣ Audiotape for Level 2
2. Copies of TRF Handout 11.7, *Old Ways and New (Expansion/Extension)*

Warm-up
Ask learners if they think that men and women have different roles in the United States than men and women in their native countries, both at home and in the workplace. Ask questions about these different roles and write their responses under the names of the different countries, including the United States. Ask *What kinds of jobs are common for women/men in your native country? in the United States? Who usually does the grocery shopping in your native country? in the United States?*

Presentation
1. Have learners turn to page 117. Ask questions about the picture to elicit known vocabulary. FOR EXAMPLE: *Where are Joon and Monroe? What are they doing? Why do you think Monroe is looking at his watch?*

2. ▣ Play the audiotape and have learners listen to the conversation to find out what Monroe and Joon are talking about. Ask questions, such as *Why is Monroe making dinner? Why is Joon surprised? What does Joon mean by the phrase "women's work?" What did Kim do in Korea? Is her life the same in the United States? What makes you think that Joon still likes some of the Korean ways?*

3. Use the conversation on the audiotape to get learners' feelings about Monroe's and Joon's families and roles. Read through the checklist and ask learners how they expect the different chores to be handled in the two families. Record their responses in a chart on the board.

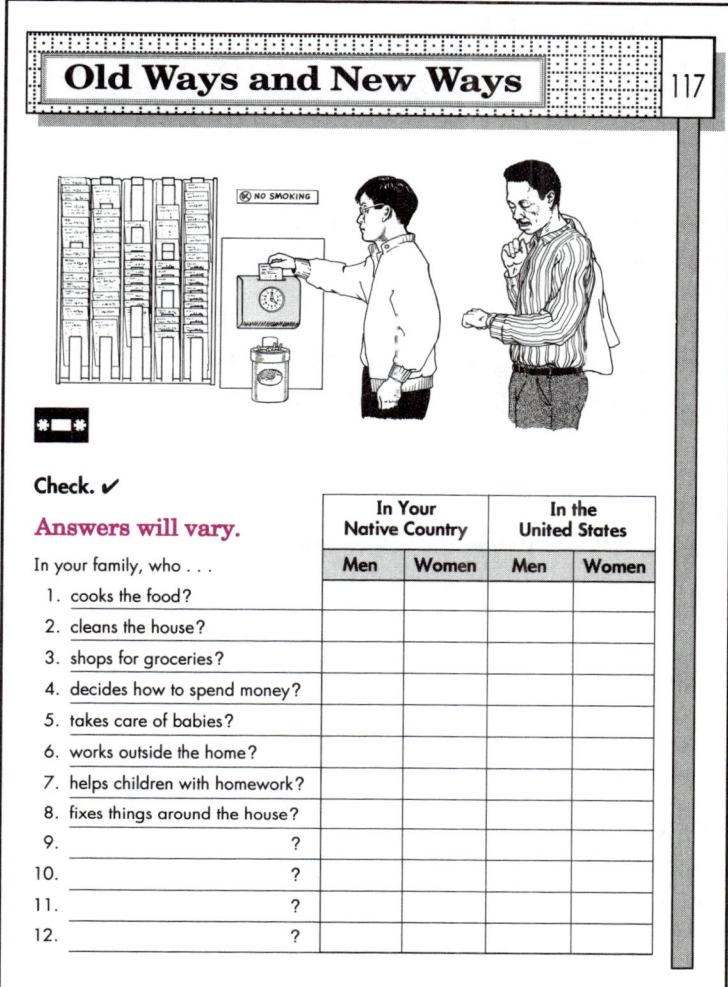

4. Brainstorm some additional chores for numbers 9–12 and write them on the board. Then have learners complete the checklist independently. Have them compare their answers in small groups. Ask about learners' own family roles and consider if these roles are based on tradition, if they are based on schedules and needs, if each person does what he or she does best, and so on.

Expansion/Extension
See TRF HANDOUT 11.7, *Old Ways and New*

- Take a class survey on who does the chores in learners' native countries. Write the answers on the board under the headings *Men* and *Women*. Tally the results. Ask *Do you think these results are fair or unfair to women? Do you follow the traditions of your native country?*

More *Expansion/Extension* on page 173

A Different Kind of Life

Purpose: To give practice in comparing and contrasting life in the United States with life in other countries

Teacher Preparation and Materials
Copies of TRF Handout 11.6, *New to the United States (Expansion/Extension)*

Warm-up
1. Ask learners if they have any family members still living in their native countries. If so, would any of these people like to move to the United States? Why?
2. Ask *How would you describe your life in the United States if you were talking to a family member still living in your native country? How is it different from life in your native country?* Write key comments on the board. If not mentioned, include the word *freedom* and have learners talk about some important freedoms people in this country have.

Presentation
1. Have learners turn to page 118. Ask questions about the picture to elicit known vocabulary. FOR EXAMPLE: *Who is in the picture? What is Kim doing? Who is she writing to? Where do you think Kim's sister is? What do you think Kim is saying in the letter?*
2. Ask volunteers to read the story aloud while learners follow along silently. Clarify vocabulary as necessary. Ask literal and inferential questions. FOR EXAMPLE: *How does Kim feel about being in the United States? How do you think her life is different here? Why might Kim think that the United States is the best place for her family to live? What is Soo Kang studying? Why does Soo Kang hope to move to the United States? Do you think it would be easy for Soo Kang to get a job in the United States?*
3. Put learners in small groups to read and discuss the questions at the bottom of the page. Remind them of the discussion in

the *Warm-up* about freedom. Tell learners to focus on freedoms for men and freedoms for women in both their native countries and in the United States.

Expansion/Extension
See TRF HANDOUT 11.6, *New to the United States*

- Take a class survey on the answers to question 3 on page 118. Ask *How many of you like the difference? How many don't?* Take note of the number of men and women who answer each way. Lead a discussion about why learners feel the way they do.
- Have learners interview family members about questions 1 through 3. Ask them to report back to the class on the results of the interviews, particularly if they found any different opinions.
- On the board write as the headings of two columns *Advantages of Living in the United States* and *Disadvantages of Living in the United States*. Have learners share their ideas in small groups and then discuss the issues with the class. Ask them which advantages or disadvantages affect them the most.

More *Expansion/Extension* on page 173

Making the Connection

Purpose: To give practice with skills, functions, and vocabulary from Unit 11

Teacher Preparation and Materials

1. Copies of the stories prepared in this lesson *(Expansion/Extension)*
2. Magazines or newspapers with pictures of life in the United States; posterboard, glue, and scissors for all *(Expansion/Extension)*

Warm-up

1. Review some of the aspects of living in the United States that were discussed throughout the unit (arrival, first few months, ideas about the United States before/after coming here, difficulties with language and customs, stereotypes, and men's/women's roles). Have learners discuss their feelings about these topics.
2. Interview a volunteer, using the questions on page 119. Use LEA techniques to write the answers on the board in story form. Read the story aloud with the class.

Presentation

1. Have learners open their books to page 119. Read the directions and questions aloud. Clarify vocabulary as necessary. Review Kim's story if necessary. Review the model story on the board and allow learners to make comments.
2. Have learners write their own stories, answering the questions and using the model story as a guide. Help with vocabulary as necessary. Put learners in small groups to read their stories aloud. Tell them to discuss ideas about life in the United States, stating agreements and disagreements with one another and offering advice.

Making the Connection | 119

A. Read Kim's story again.

B. Write a story about *your* life in the United States. **Answers will vary.**
Here are some questions to help you.
- How do you feel about living in the United States?
- What do you like about it?
- What don't you like about it?
- Do you think men and women are treated the same?
- Do you think they should be?
- Would you want a younger sister or brother to live here?

Expansion/Extension

- Distribute copies of the stories, one set to each learner. Read them aloud while learners follow along silently or have them take turns reading them in pairs. Discuss any special ideas they agree or disagree with and why.
- Ask *Does anybody want a sister or brother to move to the United States? Why?* Lead a discussion.
- Have learners make a class collage or mural about life in the United States. They may contribute magazine and newspaper pictures, photographs, real-life items (ticket stubs, labels, receipts, etc.) and anything else they might want to add. Display the finished product in a prominent place in your classroom.

UNIT 11: Getting Used to a New Land
Expansion/Extension

Arriving in a New Land
More *Expansion/Extension* for SB page 109

- Have learners write stories about their arrival in a new land. They can use their answers to the last two questions on page 109 as topic sentences for two paragraphs. Tell them to include their ideas from both the small-group and class discussions. If necessary, interview a volunteer and use LEA techniques to write his or her answers on the board in story form. Then ask learners to write individual stories to share with the class.
- Choose three or four stories to copy and cut into sentence strips. Put learners in pairs. Distribute one set of sentence strips to each pair of learners and tell them to put the story in correct order. Ask a pair of volunteers to write the story in correct order on the board. Repeat with other stories.

Ellis Island
More *Expansion/Extension* for SB page 110

- Ask for a volunteer to come to the front of the class. Ask him or her to point out on the maps his or her native country and place of entry into the United States. Mark each place with a pin of the same color or some other appropriate label. Then have each learner in the class do the same.
- Have learners take turns telling about their trip to the United States, including transportation method, the route they took, any stops made along the way, and so on. If possible, ask them to show these routes on the maps.

What's the United States Like?
Expansion/Extension for SB page 111

- Take a class survey on the answers to question 3 in exercise B. Record how many of the learners gave the same answer for their "biggest surprise" about the United States.
- Ask learners to write individual stories based on their dreams about the United States. If necessary, interview a volunteer and use LEA techniques to write his or her answers on the board in story form. Then have learners write their own stories to share in small groups.
- Put learners in pairs to create a conversation similar to Olga's and Isabel's about life before and after they came to the United States. Ask volunteers to present their conversations in front of the class.

Being Newcomers
More *Expansion/Extension* for SB page 113

- Ask a volunteer *How are you like the Lees? How are you different?* Write key comments on the board under the headings *Similar* and *Different*. Then put learners in pairs to first compare and contrast themselves to the Lees and then to one another.
- On the board, create a time line for the Lees, using the present year as the center point. Mark significant years, such as when they arrived in the United States and when they will become citizens. Then have learners make time lines for themselves.

Feeling Foolish
More *Expansion/Extension* for SB page 114

- Ask learners *What customs in the United States can make you feel embarrassed?* Have them share their ideas and then discuss how they can get used to or handle these customs.
- Put learners in pairs. Ask them to create a conversation between or story about two people involved in an embarrassing situation. It can be something that really happened or something they make up. Ask volunteers to role-play their conversations in front of the class or read their stories aloud. Have volunteers give advice to the class on what they can do in that kind of embarrassing situation.

A Parking Space

Expansion/Extension for SB page 115

- Ask learners to write their own stories titled "My Most Embarrassing Moment." You may wish to compose a model story on the board first. Afterward, have volunteers read their stories aloud.

- Choose four or five of the stories that show a clear sequence of events. Copy and cut them into sentence strips. Put learners in pairs and distribute one set of sentence strips to each pair. Have them work together to put the strips together in the correct sequence. Then have them repeat with a different set of strips.

- Review language related to apologies. (FOR EXAMPLE: *I'm really sorry, but . . . I didn't realize . . . Please forgive me, I . . . I didn't mean to . . .*) Put the class in small groups to discuss what Monroe could have said to the other driver when trying to apologize. Then have them brainstorm about what they can say when they do something embarrassing. Ask the recorder in each group to write the phrases on the board. Point out any phrases that may be considered unacceptable or rude.

Stereotypes

More *Expansion/Extension* for SB page 116

- Ask learners to describe their feelings when they heard stereotypes about their native countries and people.

- Ask learners if the stereotypes about their culture are accurate. Ask *What do you think this means? Do you think these stereotypes are fair? How can stereotypes be harmful? What can you do to get rid of stereotypes?* Lead a discussion.

- On the board, write learners' impressions of Americans now. Find out through a show of hands if the entire class agrees on any single characteristic. Ask *Is there any one way that you can describe the average American? Do you think that this is a good way to describe most Americans? Why?*

Old Ways and New Ways

More *Expansion/Extension* for SB page 117

- Ask volunteers to describe how they marked the columns for the United States. Ask learners to express agreements and disagreements, explaining their reasons for these opinions. Discuss any stereotypes that are mentioned about men and women.

- Ask learners if they think it is better to continue to do things the way they did in their native countries or to do things the way people in the United States do. Discuss advantages and disadvantages of both ways, and possible compromises.

- Have learners interview a young relative and an older one about their opinions on which is better: the old ways or the new. Ask them to report back to the class with their findings.

- Have learners name other customs from their native countries that are different from those in the United States. (customs relating to food, money, children, etc.) Ask *How do you feel about those customs? Are you trying to keep following them? Which are your favorite customs from your native country? Which are your favorite customs from the United States? Can you follow both?* Lead a discussion about the similarities and differences between these customs. Have learners look for patterns in customs that might lead them to conclusions about people's feelings in these different countries.

A Different Kind of Life

More *Expansion/Extension* for SB page 118

- Remind learners that Kim's sister is studying business. Ask learners to name different subjects women study in the United States. Ask *Can women study these subjects in your native country? What are the differences?* Have them discuss these questions in small groups and then share their ideas with the class.

12 Summary
Discovering Patterns

Objectives
- To help learners discover grammatical patterns already used in context
- To teach and give practice with those patterns

The structures covered are:
- future tense with *going to* and *will*
- conditional sentences with *if/then* clauses
- verbs + infinitives and verbs + *-ing*
- reported speech with *that*
- tag questions

Learners will require frequent practice with and reinforcement of these structures before complete mastery can be expected.

About the Structures

- **Verbs: Future–*Going to* and *Will***

Learners will practice forming and using these two forms of the future tense. They will use the two forms interchangeably. Learners may omit a form of the verb *be* before *going to* ("I going to leave."), or they may omit *to* ("I am going leave."). In the future tense with *will*, they may skip over the *'ll* in the contraction and simply say "I go" instead of "I'll go." Overcoming these tendencies will require ample pronunciation practice.

- **Conditional sentences: *If/Then* Clauses**

These are fairly simple conditional statements referring to something that might happen. Note that *then* is frequently omitted in this structure. Learners will need a lot of meaningful practice in using these statements.

- **Verb + Infinitive and Verb + *-ing***

Learners are shown two separate constructions. They practice identifying the correct form, first by choosing between two possible answers and then by forming the appropriate structure, given the simple form of the verb.

- **Reported Speech with *That***

Learners are presented with different examples of reported speech and are given practice in converting direct speech into reported speech.

- **Tag Questions.**

Tag questions are fairly straightforward in terms of usage, but the various forms can be confusing for the ESL learner. Learners are given many examples and ample practice both by choosing between two tag questions and by writing tag questions on the basis of context clues.

Verbs: Future—
Going to and *Will*

Purpose: To give practice with the formation and use of the future tense with *going to* and *will*

Teacher Preparation and Materials
1. Wall calendar
2. Index cards with parts of different sentences: *going to, she's, us, visit, call, tomorrow, I'll, you;* blank index cards

Warm-up
1. Use a calendar or time line to discuss the concept of the future. Use various dates to show the meanings of *tomorrow, next week/month; two years from now,* and so on.
2. Ask learners *What are you going to do tonight? tomorrow? next week? What will you do during summer vacation?* Write some answers on the board, using singular and plural forms. FOR EXAMPLE: *Kim will cook dinner tomorrow. Lee is going to watch a soccer game tonight. Juan and Cecilia are going to visit some friends next week.* Explain that both forms, *going to* and *will,* are used to talk about the future.

Presentation
1. Have learners turn to page 120 and look at the chart. Read one example with *going to* and ask volunteers to read others. Repeat with the examples for *will.* Ask learners what they notice about the verb forms that follow both *going to* and *will.* Lead them to conclude that *call, start,* and *study* are all simple forms.
2. Ask volunteers to read the example sentences below the chart. Point out the contractions used with *going to* and *will.*
3. Display the index cards with *going to, she's, us, visit.* Ask a volunteer to put the cards in correct sentence order and then to read the completed sentence. (*She's going to visit us.*) Repeat with cards for the sentence *I'll call you tomorrow.* For further practice, make new cards to form similar sentences. Mix the cards for a wide variety of sentences. (FOR EXAMPLE: *I'll visit you tomorrow*)
4. Have learners complete exercises A and B. Ask volunteers to read aloud the completed conversation in exercise A and then explain how they could tell that only one choice is correct for items 3 and 4. Review the correct answers for exercise B.
5. Ask questions about the exercises, mixing the use of *going to* and *will.* FOR EXAMPLE: *When is Johnny going to start school? What other classes do you think he will take? What class is Olga going to take?* Tell learners to answer with complete sentences.

Expansion/Extension
- Have learners take turns pointing to dates on a wall calendar and talking about what they are going to do tomorrow, next week, next month, and during vacation. Tell them to vary the use of *going to* and *will.*

Discovering Patterns

Verbs: Future—*Going to* and *Will*

I	am (am not)			I		
He		going to	call tonight.	He	will ('ll)	call tonight.
She	is (is not, isn't)			She		
It		going to	start at 8:00.	It	will (will not)	start at 8:00.
You				You		
We	are (are not, aren't)	going to	study tomorrow.	We	will not (won't)	study tomorrow.
They				They		

Is Olga **going to** see a doctor about that? She's **going to** have a checkup tomorrow.
Will you **be** at the party on Saturday? No, we **won't** be there.
When **will** Kim and Joon **talk** to Han's teacher? They'**ll** go to the school Monday.

A. Complete the sentences. Use *going to* or *will*.

Example: Johnny: "I ___am going to___ start school next week."
or: "I ___will___ start school next week."

1. Aunt Tessa: "So you ___will/are going to___ be in twelfth grade in September!"
2. Johnny: "That's right. I ___will/am going to___ be a senior. I think we ___will/are going to___ have a great basketball team this year."
3. Aunt Tessa: "That's good. What about your classes? What classes are you ___going to___ take?"
4. Johnny: "The usual. English, math . . . . Hey, Dad, ___will___ you let me drive to school?"
5. Tony: "What? Well, we ___will/are going to___ see about that."

B. Answer the questions. Use either *going to* or *will*.

1. Is Olga going to take another exercise class?
   No, she ___will/is going to___ take square dancing instead.
2. Will Kim and Joon sign up for evening classes?
   No, not this time. They ___will/are going to___ spend more time with Han.
3. When will you start classes?
   I ___will/am going to___ start in two weeks.

Conditional Sentences:
If/Then Clauses

Purpose: To give practice with the formation and use of conditional sentences with *If/then* clauses

Teacher Preparation and Materials
Pictures of different kinds of weather (Expansion/Extension)

Warm-up
1. Ask learners *If it rains tomorrow, what will you wear?* On the board, write *If it rains tomorrow, (then) I'll wear . . .* and write learners' comments in a list underneath. Explain that the sentences are correct both with and without the word *then*.
2. Ask learners *If it rains tomorrow, will it change your plans or plans that your family members have? What will you/they do?* Ask volunteers to describe what their family members will do. (If it rains tomorrow, I'll drive my daughter to school. If it rains tomorrow, my wife will leave for work early.)

Presentation
1. Have learners turn to page 121 and look at the chart at the top of the page. Ask volunteers to read the sentences aloud. Have learners review the first part of each sentence, noting the forms of the verbs. Repeat this procedure with the second part of each sentence.
2. Have learners describe the picture next to exercise A and then match the sentence parts. Ask two volunteers to take the parts of Tony and the doctor and to read the appropriate sentences aloud.
3. Ask a volunteer to describe the pictures next to exercise B. Ask *Who's talking? Who's listening? Why do you think Tony is lying down? What do you think he's saying?* Tell learners to read what Tony

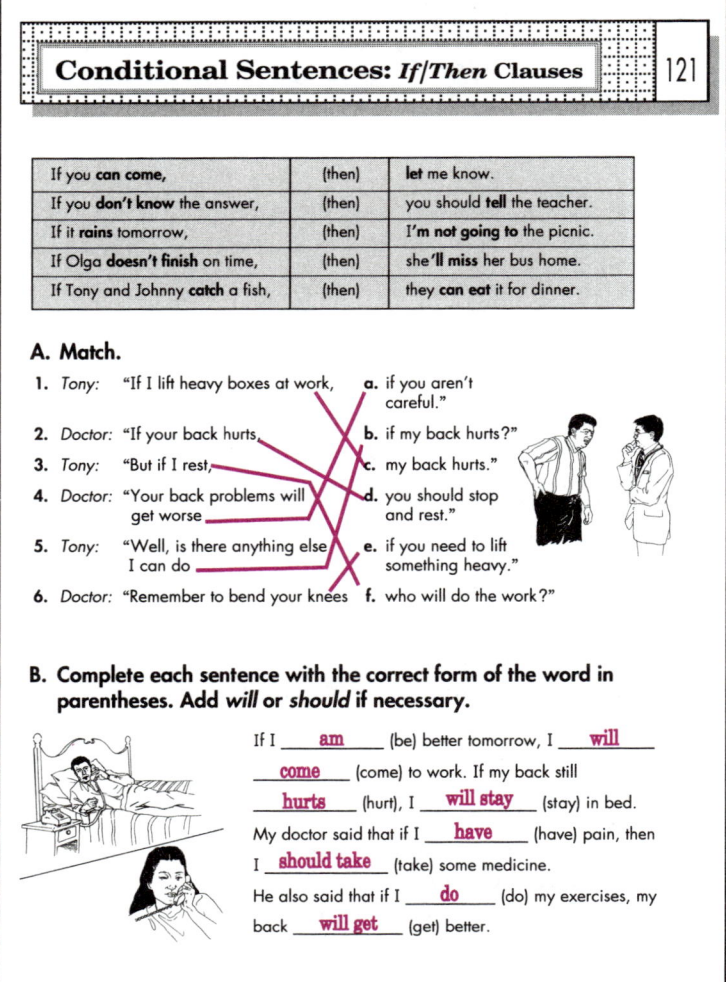

is saying and to write the missing words. Have volunteers read the completed sentences aloud.

4. Continue with a discussion of the subject matter on the page. Ask *If/then* questions (with or without *then*). FOR EXAMPLE: *If Tony's back gets worse, what will he do about work? What can you do if you have a backache? If Tony doesn't follow the doctor's advice, what will happen?*

Expansion/Extension
- Ask learners *What should you do if you want to get a better job?* Put them in small groups to brainstorm a list of things they should do. Have the reporter in each group share some of the group's ideas with the class, saying *If we want to get better jobs, we should . . .* Write some of the ideas on the board, such as *go to school* and *read more*. Continue the discussion by asking *If you want to go to school, what will you have to do?* (select classes, register, buy books)

176 • UNIT 12

Verb + Infinitive and Verb + -ing

Purpose: To give practice with the formation and use of verbs + infinitives and verbs + -ing

Teacher Preparation and Materials
Copies of menus (Expansion/Extension)

Warm-up
1. Ask learners *What do you like to do in the summer? winter?* Write some of their comments on the board. Then ask learners what follows *like*. (*to* + simple form of the verb) Repeat this procedure by asking *What do you like doing at home? at school? on vacation?* (*-ing* form follows *like*) Lead learners to conclude that both of these forms can follow the verb *like*. Elicit other verbs that can be followed by both forms.

2. Tell learners that some verbs can take only one form or the other. On the board, write the headings *-ing* and *to* + *simple form*. Give some examples and ask learners to choose which form makes the sentence correct. FOR EXAMPLE: I hope (to see/seeing you) soon. When will you finish (to work/working)? After each example, write the verb form under the appropriate heading.

Presentation
1. Have learners turn to page 122 and look at the "Verb + infinitive" column on the first chart. Ask volunteers to read the sentences aloud. Continue in this manner, having learners read the examples of verbs that can take only the infinitive or only *-ing*, or verbs that can take both forms. For additional practice, ask learners to say sentences similar to the examples, using the correct verb form or forms.

2. Have learners describe the picture next to exercise A. Then ask them to complete the exercise by choosing the correct form. Advise them to look back at the charts for help as needed. Have volunteers read the finished sentences aloud.

3. Have learners complete exercise B. Then ask two volunteers to take the parts of Ramón and Monroe and read the sentences aloud.

Expansion/Extension

- Put learners into pairs to interview each other, asking *Do you like singing? dancing? painting? cooking? Do you plan to take some classes to learn more?* Suggest that they include their own questions with examples of verb + infinitive and verb + *-ing*. Have learners report on the results of their interviews in small groups.

- Distribute copies of a restaurant menu. Put the class into small groups. Conduct a chain drill based on the menu, having learners ask and answer *What do you like to eat? drink? Do you like to eat liver? Do you enjoy drinking tea? What do you plan to eat for dinner tonight?*

Reported Speech with *That*

Purpose: To give practice in using reported speech with *that*

Teacher Preparation and Materials
Copies of simple comic strips with dialogue that focus on family relationships (*Expansion/Extension*)

Warm-up
Ask a learner *What do you like to do on weekends?* On the board, write the answer as a direct quotation. FOR EXAMPLE: *Lee said, "I like to play soccer on weekends."* Then, underneath, write the indirect quotation *Lee said that he likes to play soccer on weekends.* Repeat the procedure with other learners. (**Note:** In an indirect quotation, the subject and verb change according to the point of view of the speaker. *That* is added optionally after the first verb, and the quotation marks are deleted.) Tell learners that they will often hear this kind of reported speech in conversation.

Presentation
1. Have learners turn to page 123 and look at the chart at the top of the page. Ask volunteers to read the sentences aloud. Explain that the word *that* does not have to be used. Reread the first two example sentences aloud without *that*.
2. Have learners describe the picture with exercise A. Then read the nurse's first sentence. Ask a volunteer to write on the board what Kim tells Joon. Read it aloud with the class and ask what changed. (*That* was added before the direct quotation, and the quotation marks in front of *Monica* were taken away.) Ask learners to complete the rest of the exercise individually or in pairs and to read the completed sentences aloud.
3. Ask learners to describe the picture for the first item in exercise B. Then have them complete the sentence independently. Repeat with the picture and sentence for

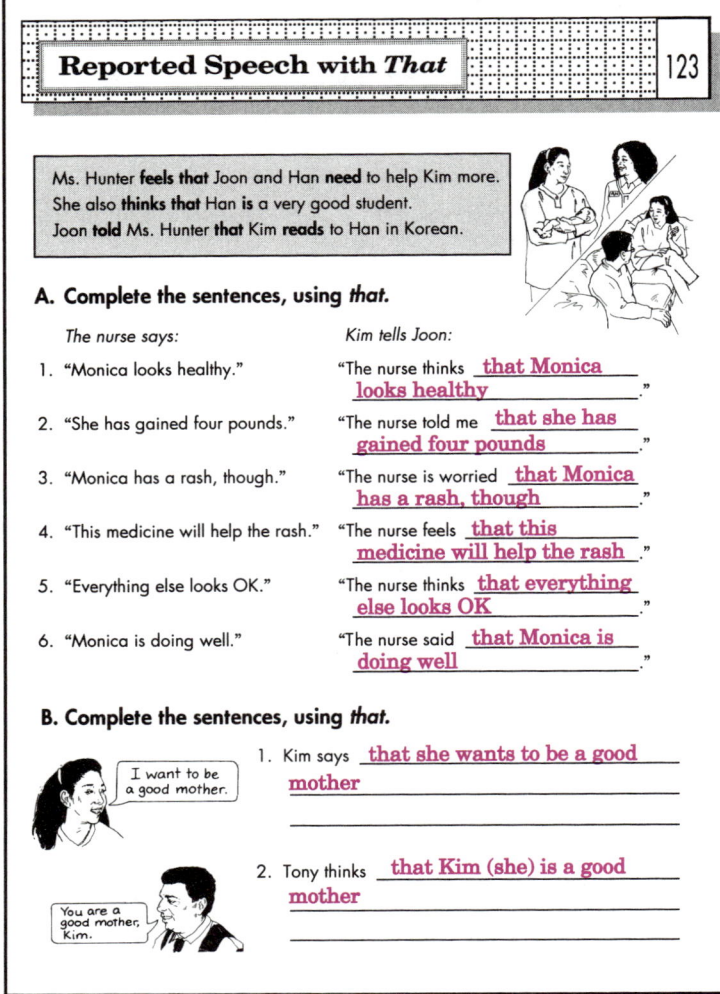

the second item. Ask volunteers to read the completed sentences aloud.

Expansion/Extension
- On the board, write the words *that, said, she, she'll, tomorrow, come.* Have a volunteer put the words together to form a sentence. (*She said that she'll come tomorrow.*) Repeat with other examples that use reported speech.
- Distribute copies of comic strips. Have learners rewrite the comic dialogues, using reported speech. They can present their finished sentences in small groups.
- Ask five volunteers to come to the front of the room to play Telephone. Seat them in a row with their backs to the board. Whisper a statement into the ear of the first volunteer, such as *I like to go horseback riding.* Write it on the board behind their backs. The first learner reports your statement to the next one, saying *The teacher says that she likes to go horseback riding.* Have them continue down the line until the final learner says the statement aloud. Compare the final statement with the one on the board.

Tag Questions

Purpose: To give practice with the formation and use of tag questions

Teacher Preparation and Materials

1. Index cards with words: *I, you, he, she, it, we, they*
2. Blank index cards (at least 14 for each group of 3–4 learners) *(Expansion/Extension)*

Warm-up

1. Ask learners *You like pizza, don't you?* Write the question and a few answers on the board. Explain that the first half of the question contains the information, while the ending merely asks the listener to respond *yes, no,* or *I don't know*. (**Note:** The subject pronoun in the tag question must match the subject in the first part of the sentence.)
2. Conduct a substitution drill, showing the different pronoun index cards and eliciting the correct forms for the question. FOR EXAMPLE: *He doesn't live around here, does he?* In each case, write the correct question on the board. Point out that if the verb in the main part of the question is a positive form, then the verb in the tag question is a negative form, and vice versa. Elicit additional examples and write them on the board.
3. Give additional practice with tag questions in the past and future tense and with modals, so that learners are able to recognize and comprehend the different forms of tag questions.

Presentation

1. Have learners turn to page 124 and look at the chart at the top of the page. Ask volunteers to read the examples aloud. You may wish to suggest that learners make a list of the different verbs that are used in the endings of tag questions. (*be, do, can,* etc.)
2. Ask learners to describe the picture next to exercise A and then complete the sentences with the correct tag questions. Have volunteers read the completed sentences aloud.

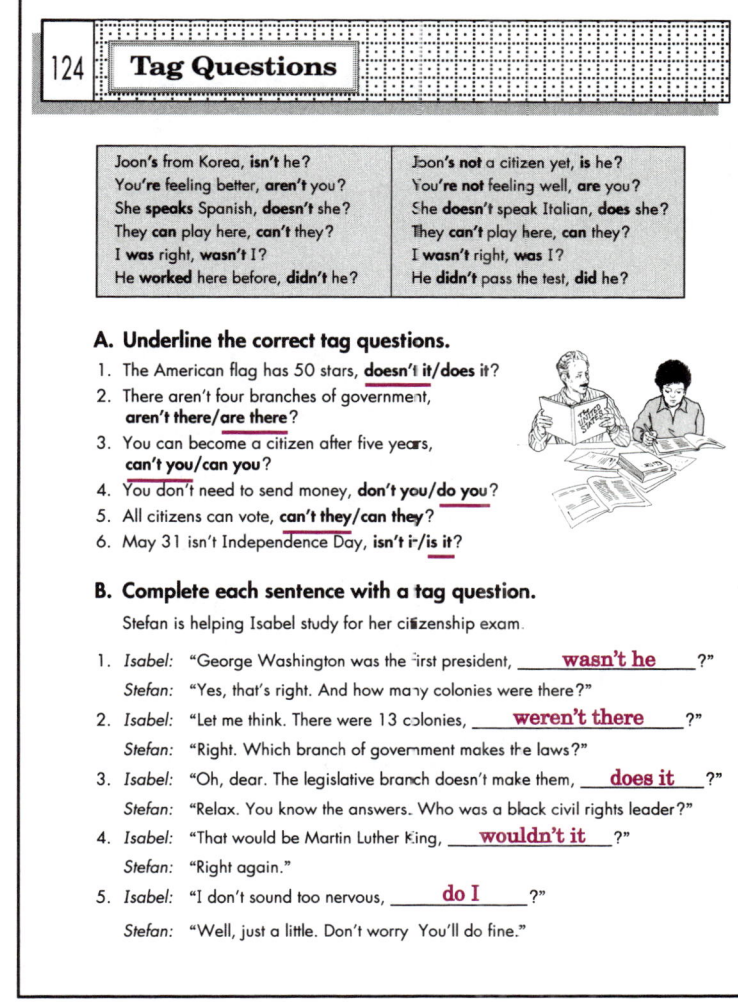

3. Have learners complete exercise B. Ask two volunteers to take the parts of Isabel and Stefan and to read the completed conversation aloud. Have learners ask other tag questions, using facts they know about the United States.
4. On the board, copy the first five sentence beginnings from the chart on page 124 in a column. In a column to the right, copy the tag questions in random order. Ask volunteers to draw a line between the appropriate sentence parts. Repeat with more examples from the chart.

Expansion/Extension

- Put the class into small groups. Distribute 14 index cards to each group. Have learners write the tag questions for *do/don't*, using different pronouns. (*do I? don't I? do you? don't you?* etc.) As you say a simple statement in the present tense, each group must choose the correct tag question and hold it up. The first group to do so wins a point. Use statements like *I like teaching, don't I? He doesn't like hot dogs, does he?*

Tapescripts

UNIT 1
Getting a Job

Page 5   Looking for Work

Narrator: Listen to the conversation between Joon Lee and Tony Martino.
Joon: I really need to find a job. I don't see any good jobs in the newspaper.
Tony: Joon, I saw some ads on the bulletin board at the Save-All Supermarket yesterday. You should go there and take a look.
Joon: That's a good idea. I haven't looked there. I'll go right now.
Tony: I hope you find something.
Joon: Thanks. I'm on my way.
Tony: Good luck. Let me know what happens.

Page 8   Community Bulletin Board

Narrator: Listen to the conversation between Joon Lee and Isabel Santos.
Joon: I found a couple of job openings on the bulletin board at the supermarket.
Isabel: That's great, Joon! What are they?
Joon: Seacoast Industries is looking for a machine operator. I'm going to apply.
Isabel: Hey, a friend of mine works there. His name is Monroe Bonner. You can ask him about the company.
Joon: That's a good idea. The other job is for a housepainter. I can paint. I think I'll call about that job too.

Page 9   Joon's First Interview

Narrator: Listen to the conversation between Joon Lee and Ned Bloom.
Joon: I'm Joon Lee. I'm here about the house-painting job.
Ned: Oh, yeah. Sit down.
Joon: Here's my résumé.
Ned: Yeah. I need another painter for my business. We're real busy, you know.
Joon: I have done some painting. I know it doesn't say so on my résumé but . . .
Ned: In or out?
Joon: Excuse me?
Ned: In or out? Have you done inside painting or outside painting?
Joon: Uh . . . Both.
Ned: Good. When?
Joon: Excuse me?
Ned: When did you do this painting?
Joon: Oh! I painted my sister's house two years ago. Last summer I painted the apartments in the building where I live.
Ned: Uh-huh . . . Well, uh, I think I need someone with more experience.
Joon: I can learn.
Ned: Well, I'll let you know.
Joon: OK. Thank you for your time.

Page 12   Joon's Second Interview
Part A.

Narrator: Listen to the conversation between Joon Lee and the personnel officer at Seacoast Industries.
Mr. Ellis: Hello, Mr. Lee. I'm Mr. Ellis. Please have a seat.
Joon: Thank you.
Mr. Ellis: Your application says that you worked as a machine operator in a bicycle factory. Tell me about that.
Joon: Well . . . That was in Korea. I worked there for five years. I learned to operate every machine in the factory.
Mr. Ellis: Did you repair the machines when they broke?
Joon: No, not really. We had a mechanic for that.
Mr. Ellis: Have you ever worked at night before?
Joon: Yes. I used to work at night in Korea sometimes.
Mr. Ellis: What did you like about the factory work?
Joon: I liked being busy. There was a lot to do.
Mr. Ellis: What didn't you like about that job?
Joon: Well . . . I hated it when the machines broke down. We couldn't get anything done.
Mr. Ellis: Hmmm . . . Why did you leave your job at Chang Industries?
Joon: The factory closed.

Part B.

Narrator: Listen to the conversation between Joon Lee and Mr. Ellis.
Mr. Ellis: Do you have any questions for me?
Joon: Yes, I do. The hours are four in the afternoon to midnight. Is that right?
Mr. Ellis: That's right. Can you work those hours?
Joon: Oh, yes. I'm looking for night work. And what's the pay?
Mr. Ellis: The pay is $280 a week.
Joon: That's fine. Do the benefits include a family health plan?
Mr. Ellis: Yes. We have an excellent health plan.
Joon: Mmmm . . . I'd really like the job.
Mr. Ellis: Good. Then I have one final question for you. Could you start Monday at four o'clock?
Joon: I sure could! Thank you.

UNIT 2
On the Job

Page 18   Punching In

Narrator: Listen to the conversation between Joon and his supervisor, Ramón Fernández.
Ramón: Make sure you punch in every day. First, you fill in your name, Social Security number, and job title on your time card.
Joon: OK.
Ramón: Then, you put your time card in this slot. Next, you press the time card down until you hear the stamp. Finally, put the card in the rack.
Joon: Are these cards collected weekly?
Ramón: Yeah. Be sure to sign and date your card at the end of the week.

Page 20   Operating Machines

Narrator: Listen to the conversation between Joon and his supervisor, Ramón.
Ramón: We always start new operators on the labeling machine. First, start the machine with this switch. Then, push this lever to load the packs. Make sure the packs are moving smoothly.
Joon: First, turn the machine on. Then, push the lever to load the packs. Next, check the packs on the belt.
Ramón: Right. This machine labels the packs. The packs go to the boxing machine automatically.
Joon: I don't understand. What happens to the labeled packs?
Ramón: They go right to the boxing machine.
Joon: I see.
Ramón: Good. Your job is to remove any unlabeled packs from the belt.
Joon: Remove unlabeled packs from the belt?
Ramón: That's right. Put the unlabeled packs in these bags. Turn off the machine if there is a problem, and call me over.
Joon: What do I do when the bags are full?
Ramón: That's a good question. Turn off the machine. Then, stack the bags on those shelves. Anything else?
Joon: No. I think I've got it.
Ramón: Good. And don't forget to turn off the machine and call me if there's a problem!

Page 22   Absent from Work

Narrator: Listen to the conversation between Helen Tran and Ramón Fernández.
Olga: Good morning. Seacoast Industries. Olga speaking. May I help you?
Helen: Hi, Olga. This is Helen Tran. May I speak to Mr. Fernández?
Olga: Sure, Helen. Just a moment.
Ramón: Fernández here.
Helen: This is Helen Tran. I can't come to work today. My son has an earache. I'm taking him to the doctor.
Ramón: OK. I hope he feels better soon.
Helen: I'll call you later if I won't be in tomorrow.
Ramón: Fine. Good-bye.

Page 23   Small Talk
Part A.

Narrator: Listen to the conversation between Monroe and Ramón.
Ramón: Hi, Monroe. Did you see the Dodgers last night?
Monroe: What a ball game! I can't believe they pulled it out in the ninth! Five runs down with two outs, and they still won!

Ramón: If they can only beat Cincinnati, they'll be in first place.

Monroe: Do you think they'll win the pennant?

Ramón: They have a shot at it if their pitching holds up, but they'll have to . . .

Part B.

Narrator: Listen to the conversation between Monroe and Joon.

Monroe: Hey, Joon. How's it going?

Joon: Fine, Monroe. How was your weekend?

Monroe: It was fantastic!

Joon: Oh, yeah? What did you do?

Monroe: We went to the lake. The weather was perfect! Blue sky, warm sun, clean air . . . Just what the doctor ordered. What about you?

Joon: Not much. The smog was so thick we stayed indoors and watched movies all weekend . . .

Part C.

Narrator: Listen to the conversation between Tony and Kim.

Tony: How's your son Han doing these days, Kim?

Kim: Oh, he's fine, Tony. Did you know we're going to have a baby? Han is very proud that he'll be a big brother.

Tony: You're having a baby? That's great news! I'll have to tell Johnny.

Kim: How is Johnny?

Tony: He's a good boy. He loves school. All A's and B's on his last report card. His math teacher wants him to join the math team. But they grow up too fast! He already wants to drive a car!

Kim: They do grow up fast. That's why I'm happy I'm having another baby . . .

UNIT 3
Making Choices about Money

Page 33 Talking to a Salesclerk

Narrator: Listen to Monroe and Althea talking to a salesclerk.

Salesclerk: May I help you?

Althea: Could you show us the Focus TV that's on sale?

Salesclerk: I'm sorry. We're all sold out of that model. Anyway, that model's too small for you. I think you'd do better with a 27-inch MEGA deluxe. It has 181 channels, remote control—

Monroe: How much is it?

Salesclerk: It's a very good buy at only $579.99 on sale.

Monroe: No, thanks. It's too big and it's too expensive. What about the Silverstar? Isn't that on sale?

Salesclerk: Oh, yes. The Silverstar's on sale too. It's a 20-inch color set for $349.99.

Monroe: That sounds like a good price.

Althea: I think so too. It's not too big, either.

Monroe: Good. Let's take it.

Salesclerk: Will that be cash, check, or charge?

Monroe: Hmmm. I don't have a charge account here—but could I open one . . . ?

Page 35 Monroe's Choice

Narrator: Listen to the conversation between the salesclerk and Monroe.

Salesclerk: Thank you for waiting, Mr. Bonner. You've been approved for Royal's instant credit card. Here's your temporary card. Please sign it immediately. Your permanent card will be mailed to you. Also, if your credit card is ever lost or stolen, please call us right away. If you have any questions, please call the Customer Service Department. Take this slip to the pick-up window to get your TV. Thank you for shopping at Royal's.

Monroe: You're welcome.

UNIT 4
Driving a Car

Page 39 Applying for a Learner's Permit

Narrator: Listen to the conversation between Johnny and the clerk in the Department of Motor Vehicles.

Johnny: I want to get my learner's permit. I'd like to make an appointment for my written test.

Clerk:	Fine. You'll need to fill in this form and have your parents sign it.
Johnny:	All right.
Clerk:	Now I'll set up a time for you to take the test. Let me look at the schedule and see where I can fit you in.
Johnny:	OK. Do you have Saturday appointments?
Clerk:	No, I'm afraid not. We're only open Monday through Friday.
Johnny:	Oh.
Clerk:	How about Monday, May 9th at 3:00 p.m.?
Johnny:	What day of the week did you say?
Clerk:	The ninth. It's a Monday.
Johnny:	I guess that sounds OK. I should be able to leave school and get here by 3:00.
Clerk:	Please be on time.
Johnny:	What do I need to bring with me?
Clerk:	Bring back this application form, along with your Driver's Education completion certificate, your birth certificate, and your Social Security card. You'll also need a check or money order for $15.
Johnny:	OK.
Clerk:	Here's your driver's manual. Be sure to study it.
Johnny:	Thanks.
Clerk:	See you on May 9th.

Page 40 Car Insurance

Narrator:	Listen to the conversation between Isabel and the insurance agent.
Isabel:	This is my first car. Can you tell me what insurance I need?
Agent:	There are two kinds of car insurance. The first kind is compulsory coverage. You must buy this kind. There are two things that this covers. First of all, you need it in case you are in an accident and have injuries. It will pay for your medical bills. It also covers some of the wages you may lose if you can't work because of an accident.
Isabel:	What else does compulsory insurance cover?
Agent:	Well, it pays for medical expenses if someone is injured by your car. It also pays for damage that is caused by your car to another person's car or property.
Isabel:	Oh, I see. And what's the other kind of insurance? Do I need it?
Agent:	The other kind is optional coverage. You may buy it, but you don't have to buy it if you don't want to.
Isabel:	What does it cover?
Agent:	Let's say you have a collision, or crash. This optional coverage pays for most of the damage to your car no matter who causes the accident.
Isabel:	Hmmm . . . That's interesting.
Agent:	You can also get optional coverage that will take care of additional medical payments for you, family members, and passengers if your compulsory coverage isn't enough.
Isabel:	Thanks for all the information. Now I have to decide what I should do!

Page 45 Taking the Road Test

Narrator:	Listen to the conversation between the examiner and Johnny.
Examiner:	Pull out of the parking lot and turn right. Then take a left onto Main Street.
Johnny:	Left at the lights?
Examiner:	Yes, that's correct.
Johnny:	OK.
Examiner:	Now I want you to take another left at the next set of lights.
Johnny:	Here? At Carter Avenue?
Examiner:	Yes. OK. Now pull over to the side and park behind that big truck you see up ahead . . .
Johnny:	OK. What next?
Examiner:	When the traffic clears, pull out and take your next left.
Johnny:	Yes, ma'am.
Examiner:	Now you'll have to take one more left and go back to the parking lot.
Johnny:	OK . . .
Examiner:	You did very well.
Johnny:	Thank you.

Page 46 Getting Pulled Over

Narrator:	Listen to the conversation between the police officer and Tony.
Tony:	What's the problem, Officer?
Officer:	Did you know that the speed limit here is 25 mph?

Tony:	Is it? How fast was I going?
Officer:	I clocked you at 35 mph. What's the hurry?
Tony:	I'm sorry, Officer. My son just passed his road test. We're very excited!
Officer:	Well, if your son's in the car, all the more reason to drive carefully.
Tony:	I know. I guess I wasn't watching my speedometer.
Officer:	Well, you should have been watching it. Let me see your driver's license and car registration.
Tony:	Sure. Here they are.
Officer:	I'm writing you a ticket for 35 mph. From now on, pay attention. The speed limit is there for a reason.
Tony:	Yes, Officer.
Officer:	You can pay the fine by mail or in person at the courthouse.
Tony:	OK.
Officer:	Or you can plead not guilty and go before the judge.
Tony:	OK. Thank you, Officer.

UNIT 5
Having a Good Time

Page 51 Inviting Friends

Narrator:	Listen to the conversation between Olga and Isabel.
Isabel:	Hello?
Olga:	Hi, Isabel. This is Olga.
Isabel:	Hi, Olga. How are you doing?
Olga:	Oh, fine, for an old lady like me. I haven't seen you since the last class we took together. Would you like to go to the movies this evening?
Isabel:	Oh, thanks for asking, but I can't. I just made plans. I'm going out with Stefan tonight.
Olga:	Oh, that's wonderful. He's such a nice young man.
Isabel:	Maybe we can get together another time.
Olga:	OK. How about dinner next week? You can bring Stefan too. He looks like he could use a good home-cooked meal.
Isabel:	Oh, thanks for the invitation.
Olga:	How's Thursday night?
Isabel:	Sounds good to me. I'll ask Stefan and I'll call you tomorrow.

Page 54 Going Away for the Weekend

Narrator:	Listen to the conversation between Johnny and Aunt Tessa.
Tessa:	Hello?
Johnny:	Hi, Aunt Tessa. It's Johnny.
Tessa:	Hi, Johnny. You and Tony are coming up here to the lake for the weekend, aren't you?
Johnny:	You bet! Dad and I are leaving after dinner on Friday. I'm just calling to see what you want us to bring.
Tessa:	Let's see . . . We're going to have a cookout on Saturday. Why don't you bring some hot dogs, a few bottles of soda, and about a dozen ears of corn? Oh, and maybe some fruit as well.
Johnny:	OK. What else?
Tessa:	Your cousins say the fish are really biting. You'd better bring your fishing pole.
Johnny:	I will. Can I bring my dog too?
Tessa:	Oh, Johnny, I'm sorry. I don't think so. We have some special plans for Sunday, and I'm afraid the dog would be a problem.
Johnny:	Oh. I see.
Tessa:	But Johnny, do remember to bring your sleeping bag, bathing suit, and a warm sweater too.
Johnny:	Yeah, OK. I hope the weather's good.
Tessa:	It's supposed to be perfect. We'll see you on Friday night.
Johnny:	OK. See you then, Aunt Tessa!

UNIT 7
Wash and Wear

Page 67 What Store Should We Go To?

Narrator:	Listen to the conversation between Monroe and Althea.
Monroe:	Well, I guess it's obvious that I need a new suit.
Althea:	Yeah, I should say so! Either your suit shrank last winter or you put on a few pounds. . . .

Monroe: A little of both, hon, a little of both!
Althea: Well, I'd like to find another nice blouse too. It's a real shame that my good blouse has a stain on it.
Monroe: And Jody needs a new outfit too. So where should we go? Any sales going on at the mall?
Althea: There's one at Royal's this week. I think that's where I'll look for a blouse.
Monroe: I'd really like to take a look at the suits at J. Taylor's. Look at this ad. They have the styles I like there.
Althea: I'll bet the prices are sky-high.
Monroe: Well, they don't show the prices here, but let's check it out. Now, what about Jody? Are there any girls' dresses on sale at Royal's?
Althea: Royal's doesn't carry a large assortment of girls' clothes. Hmmm . . .
Monroe: What about that little store on Western Avenue?
Althea: You mean the Dandelion Shop?
Monroe: Yeah, that's the one.
Althea: That closed down about six months ago.
Monroe: Shows what I know.
Althea: Jody really likes the clothes at Francie's Fashions.
Monroe: Is that in the mall?
Althea: No, it's down on Highway 35.
Monroe: Oh yeah. I know the place. How are the prices?
Althea: Not bad. Hopefully, there's a sale too.
Monroe: Yeah, that's quite a drive, so it better be worth it!

Page 69 In the Men's Department

Narrator: Listen to the conversation between Monroe and the salesclerk at Royal's Department Store.
Salesclerk: You're a 43 long? Those sizes are over here, sir.
Monroe: Thank you. I'd like a light wool suit in navy.
Salesclerk: Do you want a business suit, or something more casual?
Monroe: I'm going to a wedding, so I need a good suit—but it has to be something I can wear all year round.
Salesclerk: I see. These suits are very fine. They're our finest wool-blend suits.
Monroe: Well, I wasn't really looking for a blend.
Salesclerk: But this material is extremely durable. It will last you a long time.
Monroe: Oh, really?
Salesclerk: Oh, yes. You'll get years of wear from it. Plus there's an extra 10% off the sale price today.
Monroe: Oh . . . I do like the style. And the price is right too.
Salesclerk: You can't beat that price.
Monroe: The fitting room is over there, isn't it?
Salesclerk: Yes, it is. Let me take the suit for you. Right this way.
Monroe: Thanks.

Page 70 Choosing a Shirt

Narrator: Listen to the conversation between Monroe and Althea.
Monroe: Do you think I need a new shirt to go with this suit?
Althea: Oh, yes, honey. You could really use a new shirt.
Monroe: How about this blue one?
Althea: Well, I don't know . . . It's the wrong shade for your suit.
Monroe: This white one goes well, doesn't it?
Althea: Yeah. That looks nice. Oh, dear. It's all cotton. It may shrink, and it will definitely be a pain to iron.
Monroe: What about this one? It costs a lot less, doesn't it?
Althea: Yes. Hmmm. It's cheaper because it's an irregular. I wonder what's wrong with it? Hmmm . . . Oh, I see. There's a snag on the sleeve.
Monroe: Where? I can't see anything. Oh, you mean that? That's hardly noticeable.
Althea: It's a washable blend too, so it will be easy to take care of. You do want long sleeves, don't you?
Monroe: Oh, yes. I'll get much more use out of a long-sleeved shirt.

Page 73 Looking for Another Blouse

Narrator: Listen to the conversation between Althea and the salesclerk.
Salesclerk: May I help you?
Althea: Yes, I hope so. I bought a blouse here last year, and I really love it. I'm trying

	to find another one since my old one has a horrible fruit stain on it.
Salesclerk:	I see. What style is the blouse?
Althea:	It's an ivory, short-sleeved blouse.
Salesclerk:	Buttons down the front?
Althea:	No, actually the buttons are on the back.
Salesclerk:	Hmmm . . . I think we have some blouses like that over here, ma'am.
Althea:	Uh . . . No, these blouses are too fancy. This one here is almost the style but not quite.
Salesclerk:	How about these over here?
Althea:	No, those have the wrong kind of collar. The one I'm looking for is much more basic and simple.
Salesclerk:	Well, ma'am, we don't seem to have the kind of blouse you're looking for.
Althea:	Would any of your other stores have different blouses? I could run over to the store in Belleview if I thought they'd have the right blouse.
Salesclerk:	I doubt very much that they'd have different blouses. All of our stores get our merchandise from the same place.
Althea:	Oh, I see. I really don't know what I'm going to do. I have to go to a wedding next weekend, and I really need a blouse like that to go with my suit.
Salesclerk:	Have you tried to remove the stain?
Althea:	No, actually I haven't. I was afraid to.
Salesclerk:	What have you got to lose?
Althea:	You're right. I guess I'll try that. Thanks for all your help.

UNIT 8
What the Doctor Said

Page 78 Checkups

Narrator:	Listen to the conversation between the nurse and Kim.
Nurse:	All right, Kim. Let's continue. Do you ever drink alcohol? Wine? Beer? Anything like that?
Kim:	No, not at all.
Nurse:	That's good . . . especially for your new baby. Now I need to ask a few more questions about you and members of your family. Do you or anyone in your family have high blood pressure?
Kim:	Yes, my grandfather and one of my aunts.
Nurse:	What about heart problems?
Kim:	My father had open-heart surgery . . . and so did my uncle.
Nurse:	How about diabetes, tuberculosis, or anemia?
Kim:	No, none of those.
Nurse:	And have you or any of your relatives had any operations?
Kim:	Not me, but as I said before, my father and his brother have both had heart surgery.
Nurse:	All right, Kim. Do you currently take any medication?
Kim:	Yes, I take two aspirin when I have headaches . . . and I usually take an antacid for stomachaches.
Nurse:	Are you allergic to any medication?
Kim:	Yes, to penicillin.

Page 79 Taking Medication

Narrator:	Listen to the conversation between Kim and her doctor.
Doctor:	I've checked the tests you had today. Most of them are fine. But your blood test shows that you are slightly anemic.
Kim:	What does that mean?
Doctor:	It means that you need extra iron. It's a common problem for women, especially pregnant women.
Kim:	What can I do?
Doctor:	You should take iron tablets. You don't need a prescription.
Kim:	If I'm anemic, that won't hurt my baby, will it?
Doctor:	Your baby should be fine. Your weight and blood pressure are normal. You don't smoke. You don't drink alcohol . . .
Kim:	And I stopped drinking coffee and tea too.
Doctor:	Excellent. Your baby doesn't need caffeine. But it does need more iron.
Kim:	When do I take the pills?
Doctor:	Take one iron pill every morning with breakfast.
Kim:	Are you sure that one is enough?
Doctor:	Oh, yes. Don't take more than one a day. Too much medicine can be bad for you too.

Kim: Thank you, Doctor. I'll see you in two weeks.

Page 80 Olga's Exam

Narrator: Listen to the conversation between Olga and her doctor.
Doctor: First, try to use less salt in your food.
Olga: No salt? I can't eat eggs without salt. Or soup. There's no taste.
Doctor: I didn't say no salt; I said less salt. Next, you'd better stop smoking. Your lungs sound—
Olga: Stop smoking! Oh, that's so hard! I've been smoking for years!
Doctor: I know it's hard. But your lungs really don't sound healthy. I'll give you some information about ways to stop. Then, you'd better lose about 20 pounds. Being overweight affects your—
Olga: Excuse me, doctor. You want me to lose 20 pounds? Are you saying I'm 20 pounds overweight?
Doctor: I'm afraid so, Ms. Kovacs. As I was saying, extra weight is bad for your heart. The nutritionist can help develop a healthy diet for you. Do you ever exercise?
Olga: Exercise? I walk home from work every day. Ten blocks! Even in the rain!
Doctor: Ten blocks is a good walk. Maybe you should try walking to work too. That's almost a mile a—
Olga: Walk to work? I'd be late every day!
Doctor: Well, maybe you could get up a little earlier. Walking is excellent exercise. It would help you lose weight and reduce stress too.
Olga: Reduce stress? Maybe I should quit my job?
Doctor: That's a bit drastic. You might try meditating . . .
Olga: Me? Meditate?
Doctor: Just think about it, Ms. Kovacs. In the meantime, we can control your high blood pressure with medication.

Page 85 It's a Girl!

Narrator: Listen to the conversation between Olga and Joon.
Olga: Good morning. Seacoast Industries.
Joon: Olga? It's Joon Lee. I won't be in today. Kim and I have a baby girl!
Olga: Oh, how wonderful! How are they? When was she born? Give me details! Everyone will want to know!
Joon: Kim's fine! The baby's perfect! Kim woke me up at two in the morning and said it was time to go to the hospital.
Olga: What about Han?
Joon: We took him over to Tony's like we planned. Then I drove to the hospital in record time.
Olga: Has Han seen the baby?
Joon: Yes. Tony brought him here this morning. He's in with Kim now.
Olga: I'm so happy for you! Have you named her yet?
Joon: Her name is Monica. We're so glad we have a baby girl.

UNIT 9
Going to School

Page 91 Meeting Ms. Hunter

Narrator: Listen to the conversation between Joon and Lizette Hunter.
Lizette: I'm glad you could come in before school, Mr. Lee. As I mentioned in my note, I think it's important that we talk about Han.
Joon: But he's a good boy. He never gives us any trouble.
Lizette: He's not giving me trouble either, Mr. Lee. I'm just worried he's not doing as well as he could.
Joon: Well, his mother and I really haven't been able to talk to him about his schoolwork much since the baby was born.
Lizette: Oh, your wife just had a baby! Han never mentioned it.
Joon: He didn't? I'm surprised. I wonder why he didn't tell you.
Lizette: You know, sometimes children have a hard time adjusting to a new baby in the house.
Joon: What do you mean? Han loves his little sister. He plays with her all the time.

Lizette: Oh, I'm sure he loves her. But sometimes new babies get most of the attention. Han was your only child for seven years. He might feel a little left out of things.

Joon: I think I see what you mean. What can we do?

Lizette: Maybe you can spend some special time with him every day. Help him do his homework. Read to him at bedtime. Take him to the store with you. That sort of thing.

Joon: I'll talk this over with Kim. We want Han to do well in school.

Lizette: Of course you do. So do I. I'll let you know how he's doing.

Joon: Thank you.

Page 95 At Registration

Narrator: Listen to the conversation between Olga and Isabel.

Olga: Hi, Isabel. How have you been?

Isabel: Hi, Olga! Oh, I've been pretty busy lately.

Olga: Spending a lot more time with Stefan, huh?

Isabel: Well, yes. But I've been studying for my citizenship exam also. In fact, I'm signing up for my last course tonight—American History!

Olga: Oh. I thought you took that last term.

Isabel: No, that was American Civics.

Olga: Oh, yeah! Well, I'm signing up for Stress Management and Yoga! On my doctor's advice, no less. I'd rather take Perfect Pasta!

Isabel: Yoga? That sounds interesting. When is it?

Olga: Thursday night at 6 o'clock. Why don't you come? I'm trying to get Monroe and Althea to come too. Misery loves company, you know.

Isabel: Yoga's a good idea. And I'm here on Thursday nights anyway. Are Monroe and Althea taking classes too?

Olga: Yes. They drove me here. Althea is checking out a computer course she needs for her job. Monroe wants to learn how to make healthy desserts!

Isabel: Hmmm . . .

Olga: Isabel, I hope you'll keep taking courses here after you become a citizen.

Isabel: Oh, yes. I love learning new things.

Olga: Me too. My mother always said, "When your mind isn't growing, it's shrinking." Even my doctor agrees. The rest of me should shrink, but not my mind! Oh, it's your turn at last.

Isabel: Talk to you later.

UNIT 10
Becoming a Citizen

Page 103 Learning American History

Narrator: Listen to the history teacher talking to the class.

Teacher: I'm going to read a passage on American history. Listen and take notes. The words on the board should help you. The United States began as 13 colonies that belonged to England. The colonists had to pay a lot of money in taxes to England. They wanted to be free of England and English taxes. Finally, the colonists rebelled and fought the Revolutionary War. George Washington was the leader of the rebel army. He later became the first president of the new country. He was called "the Father of Our Country." The capital of the United States is Washington, D.C. It was named after George Washington. Thomas Jefferson, who later became the third president, wrote the Declaration of Independence. This document proclaimed America's independence from England. It was signed by many important American leaders on July 4, 1776. The Fourth of July is also called Independence Day.

Page 106 Before the Interview

Narrator: Listen to the conversation between Tony and Isabel.

Tony: Isabel! That's the third time you gave the wrong change! What's the matter with you?

Isabel: Oh, Tony. I'm sorry. My mind's not here today.

Tony: What the matter? You look worried.

Isabel: Well . . . I'm taking my citizenship test next week. I'm very worried about it.

Tony: My teacher says that I'm ready, but I don't feel ready.

Tony: I didn't know it was so soon. I know how you feel. I remember when I became a citizen.

Isabel: That was a long time ago, wasn't it?

Tony: Almost 25 years ago. I went to school just like you, and I studied hard. But I was scared when I had to take the test. I was a little sad too.

Isabel: You missed Italy, didn't you?

Tony: Yes. But my family was here and I knew I wasn't going back. I've never been sorry.

Isabel: I left El Salvador a long time ago, but I still miss it. I miss my parents and I worry about my friends. But I'm not going back either. I want to be an American.

Tony: After you're a citizen, you can go back to school and get your teaching certificate.

Isabel: Yes. That's true. I really want to be a teacher.

Tony: You'll be able to vote too.

Isabel: And serve on a jury. And I could even run for political office.

Tony: See? You know the answers. You'll do fine.

Isabel: Thanks, Tony. Now if I can just remember how to make change for our customers . . .

Page 107 Famous Americans

Narrator: Listen to the conversation between Isabel and the examiner.

Examiner: Well, Ms. Santos, now that we've gone over your application, I must ask you some questions about American history.

Isabel: Yes, sir.

Examiner: My questions have to do with famous Americans in our history. Please answer briefly. If you don't know the answer, tell me so. Do you understand?

Isabel: Yes, sir.

Examiner: OK. Who was president during the Civil War?

Isabel: Abraham Lincoln.

Examiner: Yes. Who wrote the national anthem?

Isabel: Do you mean "The Star-Spangled Banner?"

Examiner: That's right.

Isabel: Uhhh . . . Francis Scott Key.

Examiner: Good. Who was the Reverend Martin Luther King, Jr.?

Isabel: He was a major civil rights leader.

Examiner: Yes. Name two things that Thomas Jefferson was famous for.

Isabel: He was the main writer of the Declaration of Independence. Did you say two things he did?

Examiner: Yes, I did.

Isabel: He was the third president of the United States too.

Examiner: Good. You did very well, Ms. Santos. You answered all the questions correctly.

Isabel: Oh, thank you.

UNIT 11
Getting Used to a New Land

Page 111 What's the United States Like?

Narrator: Listen to the conversation between Olga and Isabel.

Olga: Isabel, did I ever tell you what it was like when I first came to the United States?

Isabel: No, I don't think so. I know you came here from Hungary when you were very young.

Olga: My parents couldn't wait to come here. They kept getting letters from my uncles and aunts. The letters made it sound like they were living like kings and queens. But I can't begin to tell you how poor we were when we first came.

Isabel: Where did you live then?

Olga: Oh, you wouldn't want to know. It was pretty bad, and it cost so much more than in Hungary. Everything was so expensive, even back then. No one ever tells you how hard it will be.

Isabel: I know what you mean. When I was still in El Salvador, my cousin, Tomás, moved to the United States. He wrote to me and said, "Izzy, you've got to come here. It's a fantastic place! There are plenty of jobs, and you can go anywhere you want, anytime you want!"

Olga: Ah, your cousin probably had no idea how expensive it is to travel across this huge country!

Isabel: Yeah, and he also had no idea how difficult it can be to find a job.

Olga: I know. My father thought he'd get the job of his dreams as soon as he arrived here. And all he could get was a job sweeping floors. Would you believe that it took over a year for my father to get a good job working in a factory?

Isabel: Well, it sounds like jobs were as hard to find then as they are now. But I'm still glad that I came here.

Olga: I have to agree with you, Isabel. In the end, things worked out pretty well for us.

Page 114 Feeling Foolish

Narrator: Listen to the conversation between Joon and Monroe.

Joon: A terrible thing happened to me yesterday. I was buying some groceries. The bill came to $24.97. When I opened my wallet, I only had $20! I felt so dumb!

Monroe: Yeah. I've done that myself. It's so embarrassing.

Joon: That happened to you? I never thought it could happen to an American.

Monroe: Sure. It could happen to anyone. It probably happens in the supermarket all the time. I hope you explained it to the checkout clerk.

Joon: Explained it?

Monroe: Sure. You could have put some things back.

Joon: I never thought of that.

Monroe: What did you do?

Joon: Well, I . . .

Page 115 A Parking Space

Narrator: Listen to the conversation between Monroe and Joon.

Monroe: You wouldn't believe what happened when I went shopping the other day.

Joon: Oh, no! Did you get in an accident?

Monroe: No, it wasn't that bad. I finally spotted a parking space. I noticed another car coming towards me, but I wasn't paying too much attention. When I got out of the car, I heard the driver yelling at me. At first I wondered why he was so mad, and then I realized what I had done.

Joon: What *had* you done?

Monroe: Well, that other driver had wanted the parking space, and he was mad because I took it.

Joon: So what did you do then?

Monroe: I started to walk toward the guy's car because I wanted to apologize, but the guy just kept yelling and drove away. Boy, did I feel dumb.

Joon: Yeah, I hate it when things like that happen.

Page 117 Old Ways and New Ways

Narrator: Listen to the conversation between Monroe and Joon.

Monroe: Wow. It's getting late. I should be going soon. Althea is working late tonight. I've got to make dinner.

Joon: You cook?

Monroe: Oh, yes. I cook almost as much as Althea. I like cooking. What I'll never like is going to the grocery store. Thank goodness I don't have to do it very often.

Joon: You shop for food?

Monroe: Sure, sometimes.

Joon: In Korea a man would never do woman's work. Kim didn't work in Korea. She had all day to do her housework. It's harder now.

Monroe: I only started cooking because I had to. Althea's income is important to us. It wouldn't be fair to expect her to do all the housework too.

Joon: I know. I feel bad that Kim has so much to do. I help take care of Han and Monica when I can, and I like doing that. I probably wouldn't do it so much if we were still in Korea. But I still don't like to do housework or cooking.

Monroe: I bet no one likes to do housework—not even women! Things must seem very different here.

Joon: Oh, yes. I like some of our new ways, but I like the Korean ways too.

Index of Functions

NOTE: The functions in boldface type are introduced in Level 2.

	Unit(s)
accepting/declining invitations	5
asking for/giving advice	3
asking for/giving information	1, 7
clarifying	Preliminary Lessons, 2, 8, 9, 10
comparing/contrasting	3, 5, 7, 11
dealing with numbers (budgets, costs)	3
describing (objects, events, problems, symptoms)	4, 5, 8, 9
expressing abilities/skills/responsibilities	1
expressing agreement/disagreement	9, 10
expressing concern	9
expressing embarrassment	11
expressing emotions	5, 11
expressing greetings	Preliminary Lessons
expressing intention	4
expressing likes/dislikes/preferences	1, 5, 7
expressing needs	4, 7
expressing surprise	11
giving/following oral and written directions	2, 4, 7, 8
giving/getting personal information	Preliminary Lessons
giving reasons/explanations	2, 3
identifying (causes)	8
interrupting	8
introducing oneself/others	Preliminary Lessons
inviting	5
making small talk	2
persuading	10
reporting (problems, successes, past events)	4, 8, 9, 10, 11
requesting assistance	2
sequencing	8
understanding safety requirements	2

Index of Structures

NOTE: The structures in boldface type are introduced in Level 2.

	Unit(s)
adjectives: comparative	3, 6, 7
adjectives: descriptive	5, 11
adverbs of frequency	3, 8, 11
adverbs of time	11
conditionals: *if/then* statements	3, 9, 12
conjunctions: *but*	4
demonstratives: *these, those*	5
future tense: *going to, will*	5, 7, 9, 12
imperatives	2, 4, 7, 8
intensifiers: *too, very*	3
irregular past tense	6
modals: *can/can't*	1, 2, 3, 6, 10
modals: *could, should, would*	3, 6
modals: *may, must*	9, 10
past continuous tense	4, 6, 10
past tense	Preliminary Lessons, 1, 2, 4, 5, 6, 8, 10
prepositions of direction	4
prepositions of place	4, 11
present continuous tense	Preliminary Lessons, 2
present tense	Preliminary Lessons
questions: *Have you . . . ?*	1
questions: negative	3
questions: *wh-*	Preliminary Lessons, 1, 8, 10
reported speech with *that*	10, 12
sequence words	2, 8
tag questions	5, 10, 12
used to + verb	1
verb + infinitive	12
verb + *-ing*	12
***when* clauses**	11
***while* clauses**	5